Culture Wise ENGLAND

The Essential Guide to Culture, Customs & Business Etiquette

David Hampshire

&

Liz Opalka

SURVIVAL BOOKS • LONDON • ENGLAND

First published 2007

Other photographs – see page 254

Survival Books Limited
26 York Street, London W1U 6PZ, United Kingdom
☎ +44 (0)20-7788 7644, ▤ +44 (0)870-762 3212
✉ info@survivalbooks.net
💻 www.survivalbooks.net

British Library Cataloguing in Publication Data.
A CIP record for this book is available from the British Library.
ISBN 10: 1-905303-24-6
ISBN 13: 978-1-905303-24-3

Printed and bound in India by Ajanta Offset

ACKNOWLEDGEMENTS

The authors would like to thank their many friends, family members and colleagues – unfortunately too many to mention – who provided information for this book. We would also like to thank Joanna Styles for editing, Lilac Johnston for proof-reading, Grania Rogers for photo selection and editing, Di Tolland for DTP, and Jim Watson for the book and cover design, maps and cartoons. Finally a special thank you to all the photographers – the unsung heroes – who provided the superb photos, without which this book would be dull indeed.

THE AUTHORS

David Hampshire was born in England and after serving in the Royal Air Force, was employed for many years in the computer industry. His work has taken him around the world and he has lived and worked in many countries, including Australia, France, Germany, Malaysia, the Netherlands, Panama, Singapore, Spain, and Switzerland. David starting working as a technical author in Australia in the '80s and he became a full-time, freelance writer in 1990. He is the author or co-author of over 15 titles, including *Living and Working in Britain* and *Buying or Renting a Home in London*. David lives with his partner in England and Panama.

Liz Opalka was born in England of Hungarian parents. She trained as a journalist and was initially worked for local newspapers in west London, but is now employed in public relations. She has travelled extensively throughout Asia, South America and Europe, and after graduating, spent a year living in Italy teaching English. In her spare time, Liz enjoys watching her football team, Queen's Park Rangers (at least on the rare occasions when they win). Liz lives in London, but helps keep the railway network afloat with frequent visits to the north-west of England, where her partner is based. This is her first book.

WHAT READERS & REVIEWERS HAVE

'If you need to find out how France works then this book is indispensable. Native French people probably have a less thorough understanding of how their country functions.'

Living France

'It's everything you always wanted to ask but didn't for fear of the contemptuous put down. The best English-language guide. Its pages are stuffed with practical information on everyday subjects and are designed to compliment the traditional guidebook.'

Swiss News

'Rarely has a 'survival guide' contained such useful advice. This book dispels doubts for first-time travellers, yet is also useful for seasoned globetrotters. In a word, if you're planning to move to the US or go there for a long-term stay, then buy this book both for general reading and as a ready-reference.'

American Citizens Abroad

'Let's say it at once. David Hampshire's Living and Working in France is the best handbook ever produced for visitors and foreign residents in this country; indeed, my discussion with locals showed that it has much to teach even those born and bred in l'Hexagone. It is Hampshire's meticulous detail which lifts his work way beyond the range of other books with similar titles. Often you think of a supplementary question and search for the answer in vain. With Hampshire this is rarely the case. He writes with great clarity (and gives French equivalents of all key terms), a touch of humour and a ready eye for the odd (and often illuminating) fact. This book is absolutely indispensable.'

The Riviera Reporter

'A must for all future expats. I invested in several books but this is the only one you need. Every issue and concern is covered, every daft question you have but are frightened to ask is answered honestly without pulling any punches. Highly recommended.'

Reader

'In answer to the desert island question about the one how-to book on France, this book would be it.'

The Recorder

'The ultimate reference book. Every subject imaginable is exhaustively explained in simple terms. An excellent introduction to fully enjoy all that this fine country has to offer and save time and money in the process.'

American Club of Zurich

SAID ABOUT SURVIVAL BOOKS

'The amount of information covered is not short of incredible. I thought I knew enough about my birth country. This book has proved me wrong. Don't go to France without it. Big mistake if you do. Absolutely priceless!'

Reader

'When you buy a model plane for your child, a video recorder, or some new computer gizmo, you get with it a leaflet or booklet pleading 'Read Me First', or bearing large friendly letters or bold type saying 'IMPORTANT – follow the instructions carefully'. This book should be similarly supplied to all those entering France with anything more durable than a 5-day return ticket. It is worth reading even if you are just visiting briefly, or if you have lived here for years and feel totally knowledgeable and secure. But if you need to find out how France works then it is indispensable. Native French people probably have a less thorough understanding of how their country functions. Where it is most essential, the book is most up to the minute.

Living France

A comprehensive guide to all things French, written in a highly readable and amusing style, for anyone planning to live, work or retire in France.

The Times

Covers every conceivable question that might be asked concerning everyday life. I know of no other book that could take the place of this one.

France in Print

A concise, thorough account of the do's and don'ts for a foreigner in Switzerland. Crammed with useful information and lightened with humorous quips which make the facts more readable.

American Citizens Abroad

'I found this a wonderful book crammed with facts and figures, with a straightforward approach to the problems and pitfalls you are likely to encounter. The whole laced with humour and a thorough understanding of what's involved. Gets my vote!'

Reader

'A vital tool in the war against real estate sharks; don't even think of buying without reading this book first!'

Everything Spain

'We would like to congratulate you on this work: it is really super! We hand it out to our expatriates and they read it with great interest and pleasure.'

ICI (Switzerland) AG

SCOTLAND
North Sea
Atlantic Ocean
NORTHERN IRELAND
Newcastle
R. Tyne
Carlisle
R. Eden
R. Tees
The Lake District
Isle of Man
R. Ouse
R. Ribble
Leeds
Hull
Irish Sea
R. Humber
REPUBLIC OF IRELAND
Liverpool
Manchester
Sheffield
Chester
R. Trent
Nottingham
ENGLAND
Norwich
R. Severn
Gt. Ouse
Birmingham
WALES
Cambridge
R. Avon
Ipswich
R. Thames
Oxford
London
Bristol
Reading
Canterbury
Salisbury
Exmoor
Portsmouth
Dartmoor
Exeter
Isle of Wight
Plymouth
English Channel
Isles of Scilly

CONTENTS

Cattistock, Dorset

INTRODUCTION

If you're planning a trip to England or just want to learn more about the country, you'll find the information contained in *Culture Wise England* invaluable. Whether you're travelling on business or pleasure, visiting for a few days or planning to stay for a lifetime, Culture Wise guides enable you to quickly find your feet by removing the anxiety factor when dealing with a foreign culture.

Culture Wise England is essential reading for anyone planning to visit England, including tourists (particularly travellers planning to stay a number of weeks or months), business people, migrants, retirees, holiday homeowners and transferees. It's designed to help newcomers avoid cultural and social gaffes; make friends and influence people; improve communications (both verbal and non-verbal); and enhance your understanding of England and the English people. It explains what to expect, how to behave in most situations, and how to get along with the locals and feel at home – rather than feeling like a fish out of water. It isn't, however, simply a monologue of dry facts and figures, but a practical and entertaining look at life in England – as it really is – and not necessarily as the tourist brochures would have you believe.

Adjusting to a different environment and culture in any foreign country can be a traumatic and stressful experience, and England is no exception. You need to adapt to new customs and traditions, and discover the English way of doing things; whether it's sharing a few bevvies with your pals down the boozer after a hard week's graft, having Rosie Lee with the trouble and strife and pie and liquor, or going for a chicken masala at your local Indian. England is a land where many things are done differently: where not only do people drive on the left (which can be disconcerting if you usually drive on the right), they drink their tea with milk and their beer warm, and where 'flying the English flag' is politically incorrect and may be construed as racist.

A period spent in England is a wonderful way to enrich your life, broaden your horizons, and hopefully expand your circle of friends. We trust this book will help you avoid the pitfalls of visiting or living in England and smooth your way to a happy and rewarding stay.

Good luck!

David Hampshire & Liz Opalka
July 2007

1.

ADAPTING TO A NEW CULTURE

With almost daily advances in technology, ever-cheaper flights and knowledge about almost anywhere in the world at our fingertips, travelling, living, working and retiring abroad has never been more accessible. Current migration patterns also suggest that it has never been more popular. But, although globalisation means the world has in effect 'shrunk', every country is still a 'world' of its own, each with a unique culture.

Some people find it impossible to adapt to a new life in a different culture – for reasons which are many and varied. According to statistics, partner dissatisfaction is the most common cause; non-working spouses frequently find themselves without a role in the new country, and sometimes with little to do other than think about what they would be doing if they were at home. Family concerns – which may include the children's education and worries about loved ones at home – can also deeply affect those living abroad.

'There are no foreign lands. It is the traveller only who is foreign.'
Robert Louis Stevenson (Scottish writer)

Many factors contribute to how well you adapt to a new culture, for example, your personality, education, foreign language skills, mental health, maturity, socio-economic conditions, travel experience, and family and social support systems. How you handle the stress of change, and bring balance and meaning to your life, is the principal indicator of how well you'll adjust to a different country, culture and business environment.

ENGLAND IS DIFFERENT

Many people underestimate the cultural isolation that can be experienced in a foreign country, particularly one with a different language. Even in a country where you speak the language fluently, you'll find that many aspects of the culture are surprisingly foreign, despite the cosy familiarity engendered by cinema, television and books. England is perceived by many foreigners as an 'easy' option, because it is part of the European Union, English is spoken, it has a multicultural society, and there are well established foreign communities in all the large towns and cities.

However, when you move to England, you'll need to adapt to a totally new environment and new challenges; these may include a new job, a new home and a new physical environment, which can be overwhelming – and all this before you even encounter the local culture. In your home country, you may have left a job where you were the boss, were extremely competent, and knew everyone. In England, you may be virtually a trainee (especially if your English isn't fluent) and not know any of your colleagues. The sensation that you're starting from scratch can be demoralising.

Even if you move to a major city, many things that you're used to and take for granted in your home country may not be available in England, e.g. certain kinds of food, opportunities to enjoy your favourite hobby or sport, and books and television programmes in your own language. Over time, this lack of 'home comforts' can wear you down. You will also have to contend with the lack of a local support network. At home you have a circle of friends, acquaintances, colleagues and possibly relatives you can rely on for help and support. In England there's no such network, which, until you make new friends, can leave you feeling lost.

The degree of isolation you feel usually depends on how long you plan to spend in England and what you will be doing there. If you're simply going on a short holiday, you may not even be aware of many of the cultural differences; although if you are, it will enhance your enjoyment, and may save you from a few embarrassing or confusing moments. However, if you're planning a business trip, or intend to spend an extended period in England – perhaps working, studying or even living there permanently – **it's essential to understand the culture, customs and etiquette at the earliest opportunity.**

> **'If you reject the food, ignore the customs, fear the religion and avoid the people, you might better stay at home.'**
>
> James A. Michener (American writer)

CULTURE SHOCK

Culture shock is the term used to describe the psychological and physical state felt by people when arriving in a foreign country, or even moving to a new environment in their home country (where the

> **'When you travel, remember that a foreign country is not designed to make you comfortable. It is designed to make its own people comfortable.'**
>
> Clifton Fadiman (American writer)

culture, and in some cases language, may vary considerably by region and social class). Culture shock can be experienced when travelling, living, working or studying abroad, when in addition to adapting to new social rules and values, you may need to adjust to a different climate, food and dress. It can manifest itself in a lack of direction and the feeling of not knowing what to do or how to do things, not knowing what's appropriate or inappropriate. You literally feel like a 'fish out of water'.

Culture shock is precipitated by the anxiety that results from losing all familiar rules of behaviour and cues to social intercourse – the thousand and one clues to behaviour in everyday situations: when to shake hands and what to say when we meet people; how to buy goods and services; when and how much to tip; how to use a cash machine or the telephone; when to accept and refuse invitations; and when to take statements seriously and when not to. These cues, which may be words, gestures or facial expressions, are acquired in the course of our life, and are as much a part of our culture and customs as the language we speak, and our beliefs. Our peace of mind and social efficiency depend on these cues, most of which are unconsciously recognised.

The symptoms of culture shock are essentially psychological, and are caused by the sense of alienation you feel when you're bombarded on a daily basis by cultural differences, in an environment where there are few, if any, familiar references. However, there can also be physical symptoms, including an increased incidence of minor illnesses (e.g. colds and headache), and more serious psychosomatic illnesses, brought on by depression. You shouldn't underestimate the consequences of culture shock, although the effects can be lessened if you accept the condition rather than deny it.

Stages of Culture Shock

Severe culture shock is often experienced when moving to a country with a different language. It usually follows a number of stages. The names may vary, as will the symptoms and effects, but a typical progression is as follows:

1. The first stage is commonly known as the 'honeymoon' stage, and usually lasts from a few

days to a few weeks after arrival (although it can last longer, particularly if you're insulated from the usual pressures of life). This stage is essentially a positive (even euphoric) one, when a newcomer finds everything an exciting and interesting novelty. The feeling is similar to being on holiday or on a short trip abroad, when you generally experience only the positive effects of culture shock (although this depends very much on where you're from and the country you're visiting – see box).

Paris Syndrome

Every year, a dozen or so Japanese tourists have to be repatriated from the French capital after falling prey to what has become known as 'Paris Syndrome'. This is what some polite Japanese tourists suffer when they discover that Parisians can be rude, or that the city doesn't meet their expectations. The experience can be so stressful that they suffer a nervous breakdown, and need to be hospitalised or repatriated under medical supervision.

2. The second stage, rejection or distress, is usually completely opposite to the first; and is essentially negative and a period of crisis. It can occur as the initial excitement and holiday feeling wears off, and you start to cope with the real conditions of daily life – except of course that life is nothing like anything you've previously experienced. This can happen after only a few weeks, and is characterised by a general feeling of disorientation, confusion and loneliness. Physical exhaustion, brought on by a change of time zone, extremes of hot or cold, and the strain of having hundreds of settling-in tasks to accomplish, is an important symptom of this stage. You may also experience regression, where you spend much of your time speaking your own language, watching television and reading newspapers from your home country, eating food from home, and socialising with expatriates who speak your language. You may also spend a lot of time complaining about the host country and its culture. Your home environment suddenly assumes a tremendous importance, and is irrationally glorified. All difficulties and problems are forgotten and only the good things back home are remembered.

Spinnaker Tower, Portsmouth

London Eye

> **The transition between your old culture and customs and those of your new country is a difficult one and takes time to complete. During this process, strong feelings of dissatisfaction may emerge. The period of readjustment can last six months, although there are expatriates who adjust earlier and (although rare) those who never get over the 'flight' stage and are forced to return home.**

3. The third stage is often known as the 'flight' stage because of the overwhelming desire to escape. It is usually the one that lasts the longest, and is the most difficult to cope with. During this period, you may feel depressed and angry, as well as resentful towards the new country and its people. You may experience difficulties such as not being understood, and feelings of discontent, impatience, frustration, sadness and incompetence. These feelings are inevitable when you're trying to adapt to a new culture that's very different from that of your home country; and they're exacerbated by the fact that you can see nothing positive or good about the new country, and focus exclusively on the negative aspects, refusing to acknowledge any positive points. You may become hostile, and develop an aggressive attitude towards the country. Other people will sense this, and in many cases either respond in a confrontational manner or try to avoid you. There may be problems with the language, your house, job or children's school, transportation, driving on the 'wrong' side of the road… even simple tasks like shopping may be fraught with problems, and the fact that the locals are largely indifferent to all these problems only makes matter worse. They try to help, but they just don't understand your concerns, and you conclude that they must be insensitive and unsympathetic to you and your problems.

4. The fourth stage, recovery or autonomy, is where you begin to integrate and adjust to the new culture, and accept the customs of the country as simply another way of living. **The environment doesn't change, what changes**

is your attitude towards it. You become more competent with the language, and you also feel more comfortable with the customs of the host country, and can move around without feeling anxious. However, you still have problems with some of the social cues, and you won't understand everything people say, particularly colloquialisms and idioms. Nevertheless, you have largely adjusted to the new culture, and start to feel more at home and familiar with the country and your place in it, and begin to realise that it has its good as well as bad points.

5. The fifth stage is termed 'reverse culture shock' and occurs when you return to your home country. You may find that many things have changed (you will certainly have changed) and that you feel like a foreigner in your own country. If you've been away for a long time and have become comfortable with the habits and customs of a new lifestyle, you may find that you no longer feel at ease in your homeland. Reverse culture shock can be difficult to deal with, and some people find it impossible to re-adapt to their home country after living abroad for a number of years.

> **'The whole object of travel is not to set foot on foreign land; it is at last to set foot on one's own country as a foreign land.'**
>
> G. K. Chesterton (English writer)

Whitby Abbey, Yorkshire

The above stages occur at different times depending on the individual and his circumstances, and everyone has his own way of reacting to them. Some stages last longer, and are more difficult to cope with than others, while others are shorter and easier to overcome.

Reducing the Effects

Experts agree that almost everyone suffers from culture shock and there's no escaping the phenomenon; however, its negative effects can be reduced considerably, and there are a number of things you can do before leaving home:

- **Positive attitude** – The key to reducing the negative effects of culture shock is to have a positive attitude towards England, whether you're visiting or planning to live there. If you don't look forward to a trip or relocation, you should question why you're going. There's no greater guarantee of unhappiness

> **'Travellers never think that THEY are the foreigners.'**
> Mason Cooley (American aphorist)

in a foreign environment than taking your prejudices with you. It's important when trying to adapt to a new culture to be sensitive to the locals' feelings, and try to put yourself in their shoes wherever possible, which will help you understand why they react as they do. Bear in mind that they have a strong, in-bred cultural code, just as you do, and react in certain ways because they're culturally 'trained' to do so. If you find yourself frustrated by an aspect of the local culture or behaviour, the chances are that they will be equally puzzled by yours.

- **Research** – Discover as much as possible about England before you go, so that your arrival and settling-in period doesn't spring as many surprises as it will if you don't do your homework. Reading up on England and its culture before you leave home will help you familiarise yourself with the local customs, and make the country and its people seem less strange on arrival. You will be aware of many of the differences between England and your homeland, and be better prepared to deal with them. This will help you to avoid being upset by real or imaginary cultural slights, and also reduce the chance of you offending the locals by cultural misunderstandings. Being prepared for a certain amount of disorientation and confusion makes it easier to cope with it. There are literally hundreds of publications about England, as well as dozens of websites for expatriates (see **Appendices B** and **C**), many of which provide access to expatriates already living in England, who can answer questions and provide useful advice. There are also 'notice boards' on many websites where you can post messages or questions.
- **Visit England first** – If you're planning to live or work in England for a number of years, or even permanently, it's important to visit the country to see whether you think you would enjoy living there, and would be able to cope with the culture before making the leap. Before you go, try to find people in your home country who have visited England, and talk to them about it. Some companies organise briefings for families before departure. Rent a property before

buying a home, and don't burn your bridges until you're sure that you have made the right decision.

- **Learn English** – As well as a positive attitude, overcoming the language barrier will be the most decisive factor in combating culture shock and enjoying your time in England. The ability to speak English and understand the local vernacular (see **Chapter 5**) isn't just a useful tool – that will allow you to buy what you need, find your way around, etc. – but is the key to understanding England and its culture. If you can speak English, even at a basic level, your scope for making friends is immediately widened. Obviously, not everyone is a linguist, and learning English can take time and requires motivation. However, with sufficient perseverance, virtually anyone can learn enough English to participate in the local culture.
- **Be proactive** – Join in the activities of the local people, which could be a carnival, a religious festival or a sporting activity. There are often local clubs where you can play sport or keep fit, be artistic, learn to cook local dishes, taste wine, etc. Not only will this fill some of your spare time, giving you less time to miss home, but you'll also meet new people and make friends. If you feel you cannot join a local club – perhaps because your English isn't good enough – you can always participate in activities for expatriates, of which there are many in the major cities. You should look upon a period spent in England as an opportunity to redefine your life objectives, and learn and acquire new perspectives. Culture shock can help you develop a better understanding of yourself and stimulate your creativity.
- **Talk to other expatriates** – Although they may deny it, many expatriates have been through exactly what you're experiencing, and faced the same feelings of disorientation. Even

Culture shock is an unavoidable part of travelling, living and working abroad, but if you're aware of it and take steps to lessen its effects before you go and while you're abroad, the period of adjustment will be shortened and its negative and depressing consequences reduced.

if they cannot give you advice, it helps to know that you aren't alone, and that it gets better over time. However, don't make the mistake of mixing only with expatriates, as this will alienate you from the local culture and make it much harder to integrate. Don't rely on social contact with your compatriots to carry you through, because it won't.

- **Keep in touch with home** – Keeping in touch with your family and friends at home and around the world by telephone, email and letters, will help reduce and overcome the effects of culture shock.
- **Be happy** – Don't rely on others to make you happy, or you won't find true and lasting happiness. There are things in life which only you can change. Every day we're surrounded by circumstances over which we have little or no control, and to complain about them only makes us unhappier. So be your own best friend, and nurture your own capacity for happiness.

FAMILIES IN ENGLAND

Family life may be completely different in England, and relationships can become strained under the stress of adapting to culture shock. Your family may find itself in a completely new and possibly alien environment, your new home may scarcely resemble your previous one (it may be significantly smaller, for example), and the climate may differ dramatically from that of your home country. If possible, you should prepare yourself for as many aspects of the new situation as you can, and explain to your children the differences they're likely to encounter, while at the same time dispelling their fears.

> **'And that's the wonderful thing about family travel: it provides you with experiences that will remain locked forever in the scar tissue of your mind.'**
>
> Dave Barry (American writer & humorist)

Culture shock can affect non-working spouses and children more than working spouses. The husband - it's usually the husband - has his work to occupy him, and his activities may not differ much from what he had been accustomed to at home. On the other hand, the wife has to operate in an environment that differs considerably from what she's used to. She will find herself alone more often – a solitude intensified by the fact that there are no close relatives or friends on hand. However, if you're aware that this may arise beforehand, you can act on it and reduce its effects. Working spouses should pay special attention to the needs and feelings of their non-working partners and children, as the success of a family relocation depends on the ability of the wife and children to adapt to the new culture.

Good communication between family members is vital, and you should make time to discuss your experiences and feelings, both as a couple and as a family. Questions should always be raised and, if possible, answered, particularly when asked by children. However difficult the situation may appear at the beginning, it helps to bear in mind that it's by no means unique, and that most expatriate families experience exactly the same problems, and manage to triumph over them and thoroughly enjoy their stay abroad.

MULTICULTURALISM

The good news for newcomers to England is that it's a largely tolerant, multicultural society, where people from over 200 nationalities live, work and play in harmony (most of the time). This has not only greatly enriched the English way of life, and added to its cuisine, religions, businesses and ideas, but makes it much easier for immigrants to integrate into society. Virtually all ethnic groups in England maintain clubs and societies to which newcomers are warmly welcomed.

In England, migrants are encouraged to maintain their culture and ties with their homeland – rather than abandon them – while being urged to embrace English values.

Coined in Canada in the '70s, multiculturalism is the term used for an ideology advocating that immigrants integrate into society while retaining and valuing the most important elements of their own culture, including speaking their own language and teaching it to their children.

Consequently, England has one of the most ethnically diverse societies in the world and a relatively low level of inter-ethnic conflict, although flashpoints do occur from time to time.

A NEW LIFE

Although you may find some of the information in this chapter a bit daunting, don't be discouraged

by the foregoing catalogue of depression and despair; the negative aspects of travelling and living abroad have been highlighted only in order to help you prepare and adjust to a new life. The vast majority of people who travel and live abroad naturally experience occasional feelings of discomfort and disorientation, **but most never suffer the most debilitating effects of culture shock.**

As with settling in and making friends anywhere, even in your home country, the most important thing is to be considerate, kind, open, humble and genuine – qualities that are valued the world over. Selfishness, brashness and arrogance will get you nowhere in England – or any other country. Treat England and its people with respect, and they will do likewise.

The majority of people living in England would agree that, all things considered, they love living there – and are in no hurry to return home. A period spent in England is a wonderful way to enrich your life, broaden your horizons, make new friends and maybe even please your bank manager.

'Twenty years from now, you will be more disappointed by the things you didn't do than by the ones you did do. So throw off the bowlines. Sail away from the safe harbour. Catch the trade winds in your sails. Explore. Dream. Discover.'

Mark Twain (American writer)

2.

WHO ARE THE ENGLISH?

Historically, England is one of the world's great nations, and although it's one of the smallest countries, it also ranks among the most attractive. England boasts fine cities with centuries of history; beautiful unspoilt countryside; a wealth of diverse regions to explore; a plethora of cultural, leisure and sports attractions to enjoy; and cutting-edge music, fashion and arts.

'The funniest thing of all is that even if you love England and belong to it, you still can't make head or tail of it.'

G.K. Chesterton (English writer)

Some 30m visitors a year come to England as well as thousands of emigrants, including many English returning after a spell abroad; and although they don't come for the weather, England has a lot to offer if you don't mind a long-term relationship with your umbrella. You might be surprised to find it's one of the most multicultural nations in the world – London is officially the world's most multicultural city – and it's also a land of contradictions. England is a country with a big personality, that can laugh at itself and keep a stiff upper lip in adversity; a nation which ritually loses at most sports but follows them religiously anyway; and a land of pub-dwellers, DIY devotees and serial queuers, who would rather make a joke than a fuss.

If you're planning to come to England for any length of time, you can expect some certainties: crazy weather, a battering of your wallet from the high cost of living, and a first-class feast of scenery, history and culture, which means you'll almost certainly never be bored (even if it's raining!).

To help you get a sense of England and the English, this chapter contains information about English history, the English character and a list of English icons.

TIMELINE

Below is a brief look at the most important events in English history, from the Romans to the present day.

55BC-AD43 The Romans – Among England's many conquerors, the first were the Romans who arrived with Julius Caesar in 55BC. By AD43 they conquered the whole country, but resistance from the locals led to them building a wall from east to west, from Bowness-on-Solway, just west of Carlisle, to Wallsend on the River Tyne estuary.

The wall, large parts of which survive to this day, was named after the emperor Hadrian, and created

the kingdom of Scotland. The Romans' legacy is considerable and includes a comprehensive road network, laws and the basis for the English language.

Pre-Middle Ages – Vikings from Scandinavia (what is now Norway and Denmark) conquer most of the east of England and the northeast of Scotland.

871-899 – Alfred the Great rules England. Alfred was king of the southern Anglo-Saxon kingdom of Wessex, which he defended against the Danish Vikings, becoming the only English King to be awarded the epithet 'Great'.

The Middle Ages (commonly recognised as the period from the 5th century fall of the western Roman Empire until the Renaissance at the end of the 15th century): during this time the English monarchy strives to dominate the Scots, Welsh and Irish, and to annex territory in France.

1066 – William, Duke of Normandy, defeats King Harold II of England at the Battle of Hastings and becomes the first Norman King, known as William the Conqueror. The Normans rule until the Plantagenets take the throne in 1154 (Henry II).

1215 – The signing of the Magna Carta (see **Icons**). This document establishes a significant constitutional principle, namely that the power of the king can be limited by a written grant.

1455 to 1487 – A series of civil wars known as The Wars of the Roses (after the white rose for the Yorkists and a red rose for the Lancastrians) are fought between the Houses of Lancaster and York.

1485 – The Wars of the Roses end when the Lancastrian Henry Tudor defeats the Yorkist King Richard III at the battle of Bosworth Field and takes the throne, becoming King

Demographics

Capital: London

Population: 50.7m (estimated)

Area: 50,346mi² (130,395km²)

Population density: 389 per km² (976mi²). London has a density of 4,700 per km² (12,172mi²)

Largest cities: London (7.2m), Birmingham (970,000), Leeds (715,000), Sheffield (513,000) and Bradford (467,000)

Foreign population: 4.9m (2001 Census)

Largest expatriate groups (overseas born): India (570,000), Republic of Ireland (420,000) and Pakistan (275,000)

State religion: Church of England

Most followed religions (2001): Christian (71.6%), Muslim (2.7%), Hindu (1%), Jedi Knight (0.7%), Sikh (0.6%), Jewish (0.5%), 15.5% claim no religion.

Henry VII of England and Wales. The end of the struggle between the Lancaster and York families comes when Henry marries Elizabeth of York. As a symbol of the union, Henry creates the Tudor rose, embodying the York and Lancaster roses.

1509-1547 – The reign of Henry VIII, who was most famous for having six wives. His divorce of his first wife, Catherine of Aragon, lead to a dispute with the Pope and the end to Papal authority in England.

1559-1603 – The reign of Elizabeth I, sometimes referred to as the Virgin Queen, Gloriana or Good Queen Bess – she was immortalised by Edmund Spenser in his poem *The Faerie Queene*. Elizabeth I was the fifth and final monarch of the Tudor Dynasty for almost 45 years, during a period that saw huge increases in English power and influence worldwide, referred to as the Elizabethan era or the Golden Age.

1588 – The invading Spanish Armada of 130 ships is defeated by the English navy, under the command of Sir Francis Drake.

1603 – James VI of Scotland becomes James I of England and rules until his death in 1625.

1625 – Charles I is crowned king.

1629 – Charles I dissolves parliament following a dispute over his tax-raising powers and rules alone, but when many people refuse to pay their taxes, he's forced to recall parliament.

1642 - Civil war breaks out between Charles' army (Royalists, known as Cavaliers) and troops led by Oliver Cromwell (Parliamentarians, known as Roundheads), a prominent figure in parliament. Cromwell's troops defeat the king in 1645, but a second civil war breaks out in 1648.

'You must not miss Whitehall. At one end you will find a statue of one of our kings, who was beheaded, at the other a monument to the man who did it. This is just an example of our attempts to be fair to everybody.'

Sir Edward Appleton (English physicist and Nobel prize winner) on Charles I and Oliver Cromwell

1649 – Charles I is executed and the monarchy abolished.

1651 – Charles II raises an army but Cromwell decisively defeats him and the king flees to France. During the three civil wars (see above), a greater proportion of the English population dies than in World War I.

Tower of London

HMS Victory, flagship of Admiral Nelson

1653 – England becomes a republic, with Cromwell as Lord Protector until his death in 1658.
1660 – Resurrection of the monarchy as Charles II returns to England and is crowned king.
1665 – The Great Plague during which London loses around 15 per cent of its population.
1666 – The Great Fire of London which lasts for three days, leaving 100,000 people homeless.
1689 – The supremacy of Parliament is enshrined in the Bill of Rights.
1707 – Union of Scotland. In the 16th Century, legislation had united England and Wales, and in 1707, Acts of Union are passed by the Parliaments of England and Scotland, forming the United Kingdom of Great Britain. These Acts abolish the Scottish Parliament and transfer the Scottish parliamentarians to Westminster.
1805 – The British navy, commanded by Admiral Lord Nelson (who dies in the battle), defeats a combined French and Spanish fleet in the Battle of Trafalgar (off Cadiz, Spain), in the most significant naval battle of the Napoleonic wars.
1815 – Napoleon is defeated at the Battle of Waterloo (south of Brussels) by the combined armies of England, led by the Duke of Wellington, and it allies.
1832 – Great Reform Act. The Act is seen as a landmark in the struggle to increase the electorate, and gives the vote to men who occupy property in towns with an annual rateable value of £10.
1837-1901 – Queen Victoria is the longest-reigning British monarch. Her rule is a time of vast industrial and economic expansion – the industrial revolution – and huge expansion of the British Empire.
1914-1918 – World War I, during which several hundred thousand Britons die.
1921 – The UK agrees to an Irish Free State, but Northern Ireland (Ulster) remains part of the UK.
1924 – the Labour party is elected to power for the first time, headed by Prime Minister Ramsay MacDonald.
1939-1945 – World War II. In 1939, Britain declares war on Germany

> **'Here is a country that fought and won a noble war, dismantled a mighty empire in a generally benign and enlightened way, created a far-seeing welfare state – in short, did everything right – and then spent the rest of the century looking on itself as a chronic failure.'**
>
> Bill Bryson (American writer),

after it invades Poland. Winston Churchill becomes Prime Minister in 1940, and British troops fight in many parts of the world against the Germans and their allies, the Italians and Japanese. Around 400,000 troops die in combat and 60,000 civilians are killed in bomb attacks.

British Empire

The Rise of the British Empire
Historians disagree over when the British Empire actually began, with estimates ranging from between the 12th century and the early 1600s. At its height it was the largest empire in the history of the world, and by 1921 held sway over some 460m people and around a quarter of the world's land area. The demise of the empire was hastened by World War II, and by the '60s most of Britain's former colonies had gained independence.

1948 – The National Health Service (NHS) is established.
1953 – Queen Elizabeth II is crowned.
1957 – The Common Market (later the EEC/EU) is created and the UK declines to join.
1961 – UK application to join the EEC is effectively vetoed by the French President De Gaulle (and again in 1967).
1973 – The UK joins the European Economic Community, now the European Union.
1979 – Margaret Thatcher becomes Conservative Prime Minister.
1982 – The UK goes to war with Argentina after it invades the British colony of the Falklands, which are liberated after a brief but fierce battle lasting three months.
1990 – Thatcher resigns and John Major becomes Prime Minister.
1994 – Tony Blair becomes Labour leader.
1997 – Tony Blair becomes Prime Minister. Referendums in Scotland and Wales support national assemblies in Edinburgh and Cardiff.
1998 – Good Friday Agreement on a political settlement for Northern Ireland is approved by voters in the Republic and Northern Ireland.
2001 – Labour party wins its second successive general election victory.
2003 – Britain joins the US in a military campaign against Iraq.
2005 – Tony Blair wins a third successive term with a much-reduced majority.
2005 – 52 people are killed and around 700 are injured on 7th July in four suicide bomb attacks in central London.
2007 – Peace finally comes to Northern Ireland, when it elects its own parliament, after the two major parties representing both sides of the conflict agree to work together. Tony Blair steps down as Prime Minister in July and Gordon Brown takes over.

> **'It is a culture... somehow bound up with solid breakfasts and gloomy Sundays, smoky towns and winding roads, green fields and red pillar-boxes. It has a flavour of its own.'**
>
> George Orwell (English author)

THE PEOPLE

England is one of the few European nations without a strong cultural identity. It has no national or regional costumes, dances or music and no visible cultural symbols. Until recently, the English even felt little allegiance to their flag. The growth of the independence movements in Scotland and Wales have changed this, however, and there's now a growing sentiment of 'being English'. For the first time in several decades the English are defending their cultural identity.

But defining 'being English' isn't easy, particularly as the country has such a multi-cultural society and there are strong regional differences – southerners are traditionally viewed as aloof and reserved, while northerners are generally more friendly and apt to chat to you in shops and on the street. Participants in the *Daily Telegraph* 2005 survey on 'Britishness' ranked a sense of fair play, politeness and stoicism as the main British characteristics. The Lonely Planet UK guide defines the British as 'uninhibited, tolerant, exhibitionist, passionate, aggressive, sentimental, hospitable and friendly. It hits you like a breath of fresh air'.The main characteristics of the English people that you can expect to encounter are described below.

Eccentricity

The English are famous for their eccentricity – the countryside is littered with 'follies' (towers with no purpose, built by rich people) and gardens displaying collections of china gnomes. A Yahoo!Mail survey conducted in 2005 found that over 90 per cent of British men and women admitted to (or claimed) eccentric traits in their personality (which seems much too high). As a nation, the English celebrate unusual behaviour and anything that deviates from the norm.

This is a country where wearing red socks with a formal suit, or spending hours train spotting, is all part of daily life, three-wheeler Reliant Robin cars are national icons to eccentricity, and many households have displays of relatively useless collections, such as thimbles and royal memorabilia. Few other

nations organise the largest home-grown onion contests, crawling through mud competitions and snail races.

Hard-working

The English have a strong work ethic, and as a nation work more hours than any other country in the developed world (according to a United Nations report in 2007, over 25 per cent of Britons work over 48 hours per week). Not surprisingly, this has a detrimental effect on family life and public health. In a recent survey conducted by the trade union Amicus, almost one in five workers said they were less likely to have sex because of long hours, and a third didn't have enough time to spend with their families. Fitness, leisure time, socialising and community work were also casualties of extended working days.

Insular

In spite of increased foreign travel, a large immigrant population and the fact that mainland Europe is a mere 32km/ 20mi away across the English Channel, England and its people have a very strong island mentality. Europe feels totally foreign and the English have little affinity to it – it's often referred to as 'the Continent' as though England was not geographically part of it.

> **'I know why the sun never sets on the British Empire; God wouldn't trust an Englishman in the dark.'**
>
> Duncan Spaeth (English professor)

The UK is a member of the EU, but the British frequently disagree with European policy, have no collective wish to join the euro currency, and there's even a national debate about leaving the EU! The United Kingdom Independence Party (UKIP) campaigns for withdrawal from the EU, and achieved 16 per cent of the votes (the Labour Party won 23 per cent) and 12 MEPs in the 2004 European elections.

Many English people 'feel' more American than European, and the UK has closer political ties with the US than any EU country, despite a shared history and geographical proximity. Expect extensive media coverage of US current affairs but little of European.

Obsessive

Few nations are without their obsessions and the English are no exception. The following are among their 'pet' obsessions.

Animals

Many English are obsessed with animals, particularly dogs and cats, whose welfare is often a top priority – the fact that the National Society for the Prevention of Cruelty to Children (NSPCC) is a later off-shoot of the National Society for the Prevention of Cruelty to Animals (NSPCA) says it all. The English support countless animal charities such as the NSPCA (the largest and oldest), the Blue Cross, the Rabbit Charity and the National Canine Defence League, with branches of animal charities in even the smallest towns.

Dogs are taken everywhere with their owners – expect to come across them anywhere: shows, exhibitions, stately homes, on trains and at the beach. The UK has some of the most comprehensive legislation in the world against cruelty to animals, and the French are nationally despised for eating horse meat, although fox hunting has yet to be completely banned in England.

Celebrities

There seems little doubt that as a nation, the English have an insatiable appetite for celebrity gossip, especially if sex (see below) is involved. Pick up any tabloid newspaper or lifestyle magazine or switch on the TV, and you're bombarded with images of celebrities. An endless number of Z-List celebs queue up to give their flagging careers a boost by being filmed ballroom dancing, ice-skating, singing, eating all manner of unspeakable bugs in the Australian jungle or even swapping spouses for a week.

The most high-profile celebs, such as Victoria and David Beckham, Kate Moss and Prince William's and Prince Harry's latest girlfriends feature almost daily in the tabloids. Even the most mundane of outings – Kate Moss leaving her house to buy cigarettes, for example – rate a photo and article the following day. English newspapers feature a steady stream of 'kiss and tell' stories – people who have had sexual encounters with celebrities, and are willing to spill the beans for a fat fee.

Drink

The English have a long-standing and well-documented love affair with the demon drink. From

> **'When I read about the evils of drinking, I gave up reading.'**
>
> Henry Youngman
> (British-born American comedian).

William Hogarth's famous 1751 engraving *Gin Lane*, highlighting the abuse of spirits by the working classes, to present-day sensational *Daily Mail* headlines and shock photos of drunken teenagers lying unconscious in the street, it seems that as a nation, the English are more interested in getting 'totalled' than enjoying a civilised 'tipple'. Not for nothing are 'pub crawls' – visiting several pubs in an evening and having a drink in each one – a popular weekend activity.

Recent research also makes sober reading, revealing that a fifth of English adults drink more than double the daily recommended limit at least once a week. Almost 4m people are thought to be dependent on alcohol in England and Wales, and alcohol abuse is estimated to cost the National Health Service over £3bn a year.

Sex

'No sex please, we're British' is a well-known catch-phrase, and portrays the uneasy relationship the English have with sex. The English

> **'An Englishman, even if he is alone, forms an orderly queue of one.'**
>
> George Mikes *How to be an Alien*

tabloid media is obsessed with sex, particularly if a celebrity is involved, and it features large in English humour – sexual innuendos are an important part of comic repartee – and sex shops thrive; but for many people, anything to do with the body and sexual matters is taboo and never to be discussed frankly – even in private.

In a country with one of the highest incidences of teenage pregnancy and where the most popular newspaper, the *Sun*, publishes a daily spread of a topless woman (know as 'page 3'), it's perhaps surprising to discover that the *Kama Sutra* was banned until 1963, and that public figures involved in extra-marital affairs are expected to resign.

Queuing

You'll find yourself doing a lot of waiting while living in England. Buses never seem to come quick enough, trains are often delayed and traffic jams are a way of life. Perhaps then it's not surprising that queuing is an innate part of the culture and that the English are obsessed with queuing 'properly'. Whether it's a bus or a bag of chips you're after, you're expected to form an orderly line and wait your turn uncomplainingly. Queue-jumpers are most definitely frowned upon, and nothing marks a foreigner out faster than failure to comply with this most English of 'rules', so you're well advised to 'get in line'.

Polite

One of the overwhelming English characteristics is politeness and good manners. 'Please' and 'thank you's' punctuate all speech, and requests and commands are made with exquisite politeness rather than say "Can you open the window?", the English prefer "I'm sorry to bother you, but could you possibly open the window, please?" Among children's first words are 'please' and 'thank you' – known as 'magic words' and the only way of getting something – and foreigners who don't use 'please' and 'thank you' are frowned upon and labelled as rude.

This universal deference for others has many advantages – the English listen to you when you speak to them, and queues are strictly observed. On the other hand, politeness is carried to the extreme, and the English even apologise when someone bumps into them, treads on their feet or interrupts them.

Private

The English are essentially private people and have a reputation for being reserved, and reveal little about themselves to anyone other than family and old friends. Few English strike up casual conversations with strangers

> **'If an Englishman gets run down by a truck, he apologises to the truck.'**
>
> Jackie Mason (American comedian)

HRH Prince Charles

(although many are quite happy for others to hear their mobile phone conversations) and many dislike the easy intimacy displayed by other nationalities, such as Americans and Australians.

The English cherish their privacy and have a deeply engrained respect for the privacy of others. It isn't common for an English person to invite a casual acquaintance into his home. Even work colleagues often limit their socialising to a drink in the pub after work, but may never socialise together with their colleagues and families at weekends, or only after a considerable length of time.

Royalists

While growing sections of the English public feel the Royal Family has outlived its usefulness

> **'Englishmen will never be slaves: they are free to do whatever the government and public opinion allow them to do.'**
>
> George Bernard Shaw (Irish dramatist & literary critic)

and now merely represents a burden on their tax bills (although the Keeper of the Privy Purse claims the Royal Family costs the taxpayer a mere 62p per person, per year), there remains a powerful groundswell of support for the royals. The outpouring of grief following Princess Diana's death showed just how deep the public affection is for some members of the Royal Family. The Queen, who has reigned since 1952, is admired by many English people for her dignity and stoicism, and her popularity has been boosted by a recent Oscar-winning film, *The Queen*, starring Helen Mirren.

Rule-followers

The English like rules and, above all, they like to follow them. Signs prohibiting activities are common in public spaces – such as 'no ball games' and 'no loitering' – and English parks have (long) lists of rules and regulations, known as 'bylaws', posted at their gates. Most English are law abiding and there's generally great respect for rules and regulations, which are followed to the letter. England must be one of the few countries in the world whose inhabitants worry about not paying enough taxes, rather than working out ways to avoid paying them.

On the plus side, this means English society is generally ordered and efficient – most drivers follow the Highway Code when motoring – and procedures are invariably carried out according to the rule book (unlike on the continent where anything goes). You can also usually be sure of fair play at every turn. On the down side, there's little room for improvisation in English society – many people have an inherent fear of things not being done correctly, although if they aren't, the English rarely complain (see Stoical below).

Stoical

The English are famous for their stoicism in the face of adversity and under any circumstances. In the *Daily Telegraph* 2005 survey on 'Britishness', stoicism was an essential characteristic for almost 80 per cent of those interviewed and the English were universally praised for their stoicism and 'getting on with it' in the aftermath of the 2005 bombings in London.

The phrase 'stiff upper lip' describes the English willingness to put up with almost anything without complaining. This is a country where

families have picnics on the beach in bad weather, commuters wait hours for delayed train services in patient silence, and few diners in restaurants complain about bad service or poor food.

Stoicism leads to the English being masters of the understatement, e.g. when the temperature plummets you might hear the weather described as 'a bit fresh' or a difficult situation described as 'could be worse'. However, recent studies showed that the stiff upper lip is actually having deadly consequences for the population. According to a survey by the British Heart Foundation, almost half the people in the UK ignore chest pains that could be heart attack symptoms, preferring to wait and see if they improve before seeking medical help.

Traditional

England is a paradox when it comes to change. This is a country that spearheaded the industrial revolution, and produced scientists such as Darwin and Newton, who fundamentally changed the way we think about the world. Yet a significant and powerful section of English society dislikes and rejects change, in other words, it's traditional. This tranche of 'middle England' strongly supports the Royal Family, opposes the euro currency and almost all immigration. Its mouthpiece is the right-wing press, in particular *The Sun*, *The Daily Mail* and *The Daily Telegraph*.

> **'Imagination is a quality given a man to compensate him for what he is not, and a sense of humour was provided to console him for what he is.'**
>
> Oscar Wilde (Irish writer & wit)

SENSE OF HUMOUR

Perhaps, the most endearing quality of the English is their sense of humour, and having a sense of humour is a fundamental part of the English psyche, and runs like a vein through almost every social interaction. The English love to laugh and make others laugh, and there's probably no greater insult than to accuse someone of having no sense of humour. Few conversations are totally free of humour, which takes the form of banter, teasing, understatement, exaggeration or just plain silliness. You'll often find that lurking behind even the sternest of English countenances, there's a dry line in wit.

Essential aspects of English humour include: using words with double-meanings so the listener is confused or expects the wrong outcome; sexual innuendos – "nudge, nudge, wink, wink" signifies something a little *risqué*; bodily functions – burps and farts are considered highly funny; ridiculous or unlikely situations; and laughing at themselves. The English are perhaps unique in their ability to make fun of their own mistakes, behaviour and character: although they like to laugh at others also, particularly the Americans, French and Germans. Above all, there's irony, which is the dominant feature of English humour and permeates a lot of it; and is perhaps the most difficult aspect for a foreigner (even an English speaker) to understand, particularly Americans. Foreigners often complain they find it difficult to know when an English person is being serious.

A lot of English people use sarcasm, colloquially known as 'taking the piss' or 'taking the Mickey'. Often this is done affectionately, and if someone takes the Mickey out of you, it's usually a sign that they like you and feel comfortable with you.

THE CLASS SYSTEM

Class may seem a relatively old-fashioned concept in the 21st century, but there's no doubt that England remains a highly class-conscious nation – it has been described as a society based on privilege, inherited wealth and contacts. At the top of the heap there's the upper class (the 'blue-bloods' or aristocracy), crowned by the Royal Family, followed at a respectable distance by the middle class (which is subdivided into upper middle class, middle middle class, and lower middle class), then the working class or lower class, and lastly, the underclass.

> **'Speech is the most important indicator of class – a person with an upper-class accent using upper-class terminology will be recognised as upper-class even if he or she is living in a run-down council flat. Equally, a person with working-class pronunciation will be identified as working class even if he or she is a multi-millionaire.'**
>
> Kate Fox, *Watching the English*

People were traditionally officially classified according to their occupations under classes A to E. However, owing to the burgeoning of the middle class in the last few decades (we are all middle class now), the government has introduced no fewer than 17 new classes (including a meritocratic super class of top professionals and managers earning zillions a year).

Within the English class structure, it's the professional middle classes who are most uncomfortable about the whole idea of class. Many English working class people are proud of their roots and happy to call themselves working class, while (as you would expect) the upper class English are also pretty comfortable with the notion of class and their position at the top of the pecking order.

The average family in England now has an average of 1.64 children, the lowest since records began in 1924. (It would be even lower but has been boosted by immigrants in recent years.)

Speech

When any two English people meet for the first time, the first thing they are likely to notice about each other is their speech (as soon as an Englishman opens his mouth he announces his class). Accents and vocabulary are hugely relevant to the English and people make immediate assumptions about the class of the speaker and where they are from.

CHILDREN

The Victorian maxim that 'children should be seen, but not heard', is increasingly untrue in England. Cafés and restaurants, traditionally non family-friendly, now make an

Hoodies

'Hoodie' is a disparaging term used to describe teenagers who wear hooded tops pulled down low over their faces. Hoodies are closely associated with yob-like behaviour, and some shopping centres no longer allow people wearing hooded tops to enter.

effort to cater for younger customers by offering special children's menus, high chairs and sometimes colouring books, crayons and balloons. Children aren't allowed in pubs except in designated areas, often outdoor (and therefore cold) or in purpose-built lounges.

Children generally go to bed early, e.g. 7pm, and few go out with their parents in the evenings. In spite of the fact that English society is more child-friendly, many people disapprove of children shouting in a public place and some may even complain.

Young people

English teenagers typically spend more time with their friends than they do socialising with their families. It's common for English teenagers to stop going on family holidays at around 16 years of age. When not with their friends, they are invariably watching TV or playing on their computer or video games.

Leaving Home

Spiralling house prices have meant that it's increasingly common for young people to live at home with their parents until their late '20s or early '30s. Young people who work and live at home in England are usually expected to contribute to the family finances and pay towards their keep.

ATTITUDES TO FOREIGNERS

The English have a history of racism and xenophobia and have been trading insults with their neighbours for millennia. However, although they spend a lot of time abusing foreigners the English are just as insulting about their own countrymen, and their prejudices aren't usually personal. Newcomers – wherever they are from – are usually judged on their merits and character rather than their nationality; and if they learn English, are friendly and work hard, are accepted unreservedly in most places (but don't flaunt your wealth if you make a lot of money, as rich foreigners are despised!).

The English have an ambivalent attitude towards foreigners, although there's less distrust and suspicion towards aliens in England than in many other European countries. Despite the fact that the tabloid press spends much of its time stirring up loathing of the European Union and mistrust of foreigners who (naturally) only come to Britain to live off the state, there's very little deep-seated xenophobia in England. The English are among the most travelled people in the world, hundreds of thousands own homes abroad, and they are generally open-minded and tolerant of foreigners and foreign things. There's little prejudice towards foreigners in business, and anyone, whatever his race, creed or colour, can become a success in Britain, which is why foreigners are so keen to gain entry to the country.

The UK is Europe's most multiracial country – almost 10 per cent of the population or 5m people

> **'Dangerous foreigners begin at Calais and don't stop until you get to Bombay, where they speak English and play cricket.'**
>
> Clement Atlee (British Prime Minister)

were born overseas – and London the world's most cosmopolitan city, where residents speak over 300 different languages, and live, work and play in harmony (most of the time). Migrants are encouraged to maintain their culture and ties with their homeland – rather than abandon them – while being urged to embrace English values. However, multiculturalism has been criticised in recent years for encouraging newcomers not to integrate and learn English; and consequently many foreigners (particularly Asians) in the UK, live in segregated communities and towns, apart from white English people.

Like the inhabitants of most developed countries, the English are concerned about the impact on their culture and way of life of increasing numbers of immigrants, particularly the influx of migrants from the new European Union members in Eastern Europe in recent years. It's estimated that by mid-2007, 650,000 had already arrived, which has put a severe strain on housing, schools (some of which teach children in 'dozens' of languages) and health services in some towns, which has inevitably led to tensions. This has led to a number of towns and areas, called 'hot-spots', being 'over-whelmed' with immigrants. A survey in mid-2006 found that over two-thirds of residents in these areas thought that there were too many immigrants, and over half thought they received unfair priority with regard to social services and state handouts.

Despite the increasing pressures from immigration, the UK is one of the most ethnically diverse societies in the world and has a relatively low level of inter-ethnic conflict, although racial tensions occasionally spill over into violence. The country certainly has its share of racists, bigots and xenophobes, but no more – and probably a lot fewer – than many other countries.

ICONS

Every country has its icons – people, places, structures, food (and drink) and symbols – which are revered or unique to that country and have special significance to its inhabitants. The following is a list of some of England's icons that you can expect to see or hear reference to. (The author apologises for the many worthy people missing from this list due to lack of space; it's a tribute to England that it has so many people worthy of the title 'icon'.)

Icons – People (Historical)

An interesting insight into the qualities British people most admire can be found in a poll carried out by the BBC in 2002 to find the 100 Greatest Britons. The survey showed that Brits seem to rate science, engineering and invention very highly, with one fifth of the top 100 hailing from these industries. The greatest proportion of living Britons on the list were from the world of popular music – evidence of just how influential pop music is in the UK.

Jane Austen (1775-1817) – Jane Austen vividly evoked the drawing room dramas of women living in the 19th century. Her novels, including *Pride and Prejudice* and *Sense and Sensibility*, are still popular today, and have been recreated in countless films and TV dramas.

Isambard Kingdom Brunel (1806-1859) – Brunel is recognised as Britain's greatest engineer, one of a small group who, in the mid-18th to mid-19th centuries paved the way for the Industrial Revolution. Brunel's work included designing bridges (notably the Clifton Suspension Bridge), tunnels and viaducts, and the first propeller-driven iron ship, the *SS Great Britain*.

Geoffrey Chaucer (1343-1400) – The poet Geoffrey Chaucer was a seminal figure in English literature. His *Canterbury Tales* remains a worldwide bestseller, and is believed to have been the first ever book to be printed in England, in 1476. The *Canterbury Tales* centre on a group of 14th century pilgrims journeying to the shrine of the murdered archbishop Thomas Becket.

Statue of Winston Churchill

Winston Churchill (1874-1965) – A former Secretary of State for War and Air, and Chancellor of the Exchequer, Churchill is recognised as Britain's greatest wartime Prime Minister and also the country's most admired person. He became Prime Minister following Neville Chamberlain's resignation in May 1940, and inspired England by refusing to surrender to Nazi Germany. Throughout the war he built strong relations with US President Roosevelt and maintained an alliance with the Soviet Union.

Captain James Cook (1728-1779) – Cook served with the Royal Navy and in 1768 was appointed commander of the ship *Endeavour,* in which he charted New Zealand, sailed the east coast of Australia and

Houses of Parliament at dusk

rediscovered the Torres Strait. Cook was killed by natives in Hawaii in 1779.

Oliver Cromwell (1599-1658) – After civil war broke out between King Charles I and parliament in 1642, Cromwell created and led his powerful New Model Army, which triumphed over the king's forces at the Battle of Naseby. In 1653, he became Lord Protector until his death five years later.

Charles Darwin (1809-1882) – Darwin worked on his theory of evolution for 20 years and published his work, *On the Origin of Species by Means of Natural Selection*, in 1859. Darwin's book created a storm of controversy because it turned the prevailing belief about how the world was created on its head. However, although his theory caused outrage at the time, it's now accepted as the orthodoxy throughout the world (except by creationists).

Charles Dickens (1812-1870) – One of England's greatest popular writers. When he was a child, his father was imprisoned for his debts, and Charles was sent to work in a factory. This experience had an indelible effect on the young writer, and the appalling hardships suffered by the poor in Victorian England are described in many of his works such as *Oliver Twist* and *David Copperfield.*

Francis Drake (1540-1596) – Drake was an Elizabethan sailor and navigator and the first Englishman to circumnavigate the globe. A life-long enemy of the Spanish, Drake was a vice-admiral in the fleet that defeated the Spanish Armada in 1588.

Queen Elizabeth I (1533-1603) – The reign of Elizabeth I is often thought of as a Golden Age for England. Theatres performed the plays of her contemporaries Shakespeare and Christopher Marlowe, the English explorer Raleigh discovered potatoes and tobacco in the new world, and scientist and writer Sir Francis Bacon was experimenting using snow to preserve food (he actually died after contracting pneumonia whilst trying to freeze a chicken). However, Elizabeth's reign was also a time when there was a great deal of poverty and hardship. She knew how to get what she wanted and could be fairly ruthless, but shied away from making tough decisions, such as what to do with Mary, Queen of Scots.

Guy Fawkes (1570-1606) – History has wrongly credited Guy Fawkes with being the instigator of a plot by radicalised Catholics to blow up the Houses of Parliament. The plot was discovered on 4th

Admiral Horatio Nelson (1758-1805)

Under Nelson's leadership, the Royal Navy proved its supremacy over the French during the period 1794 to 1805. Nelson's most famous battle at Cape Trafalgar (off Cadiz, Spain) saved Britain from likely invasion by Napoleon, but also cost him his life at the hands of a French sniper. Trafalgar Square in London commemorates the battle – at the square's centre stands Nelson's Column, topped by a statue of Lord Nelson.

Nelson's Column, London

November 1605, and the plotters were subsequently caught and hung, drawn and quartered. England commemorates the Gunpowder Plot on the 5th November each year with bonfires and firework celebrations around the country. Effigies of Fawkes are placed on top of the bonfires – a practice known as 'burning the Guy'.

King Henry VIII (1491-1547) – The king with the six wives is probably the most (in)famous of all England's kings. When Henry wanted to divorce his first wife Catherine of Aragon after she failed to provide him with a male heir, the Pope refused to grant the divorce. Henry went ahead and married Anne Boleyn anyway. The Pope excommunicated him, so Henry established himself as head of the Church of England and ordered the dissolution of the monasteries.

Sir Isaac Newton (1643-1727) – Mathematician and physicist Isaac Newton was one of the greatest scientific brains of all time. Best known for the discovery of gravity, which according to legend stemmed from seeing an apple fall in his orchard, upon which Newton realised the same force governed the motion of the moon and the apple.

Florence Nightingale (1820-1910) – Born into a wealthy family, Florence Nightingale's greatest achievement was to raise nursing to the level of a respectable profession for women. In 1860, using public subscriptions to the Nightingale Fund, she established the Nightingale Training School for nurses at St Thomas' Hospital.

Emmeline Pankhurst (1858-1928) – Pankhurst was a founder member of the Women's Social and Political Union (WSPU) in 1903, whose members were christened 'suffragettes', and shocked the country with their militant actions to gain votes for women. In 1918, the Representation of the People Act gave voting rights to women aged over 30, and women were granted equal voting rights with men (at 21) in 1928, shortly before Pankhurst died at the age of 69.

William Shakespeare (1564-1616) – England's greatest playwright, the Bard's work is so deeply embedded in the English language that many of his expressions are still in daily use. Shakespeare coined an incredible 2,000 words and his plays are still performed throughout the world on an almost daily basis. (See **Chapter 5** for more on Shakespeare's legacy.)

Joseph Mallord William Turner (1775-1851) – One of Britain's greatest romantic landscape artists, Turner's masterpiece, *The Fighting Temeraire*, was voted Britain's Greatest Painting by BBC Radio Four's *Today* programme in 2007. The annual 'Turner' prize, named in his honour, is Britain's most publicised and controversial arts award.

Queen Victoria (1819-1901) – The longest serving ruler in British history, Victoria reigned from 1837 until her death in 1901. The period of her reign was a time of huge growth for the nation, in terms of the empire, industrial expansion and economic progression. Under Victoria, a series of acts broadened the social and economic base of the electorate, and direct political power moved away from the sovereign.

Arthur Wellesley, Duke of Wellington (1769-1852) – The Duke achieved considerable military success – most notably defeating Napoleon (with the help of the Prussians) at the Battle of Waterloo in June 1815. In 1828 he became a reluctant Prime Minister. Opposed to parliamentary reform, he was an unpopular political figure and was dubbed the 'The Iron Duke' when he put up iron shutters at his home to stop the windows being smashed by angry crowds.

Sir Richard Branson (b1950)

England's most famous entrepreneur, Branson laid the foundations of his empire when he set up a record shop (Virgin Records) in Oxford Street, London, at the age of 20. The Virgin Group has since mushroomed into a huge international conglomerate, conquering the market in everything from cosmetics to cola. In 1999, Branson was awarded a knighthood in the Millennium New Year's Honours List for 'services to entrepreneurship'.

Sir Richard Branson

Icons – People (Modern Day)

The Beatles (1960-1970) – the Liverpool 'Fab Four' are one of the most critically acclaimed and successful bands of all time. John Lennon (1940-1980), Paul McCartney (b1942), George Harrison (1943-2001) and Ringo

> **'David Beckham loves texting. He was going to text in his vote in the General Election but couldn't spell X.'**
>
> Lenny Henry (English comedian)

Starr (b1940) released twelve studio albums from 1963-1970, including the classics *Sgt. Pepper's Lonely Hearts Club Band* and *Revolver*, and have sold more albums than any other group in history.

Sir Timothy (Tim) Berners Lee (b1955) – Sir Tim invented the World Wide Web in 1989 as an internet-based hypermedia initiative for global information sharing. He was knighted (with the rank of Knight Commander, the second highest rank in the Order of the British Empire) in the 2004 New Year's Honours list.

David (b1975) **& Victoria** (b1974) **Beckham** – England's most famous footballer, nicknamed 'Goldenballs', has managed to achieve a level of fame which many people feel far outshines his actual ability. The Beckham brand is a global phenomenon and his image rights far outweigh his earnings as a footballer. Beckham can deliver some killer crosses and free kicks, and was part of a hugely successful Manchester United side which won numerous trophies, including the Champions League in 1999. Beckham was transferred to Real Madrid in 2003 and in early 2007 signed a five-year deal with LA Galaxy worth a possible staggering £128million ($250m).

Former Spice Girl **Victoria Beckham** is one of the most

photographed celebrities in the country, and many believe that she's the driving force behind 'Brand Beckham'. She and David have their own line of perfumes, and Victoria has also branched out into fashion design. She is rumoured to be keen on launching a career in Hollywood, which many think was a factor in her husband's decision to join the LA Galaxy soccer team.

Tony Blair (b1953) – Tony Blair was Prime Minister for a decade from 1997-2007 and presided over many significant changes, including the creation of the Scottish and Welsh Parliaments, the establishment of an elected Mayor of London post, and the removal of hereditary peers from the House of Lords. Blair's tenure was a time of huge growth and economic stability for the country, with relatively low inflation and unemployment. However, his hugely unpopular decision to go to war with Iraq has severely dented his reputation, as the public feel they were misled, especially as no weapons of mass destruction (the reason for the invasion) were discovered.

David Bowie (b1947) – Bowie scored his breakthrough in 1972 with the album *The Rise and Fall of Ziggy Stardust* and *The Spiders From Mars*, about a sexually ambiguous rock star from outer space. Ziggy Stardust made Bowie a household name in England and the US.

Michael Caine (b1933) – Star of cult films such as *Zulu*, *Alfie* and the classic comedy *The Italian Job*. After a lean spell, Caine made a comeback with *Little Voice* in 1998, and has starred in a string of films since, including *The Quiet American* and *The Cider House Rules*, for which he won an Oscar for Best Supporting Actor.

Agatha Christie (1980-1976) – The Guinness Book of Records lists Christie as the best-selling fiction author of all time. Christie created two memorable fictional detectives – the Belgian Hercule Poirot, whose canny 'little grey cells' defeated crooks in 33 novels, and the bird-like Miss Jane Marple, who featured in 12 novels.

Diana, Princess of Wales (1961-1997) – Born into one of England's historic families, shy Diana grew up in exclusive circles before marrying Prince Charles and becoming the world's most photographed woman. Even when her marriage failed, she continued to captivate the attention of the public and the media worldwide. Diana's untimely death in a car accident in Paris in 1997 prompted an unprecedented outpouring of public grief.

Lucien Freud (b1922) – Freud came to England as a boy after his family escaped Hitler's Germany. The grandson of Sigmund Freud, he's Britain's best-known portrait painter, whose trademark is gritty, realistic and often nude portraits.

Hugh Grant (b1960) – BAFTA winner Grant has turned playing bumbling Englishmen into a lucrative art form. The floppy-haired one made a string of largely forgettable films before starring in *Four Weddings And A Funeral* in 1994, which became the highest-grossing British film in cinema history, taking over $244m at the box office worldwide. Grant survived a sex scandal to bounce back with another smash, *Notting Hill*, with Julia Roberts, since when he has had a number of other international hits including *Bridget Jones' Diary* and the follow-up, *The Edge of Reason*.

Damien Hirst (b1965) – Famous for his controversial exhibits, which include a shark in a tank of formaldehyde and animals in various states of dismemberment. An exhibit consisting of a rotting cow's head complete with maggots, newly-hatched bluebottle flies and an 'Insectocutor' to electrocute them, won him the 1995 Turner Prize.

David Hockney (b1937) – Yorkshire-born minimalist painter Hockney moved to California in 1966, a move which had a deep impact on his work. In 2005, his painting *Mr and Mrs Clark and Percy* was short-listed for the title of the greatest painting in Britain by Radio 4's *Today* programme.

Elton John (b1947) – One of England's best-loved music stars, John is still going strong in his 60s. In 1973, he established his own record label, Rocket Records, and soon formed a prolific creative partnership with lyricist Bernie Taupin. Among his most famous hits are *Your Song* and *Candle in the Wind*.

Kate Moss (b1974) – Kate Moss is easily the most influential and defining British model of the last decade. The nation has a fascination with Ms Moss and you can pretty much guarantee that whatever she wears will become a must-have item. The waif-like beauty from Croydon has weathered a cocaine scandal, bouncing back stronger than ever after the requisite spell in rehab. She is the face of a large number of brands, including Agent Provocateur lingerie, Rimmel cosmetics and the fashion house Burberry.

Laurence Olivier (1907-1989) – Olivier is revered as one of the country's all-time acting greats. When he was offered the role of Hamlet in 1937, Olivier explored the idea of adapting Freudian psychology to his character. He invented a new acting style to reflect the psychological torment of the character, a performance which earned him widespread acclaim.

The Rolling Stones (formed 1960) – often dubbed the greatest Rock and Roll band in the world, the famous five-some of Mick Jagger, Keith Richards, Charlie Watts, Bill Wyman and Brian Jones (who was replaced by Mick Taylor in 1969 and died shortly after) have released 29 albums and had 37 top ten singles. They were still popular and performing in their 60s.

Twiggy (born as Lesley Hornby in 1949) – Twiggy's elfin haircut, huge eyes and endless legs earned her modelling fame across the world.

She still graces billboards around the country today as a mainstay of a high-profile Marks & Spencer advertising campaign.

Icons – Sports, Sports' Stars & Sporting Events

Roger Bannister (b1929) – Bannister sprinted his way into the history books when he became the first person in the world to run a mile in under four minutes (3min 59.4secs) in May 1954.

Ian Botham (b1955) – Botham is regarded as England's greatest ever all-round cricketer. He was an outstanding batsman, bowler and fielder, and in a test career spanning 15 years, he scored 5,200 runs, took 383 wickets and held 120 catches. His most memorable performance was in the Headingly test of 1981 when he almost single-handedly destroyed the Australians. With England on 105 for 5 in their second innings and facing defeat by an innings, Botham came to the crease and scored 149 not out; with England still staring defeat in the face and the Australians needing just 128 to win, they were bowled out for 111.

Frank Bruno (b1961) – The much-loved boxer racked up an impressive 40 wins from his 45 contests. His crowning glory was lifting the World Boxing Council crown in 1995 after beating Oliver McCall.

Sir Bobby Charlton (b1937) – A Manchester United football player for all his career, and a survivor of the Munich air crash that killed many of his team-mates in 1958, Sir Bobby was a member of the 1966 World Cup winning team and European Footballer of the Year in the same year. He remains England's highest goal scorer with 49 goals and is the third most-capped player with 106 caps.

Sebastian (Seb) Newbold Coe (b1956) – Athlete Coe won four Olympic medals (including golds at 1,500m in Moscow in 1980 and again at Los Angeles in 1984 – the only person to win back-to-back golds at this distance). Seb Coe headed London's successful bid to host the 2012 Olympics, and is now the chairman of the London Organising Committee for the Olympic Games. He became a Member of Parliament in 1992 and was given a peerage in 2000.

Cricket – A mystery to many foreigners who don't hail from Commonwealth countries (and probably to most of England's females), cricket is essentially a bat and ball game played with two teams of 11 players. The winning side is the one that scores the most

Tim Henman (b1974)

Although he has never been able to realise the nation's dream of winning Wimbledon, the tennis pro from Oxford is much loved for his heroic performances on centre court. For the past decade, the nation has been gripped by a strange fervour dubbed 'Henmania' during Wimbledon fortnight, as Tim's every serve, slice and volley has been watched with bated breath.

Tim Henman

runs, usually the aggregate of two innings. Batsmen must protect their wicket, a set of three parallel wooden stakes known as stumps, driven into the ground with two small crosspieces (bails) laid on top. Test Matches are played over up to five days.

Desert Orchid (1979-2006) – One of England's most legendary and popular racehorses, the grey won 34 races in total, including the Cheltenham Gold Cup. Desert Orchid was so popular that he received hundreds of birthday and Christmas cards. He died at the age of 27.

FA Cup – The most famous club competition in the world of football, the first FA Cup competition took place in 1871-72 and had 15 entries – in 2007 over 600 teams participated. Manchester United have won the Cup the most times (ten), followed by Arsenal and Tottenham Hotspur (eight). In total, forty-two different clubs have won what is one of England's best-loved sporting institutions.

Gary Lineker (b1960) – Footballer who won the golden boot for scoring the most goals in the 1986 World Cup, Lineker is England's second-highest goal scorer on 48 goals (he also achieved the rare feat of never being booked throughout his career). 'Nice guy' Lineker, an image he lampoons in a long-running series of advertisements for a brand of crisps, fronts the BBC's flagship football highlights' programme, *Match of the Day*.

Ellen McArthur (b1976) – The diminutive yachtswoman sailed into the record books after becoming the youngest person and fastest woman to sail around the world in 2001, which she followed up in 2005 with the record for the fastest solo circumnavigation of the globe.

Bobby Moore (1941-1993) – Footballer Bobby Moore is best remembered for captaining England to World Cup victory in 1966, although he was also an FA Cup winner in 1964 and a European Cup-Winners' Cup winner a year later. When Moore retired at the age of 36, he had won a record 108

> **'We haven't had any more rain since it stopped raining.'**
>
> Harry Carpenter (BBC commentator at Wimbledon)

England caps, and made exactly 900 appearances for his two clubs and his country. In 1991, he was diagnosed with cancer and died in 1993, aged just 51.

Paula Jane Radcliffe (b1973) – Long-distance runner Radcliffe is the current world record holder for the women's marathon, which she set during the 2003 London Marathon with a time of 2:15.25. Radcliffe has set numerous records, official and unofficial, on the track, in cross country and on the roads.

Steve Redgrave (b1962) – The greatest ever Olympian rower, Steve Redgrave won five consecutive Olympic gold medals (he also won a bronze that he prefers to forget about). After striking gold in Sydney in 2000, he became the nation's only athlete ever to have won gold medals at five consecutive Olympic Games.

Wayne Rooney (b1985) – Footballer Rooney became England's youngest ever player (at 17 years 111 days) against Australia in February 2003. One of England's most exciting players, he's capable of single-handedly changing games, and has scored many spectacular goals. Rooney is equally famous off the football field, and he and his fiancée, the free-spending Colleen McCoughlin, sold the rights to their wedding to a magazine in 2007 for a reported fee of £1.5m.

Wimbledon – The first Lawn Tennis Championships at Wimbledon took place in 1877, attracting a few hundred spectators; nowadays around 500,000 people stream through the gates during Wimbledon fortnight (June/July), and a global TV audience of millions watch players from over 60 nations compete for what many believe is the world's premier tennis tournament (and the only one still played on grass).

The Angel of the North

Unveiled in 1998, Antony Gormley's angel (overlooking the A1 and A167 roads in Gateshead) is one of England's most famous works of public modern art. Made of steel and standing 20m (66ft) tall, with wings of 54m (178ft) and weighing 200 tonnes, it's one of the world's largest sculptures.

Angel of the North

Stonehenge

Stonehenge is one of the most recognisable monuments in the world – the 5,000-year-old structure became a World Heritage Site in 1986. However, despite extensive research, the reason behind its construction remains a mystery.

Icons - Places & Structures

Big Ben – A common misconception is that Big Ben is the name of the famous clock tower that's part of the Houses of Parliament. It is, in fact, the popular name for the 13-ton bell inside the tower, which is actually called St Stephen's. The BBC first broadcast Big Ben's New Year's Eve chimes to welcome in 1924 and has been doing so ever since.

Oxford & Cambridge Universities – At the ripe old age of over 800, Oxford is the oldest university in the English-speaking world. In 1209, scholars fleeing Oxford found themselves in Cambridge, where they set up another university to rival the first. Oxford and Cambridge (collectively called 'Oxbridge') are the most prestigious universities in the country, and between them educate some 35,000 students (two-thirds of them undergraduates) spread over a total of 70 colleges.

Tower of London – During its 900-year history, the Tower has served as a royal palace, a prison, a place of execution and a jewel house (it houses the Crown Jewels). In the 15th century, Henry VI and the two 'Princes in the Tower' were murdered within its walls.

Westminster Abbey – In the 1040s, Edward the Confessor, last of the Anglo-Saxon kings, decided to build a large church near his royal palace, in honour of St Peter the Apostle. This church became known as the 'west minster' to distinguish it from St Paul's Cathedral (the 'east minster') in the City of London. Westminster Abbey has been the place of the coronation, marriage and burial of every British monarch except Edward V and Edward VIII since 1066. The current building dates largely from the 13th to 16th centuries.

White Cliffs of Dover – The 350ft chalk cliffs of Dover are a great symbol of England. Facing towards Europe across the narrowest part of the English Channel, an historical entry route for invaders and visitors alike, the cliffs are seen both as a bulwark against foreign invasions, and as the first glimpse of home for returning Englanders.

Icons – Symbols

The Archers – The world's longest running radio soap opera (with more than 15,000 episodes), since 1950, *The Archers* was originally billed as an 'everyday story of country folk' (even though it's recorded in Birmingham). It's the most popular BBC Radio 4 programme, and also attracts 750,000 internet listeners.
BBC – The British Broadcasting Corporation (BBC) was founded in 1922, and is the largest broadcasting (radio, television and internet) corporation in the world, and the most respected. It's a quasi-autonomous public corporation operating as a public service broadcaster, funded mainly through TV licence fees, commercial businesses and grants.
John Bull – The fictional character of John Bull was invented by the satirist Dr Arbuthnot in 1712. He appears as the personification of England in a series of allegorical stories about contemporary politics. Often accompanied by his trusty bulldog, John Bull was a man of the people, with lots of common sense, good intentions and a very English fondness for beer.
Britannia – Like Lady Liberty for the United States, Britannia is a female personification of Great Britain. Since Victorian times she has been depicted as a goddess, holding Poseidon's three-pronged trident, representing Britain's naval power. She has been depicted on the 50 pence coin since 1969.
Bowler Hat – The bowler hat was originally created as a hard hat (in 1850) for Sir William Coke's game wardens to wear when patrolling his estate on horseback. It subsequently became a ubiquitous piece of headgear worn by people of all social classes, but is most famously associated with 'city gents'.

The Domesday Book – A record of the great survey of England, completed in 1086 for William the Conqueror. William's inspectors surveyed England to discover who owned the land and their possessions in order to levy taxes. His inspectors' findings are painstakingly recorded in two books – Little Domesday and Great Domesday, which are preserved to this day in the National Archives at Kew.
Gardens – England is famous for its gardens, which include the world-famous Royal Botanic Gardens Kew (Kew Gardens), and a wealth of formal gardens maintained by the National Trust (see below). The typical English landscape garden originated in the 18th century, containing statues, water and formal

elements; one of the most famous designers was Capability Brown (1716- 1783)

Jerusalem – A patriotic song, much based on William Blake's poem (1804) of the same name, which was an excerpt from the preface to one of his 'prophetic books', *Milton*, and set to music by composer Hubert Parry in 1916. Much loved by football fans, prom-goers (it's traditionally sung by the audience on the last night), and Women's Institute members across the nation, many people would like *Jerusalem* to replace *God Save the Queen* as the national anthem.

Jerusalem
(William Blake, 1757-1827)

And did those feet in ancient time
Walk upon England's mountains green?
And was the holy Lamb of God
On England's pleasant pastures seen?

And did the Countenance Divine
Shine forth upon our clouded hills?
And was Jerusalem builded here
Among these dark Satanic Mills?

Bring me my bow of burning gold!
Bring me my arrows of desire!
Bring me my spear! O clouds, unfold!
Bring me my chariot of fire!

I will not cease from mental fight,
Nor shall my sword sleep in my hand,
Till we have built Jerusalem
In England's green and pleasant land.

The London Tube Map – The famous, award-winning tube map with its interlocking bold-coloured lines, was designed by a London

Underground electrical draughtsman named Harry Beck in 1931. Beck based the map on the circuit diagrams he drew for his day job.

Magna Carta – An English charter originally issued in 1215, the Magna Carta (latin for 'Great Charter', literally 'Great Paper') was the most significant early influence on the extensive historical process that led to the rule of constitutional law today. It's considered one of the most important legal documents in the history of democracy.

Miniskirt – The stuff of nightmares for anyone who isn't a long-legged beauty, or indeed anyone over the age of 25, miniskirts traditionally fall no lower than eight inches above the knee. The mini was created by designer Mary Quant and was the defining fashion symbol of the '60s.

National Trust – The Trust, which has 3.5m members and over 40,000 volunteers, is a charity which preserves over 300 historic houses and gardens (all of which are open to the public), and also maintains many important natural habitats, including forests, beaches and farmland.

The Pub – The name 'pub' is an

abbreviation of 'public house', of which there are over 60,000 in the UK. The Romans introduced the earliest pubs (or 'taverns') to provide food and refreshment for their soldiers, and they were built throughout England. In 965, King Edgar decreed that there should be one Ale House per village. The reason pictorial signs were first introduced was to help the largely illiterate population find their way to drinking establishments! The most common pub name in England is the 'Red Lion'.

Punch & Judy – A popular puppet show featuring Punch and his wife Judy, consisting of a sequence of short scenes, each depicting an interaction between two characters, most typically the anarchic Punch and one other character. A *Punch & Judy* show is traditionally performed by a single puppeteer, known as a *Professor*.

The Routemaster Bus – The AEC Routemaster is a model of double-decker bus that was unveiled in 1954 and introduced in London in 1956. The red buses became one of the most famous symbols of London until they were withdrawn from service in 2005.

Shops – It's said that Napoleon dubbed England a nation of shopkeepers (unfit to wage war against France), and while this may no longer be true, it's certainly a nation of compulsive shoppers. Among the nations most popular stores, are Fortnum & Masons and Harrods (London), and the chain stores Boots, John Lewis, Marks & Spencer and WH Smith.

The Red Telephone Box

Designed by Sir Giles Gilbert Scott in 1924, the red telephone box is a familiar sight on the streets of England, despite a reduction in their numbers in recent years due to the introduction of mobile phones. The wet climate necessitated protecting callers from the elements and the colour red was chosen to make them easy to spot.

Women's Institute – The National Federation of Women's Institutes (NFWI), known simply as the WI, is the largest voluntary organisation for women in the UK with over 200,000 members and almost 7,000 groups. Founded in 1915, the WI plays a unique role in providing women with educational opportunities and the chance to build new skills, take part in a wide variety of activities and campaign on issues that matter to them and their communities.

> 'The only way to eat well in England is to have breakfast three times a day.'
> Somerset Maugham (English writer)

Icons – Food & Drink

Ales – Britain is famous for its beers (or ales), notably bitter and stout (formally porter). Bitter is a well-hopped draught ale, usually copper-coloured, with a slight but distinctive bitter taste. In recent years there has been a resurgence of traditional (cask-conditioned – the yeast is still present in the barrel) beers, called 'real ale', spear-headed by the Campaign for Real Ale (CAMRA) and often made by micro breweries. Stout is a sweet or dry, black beverage made from roasted barley, the most famous being Guinness (which is actually Irish but is popular throughout Britain).

Afternoon Tea – Anna, the Duchess of Bedford, is credited with starting the tradition of afternoon tea in 1830, when she began eating a light afternoon meal to tide her over the period between lunch and dinner. A decade later, and ladies across London were chatting over wafer-thin sandwiches, cakes and pots of tea, which remains a tradition among the upper and middle classes to this day.

Bangers & Mash – An English favourite, especially in colder months, bangers and mash is a simple dish of sausages and mashed potato, often served with rich gravy. The term 'bangers' stems from World War II, when sausages contained so much water that, when fried, they exploded with a bang!

Cheddar Cheese – Legend has it that Cheddar cheese was discovered by chance in the 16th century, after a village milkmaid left a pail of milk in the Cheddar Gorge caves. When she returned, she found that the milk had turned into cheese, and the world-famous brand was born. To make true Cheddar, it must be cut into blocks after its first churning, while still soft and just starting to set.

Curry – The English love their curry, and many now consider it the national dish. However, the type of fare you'll find in curry houses has been tailored to English tastes and bears little resemblance to anything you'll find in India (although many claim English curry is better). Indian restaurants in England are also strangely homogenous; order a chicken korma or lamb rogan josh and it will pretty much taste, the same, whether you're in Derby

English Breakfast

The traditional English breakfast is an artery-clogging confection comprising some or all of the following items: sausage, bacon, eggs (usually fried or scrambled), fried bread, tomatoes, mushrooms, sauté potatoes, black pudding and baked beans. It goes without saying that prolonged exposure to such calorific fry ups could serious damage your health. Not surprisingly, few English people start their mornings with a full English breakfast nowadays, although fry-ups remain popular at weekends.

or Devon, Dundee or Darlington. Chicken tikka masala is now officially recognised as the national dish, having overtaken fish and chips in popularity.

Fish & Chips – In 1860, Joseph Malin opened the first business in London selling fried fish and chipped potatoes. Ever since, fish and chips have been a cornerstone of English cuisine. Nowadays there are around 8,600 fish and chip shops in Britain, and the nation munches its way through millions of portions a week.

Marmite – A savoury spread made from yeast extract, a by-product of brewing, Marmite has been a favourite with the British since it was first produced in 1902. Today it's an institution among Britons, and is traditionally eaten as a savoury spread on bread, toast and savoury biscuits. It has a number of imitators, foremost of which is Vegemite, made in Australia.

Pork Pie – A traditional British food, a pork pie (called a 'growler' in Yorkshire) consists of pork and pork jelly in a hot water crust pastry, and is normally eaten cold. The original and best pork pies are made in and around Melton Mowbray, using uncured meat, while the more common commercial pies use cured meat.

Roast Beef & Yorkshire Pudding – One of England's favourite meals, traditionally eaten for Sunday lunch. Yorkshire pudding is made by mixing eggs, plain flour, milk, a pinch of salt and water. This batter is then poured into a very hot, greased baking tin, and baked at a high heat until it has risen. Yorkshire pudding is traditionally served with roast beef, or baked with sausages, when it's known as 'toad in the hole'. Sandwiches – The lunchtime

> **'Even today, well-brought up English girls are taught to boil all vegetables for at least a month and a half, just in case one of the dinner guests comes without his teeth.'**
>
> Calvin Trillin (American journalist & humourist)

Sandwiches – The lunchtime choice for many English people, the sandwich was named after the 18th century fourth Earl of Sandwich, John Montagu. The Earl was an obsessive gambler and would ask his servants to place meat between slices of bread, so that he could carry on playing cards without getting his hands grubby. In the north of England, sandwiches may be called 'sarnies' or 'butties'.
Stilton cheese – The only British cheese with its own certification trademark, Stilton was first made in the early 18th century in the midlands of England. It is made by just six dairies in the counties of Leicestershire, Nottinghamshire and Derbyshire (using the original recipe), who are licensed to produce the creamy, blue-veined cheese.
Tea – For the English, tea is the band-aid of beverages, an instant restorative which is offered as the cure-all for everything from a broken heart to a broken-down car. Most English people take their tea with milk (and possibly sugar) rather than with lemon or herbs (or black), although herbal teas and green tea are increasingly popular. Tea is drunk at almost any time of the day or night, and the English drink around 200m cups a day.
Toast – Whether it's beans (or eggs) on toast, cheese on toast or simply a good wedge of white bread with a generous coating of butter and jam, toast is a much-loved English comfort food at any time of the day.

Lacey Green Windmill, Bucks

9
BED
BREAKFAST
9
BED
BREAKFAST

3.

GETTING STARTED

One of the most difficult stages of adjustment to a new country are those first few days when you have a million and one things to do. This is stressful enough without the addition of cultural differences. This chapter is designed to help you overcome the challenges of arriving and settling in England, including those posed by obtaining a visa, finding accommodation, renting or buying a car, obtaining healthcare, council services and utilities, finding schools for your children, opening a bank account, getting online and staying informed – and English bureaucracy.

'It is good to have one foot in England; it is still better, or at least as good, to have the other out of it.'

Henry James (American author & literary critic)

IMMIGRATION

Immigration controls, when you arrive in England, are usually straight forward, although the procedures may be longer for some non-European Economic Area (EEA) nationals because their passports and visas are thoroughly checked and stamped. All visitors' passports are screened and recorded and your luggage can also be searched. Young travellers may find themselves under more scrutiny than others, particularly visitors from 'exotic' regions, e.g. Africa, South America, the Middle East and Far East, who may find themselves under close scrutiny from customs officials looking for illegal drugs.

Immigration and customs officials are generally polite, but the onus is on you to prove your visit is *bona fide* and you should remain calm and civil, however long the entry procedure takes (carry a good book or a few magazines).

Visas

Non-EEA nationals may require a visa, officially known as entry clearance, to enter England, irrespective of the reason for your visit. To find out whether you need a visa, visit the Government-run UK Visas website (💻 www.ukvisas.gov.uk) and complete an online questionnaire. This tells you if you need a visa, which application form to use and where to make your application.

Visa Applications

Visa applications must be made at the British embassy, high commission or consulate in your

country of residence, and should be made several months in advance. You can usually apply for a visa online or make an application by post or in person.

Applications are judged on a number of factors, including whether you can support yourself and your family financially without help from the government, whether you have a criminal record, and, if you want to study in England, whether you've been accepted on a course with a registered education provider. Fees for processing visa applications range from £30 to £260.

If you require a work permit (most non-EEA nationals planning to work in England do), the application is now combined with the visa application. See the Home Office website (💻 www.homeoffice.co.uk), UK Visas (💻 www.ukvisas.gov.uk) or Passport (💻 www.passport.gov.uk) for further information.

During Your Stay

If you plan to leave and enter England more than once, you must ensure that you have a multiple-entry visa. If you don't and you try to re-enter England, you will be refused entry even if you have 'leave to remain' (the right to live) in England. Your stay in England is only legal for the duration of your visa or permit. If applicable, you must make sure that you renew your visa well in advance of its expiry date, preferably by applying in person, as postal applications can take a long time to be processed. For more information, contact the Immigration and Nationality Directorate (💻 www.ind.homeoffice.gov.uk).

If your 'leave to remain' expires while you're in England and you haven't applied for an extension, you're committing a criminal offence and can be fined up to £2,000, imprisoned and/or deported, in which case it's extremely difficult, if not impossible, to return to England.

Non-visa nationals

If you don't need a visa to enter England, you're classed as a non-visa national. Under new legislation, all non-visa nationals (except British nationals), without the right of abode in the UK, now require entry clearance for a stay of over six months. For more information, visit the Home Office website (💻 www.homeoffice.co.uk).

BUREAUCRACY

England is by no means the worst country when it comes to

If you need a visa but arrive without one, you will be sent back to your home country at your own expense.

> **Red Tape**
>
> **The phrase 'red tape' dates back to the early 19th century, when English lawyers and government officials tied their legal documents together with red ribbon or tape. It became a metaphor for bureaucracy after Charles Dickens coined the phrase in his novel, *The Pickwick Papers***

bureaucracy, and nationals from many countries, e.g. India, Mexico and Spain, will find the lack of paperwork positively refreshing. But bureaucracy still rears its ugly head in many aspects of English life, and numerous procedures still require more than their fair share of form-filling. Red tape is particularly visible in business – small and medium businesses are required to follow nearly 80 sets of regulations, and the British Chambers of Commerce (BCC) estimate that the collective cost of regulations on British business in 2006 was over £55bn! Public sector workers such as schools and university staff, police officers and National Health Service (NHS) employees, all complain about being weighed down and overwhelmed by unnecessary bureaucracy.

Paperwork obligations often mean they cannot get on with their real jobs – a report by the Academy of Medical Sciences claimed that thousands of lives are lost because medical researchers are hampered by bureaucracy in obtaining patient data. The Government has pledged to reduce red tape by a quarter by 2010. However, history has shown that when the Government reduces paperwork in one area, a slew of new requirements often follow closely behind.

ACCOMMODATION

The hackneyed expression 'An Englishman's home is his castle' still has resonance today – there's no doubt that property is a prized commodity in England, and owning your own home is seen as very important and the safest investment you can make. Around 70 per cent of the country's homes are owner occupied and 30 per cent rented. Of the rented homes, only a third are rented from private owners, with the rest rented from social landlords, councils and housing associations.

> **The average number of people living in a household in England and Wales is around 2.3, down from 2.5 in 1991.**

> In England, some 80 per cent of households are houses or bungalows and only 20 per cent are flats, maisonettes or apartments.

Rented Property

Rental property is a good option if you're planning to stay in England for less than three years, or you don't want the trouble, expense and restrictions involved in buying a house. Most parts of England have a good choice of rented property, but you should start your search at least a month in advance of your move.

Most rented property in England is let through letting agents or estate agents. Bear in mind that letting agents are totally unregulated in England, and you need to be on your guard when dealing with them. If possible, choose an agent who's a member of the Association of Residential Lettings Agents (ARLA – 💻 www.arla.co.uk) or the National Association of Estate Agents (NAEA – 💻 www.naea.co.uk), both of whose members have a bonding scheme or professional indemnity insurance to safeguard rental income and deposits. Although letting agents act on behalf of landlords (who pay their fees), be aware that many agents also charge tenants a fee. This practice is illegal under the Accommodation Agencies Act 1963, but agencies get round this by calling fees 'administration charges', which range from around £30 to £200 for checking references, drawing up tenancy agreements and preparing an inventory.

Also bear in mind the following when renting property:

- **Payment:** Don't make any payments in cash without obtaining an official receipt.
- **Furnished or unfurnished:** Around 90 per cent of English properties are let furnished, but the quality ranges from reasonable to stuff you'll probably want to throw straight into a skip.
- **Deposits:** You must usually pay one month's rent in advance plus a deposit against damages equal to another month's rent. These can both be **much** higher for furnished and luxury properties.
- **References:** Most letting agents require a reference from your employer, plus bank and credit references.

Landlords

English landlords are no better or worse than those in most other countries, but there's no guarantee

your landlord will be a good one. Some tenants find that properties managed by a letting company rather than an individual landlord are better maintained and repairs carried out more quickly, while others find that letting companies let them down.

As a tenant, you aren't permitted to sub-let a property without the landlord's permission, make any improvements or repairs, cause a nuisance to neighbours, or carry out any dangerous or illegal activities in a property or on its land.

Property Checks

What to look out for when viewing a property to rent or buy:

- Choosing a property with gas central heating and double-glazing will help cut down on your fuel bills, while storage heaters and other electric heating are expensive to run.
- Check that the front and rear doors are solid with secure locks, and that there are locks on all ground-floor windows.
- If a property has any gas appliances, the landlord must give you a copy of the Gas Safety Certificate. Under English law, all rented houses must have an annual gas safety inspection by a Council Of Registered Gas Installers (CORGI) engineer.

London is easily the most expensive place in England to rent – average rental costs in the capital are around £1,600 per month, compared with just £700 nationwide.

Buying a Home

Buying a property in England is generally safe, with full legal guarantees, but the following aspects of the purchase process may surprise you:

Estate Agents

Estate agents (real estate agents or brokers) in England have a poor reputation, and finding a good one is a bit like winning the lottery! However, the following tips should help to ensure that you don't end up with a cowboy:

- Use an agent who belongs to an Ombudsman's scheme (Ombudsman for Estate Agents Scheme: ☎ 01722-333306) – your right to complain depends on whether your estate agent is a member of a scheme, or the National Association of Estate Agents (NAEA – ☎ 01926-496800, 💻 www.naea.co.uk);
- Obtain a copy of the Office of Fair Trading's (OFT) guide, *Using an Estate Agent* (☎ 0800-389 3158, 💻 www.oft.gov.uk);

- **Never forget that the agent is working for the seller, not the buyer.**

Purchase Procedure

Unlike most other countries, buyers aren't required to pay a deposit under English law, and may pull out of a purchase process at any time with no penalty; therefore, not surprisingly, many buyers pull out at the last minute. Only when contracts are exchanged is the sale complete and irrevocable. The process of buying a home is long and takes an average of around 12 weeks. **It is easily the worst system in the world!**

Chains

Most home purchases in England are part of a chain of sales, and when one sale fails everybody in the chain is affected – a common ocurrence. Sales fail for numerous reasons, e.g. lack of finances, a survey shows serious issues or a party simply changes their minds. In an attempt to avoid breaks in the chain, the government has introduced mandatory Home Information Packs (HIPs – see www.homeinformationpacks.gov.uk), which require all homeowners or their agents to provide prospective buyers with certain information.

To give a purchase or sale the best possible chance of succeeding, keep in close touch with your solicitor and estate agent to make sure that everything possible is being done to speed things along. It also helps to stay flexible, for example being prepared to rent as a short-term measure, if it means you can keep the chain going and complete a sale.

Gazumping

The term 'gazumping' means to outbid rivals at the last minute. Despite being an exasperating and heartbreaking practice, gazumping is perfectly legal in England. Even when an offer you've made on a property has been accepted, the estate agent has a legal duty to tell the seller about any other offers received. However, these offers must be real (the estate agent cannot invent a bid or potential buyer), and if you suspect foul play, the OFT advises buyers to ask the estate agent for evidence of higher offers.

Mortgages

Mortgages are available from a huge number of lenders in England, including building societies, high

> 'The fact that English people choose to burden themselves with a massive commitment (mortgage), of which many fellow Europeans are free, illuminates something. It has to do with a sense that they are making an investment...but it speaks to some deep sense of the importance of individual possession too.'
>
> Jeremy Paxman (English writer and broadcaster), *The English*

street and foreign banks, direct lenders and insurance companies.

- **Applying for a mortgage**: In England, you can only apply for a mortgage after an offer on a property has been accepted.
- **Your income:** Three factors determine whether you can get a mortgage and for how much: income, credit history and the property itself (you're unlikely to get a mortgage on a ruin.)
- **How much you can borrow:** You can usually borrow up to 3.75 times your gross (pre-tax) salary, or 2.75 times the joint income of a couple. However, lenders are flexible, and some lend professionals up to five times (or more) their annual salary. The amount you can borrow also depends on how large a deposit you can put down. If you're self-employed, you may be able to get a self-certification mortgage, which allow borrowers to estimate their earnings rather than provide proof of income.In order to agree a mortgage, lenders need to value a property, although this is just a cursory inspection which won't show any serious problems. It's important to have an independent, more detailed survey carried out, such as a Home Buyers Report or a Building Survey.

BUYING OR HIRING A CAR

Car Hire/Rental

The largest car hire companies in England are Avis, Budget, Europcar and Hertz, all of which have offices throughout the country and at most airports. To hire a car in England, you must have a full British, European or international driving licence, and have held it for a minimum of one year (two years if you're under 23). The minimum age for car hire is usually between 18 and 23.

Buying a car

- is registered with the DVLA;
- has a valid tax disc and holds a current test certificate (MOT) if it's over three years old;

- has third party insurance, which covers your use of the vehicle;
- doesn't have outstanding finance (time payments).

If you unwittingly buy a stolen car from a private buyer, you may lose the car and the money you paid for it. To make sure you buy a vehicle from the legitimate owner (or someone authorised to sell it), you should take an independent qualified examiner with you to check that:

- the registration certificate is genuine (hold the certificate up to the light to check you can see the DVLA watermark);

Don't be afraid to try out your bartering skills with a car dealer who will often, but only if asked, lower the price or include extras in the list price.

- the 17-character vehicle identification number (VIN) matches the VIN on the registration certificate.

All of the above checks and more can be carried out online at various websites such as Car Data Checks (www.carchecksupermarket.co.uk/vehicle-check.html).

The organisation which registers drivers and vehicles and collects vehicle taxation in England is the Driver and Vehicle Licensing Agency (DVLA, www.dvla.gov.uk).

New Cars

Many new cars are sold at list price, but shop around for the best deal as dealers often compete in offering discounts, guarantees, financing terms (beware of high interest rates) and special deals.

Used Cars

Used car dealers have the same dubious (and usually well deserved) reputation in England as in other countries, and caution must be taken when buying from them. It's generally better to buy from an authorised main dealer, even if you pay a bit more, and obtain a warranty.

EMERGENCY SERVICES

The national emergency service (dial 999) covers police, fire and ambulance emergencies, plus coastguard, cave and mountain rescue services. 999 calls are free from all telephones, including payphones. When you dial 999, the operator asks "Emergency, which service please?" and you should

Emergency Telephone Numbers

The emergency telephone number in the UK is 999 for any emergency. You can also dial 112, which is the Europe-wide emergency number and the international emergency telephone number for GSM mobile phone networks.

state the service you need. You're immediately switched through to that service, and need to clearly state your name, location and give a brief description of the emergency.

Other services such as counselling in times of personal crisis (the Samaritans offer free and confidential counselling), and organisations offering free help and advice (e.g. Alcoholics Anonymous) are listed in telephone directories.

- **Ambulance service:** As well as providing an emergency transport service for those in urgent need of medical attention, the ambulance service also deals with the victims of accidents such as drowning, asphyxiation, choking, electrocution, serious burns and hanging.
- **Fire service:** The fire service attends fires, traffic accidents, natural and man-made disasters, and extricates people who are trapped, e.g. in buildings. The fire brigade may charge for special services, such as supporting a house that's in danger of collapse as a result of subsidence, or rescuing a cat from a tree.

HEALTH SERVICES

Health services in England are generally good, although patients complain of long waiting lists in the state health scheme, and those who can afford it choose private healthcare.

State Healthcare

Healthcare is provided free to all residents in England by the National Health Service (NHS), one of the first in the world to provide universal free healthcare.

Visitors eligible for NHS treatment

All visitors are entitled to free emergency treatment. If you're an EEA national, you're entitled to free National Health Service (NHS) treatment. Non-EEA nationals don't usually qualify for free medical services, unless their home country has a reciprocal agreement with the UK. Contact the social security authorities in your country, or the Department for Works and Pensions, Pensions and Overseas Benefits in England (☎ 0191-218 7777, 💻 www.dwp.gov.uk) for further

NHS Direct

NHS Direct is a telephone and internet (☎ 0845-4647, 💻 www.direct.co.uk) service staffed by National Health Service (NHS) nurses. If you're feeling unwell, you can call NHS Direct for advice as an alternative to visiting a doctor. NHS Direct staff can also tell you where to find your nearest doctor, pharmacist, dentist or support group. Calls are charged at the local rate. A textphone service (☎ 0845-606 4647) is also available for people who have difficulties with hearing or speech.

details. Even if your country doesn't have such an arrangement, you're entitled to free medical services if you're ordinarily resident in England.

Registering with a Surgery & Doctor

Doctors' surgeries are run by the member doctors themselves, and services provided vary from practice to practice; but as a general rule, all surgeries provide a wide range of services, including physical examinations, diagnosis of symptoms, prescribing medication and other treatments, and advice on health problems.

To register with a local doctor and surgery, either telephone or visit in person. Surgeries operate through catchment areas, i.e. residents living within a certain radius are eligible to join. If you aren't sure whether you're eligible, ask the receptionist. You also need to find out whether the surgery is accepting new patients, as some are full.

Making an Appointment

You can make an appointment in person or by telephone. Expect to see a doctor within two working days if your condition isn't urgent, although waiting times will depend upon the size of the practice. All doctors' surgeries have an out-of-hours emergency service.

Medicines

Medicines and drugs are obtained from a chemist (pharmacy), most of which provide free advice regarding minor ailments, and suggest appropriate medicines. Some medicines can be bought over the counter without a prescription. Supermarkets sell certain medicines such as painkillers and cold remedies.

Medicines that can only be prescribed by a doctor are called prescriptions. NHS prescriptions for medicines are charged at a fixed rate, irrespective of the actual price of the medicine. Certain people (e.g. students, pensioners, expectant mothers, the unemployed, etc) qualify for free prescriptions.

Childbirth

Childbirth usually takes place in a hospital, where a stay of two days is usual. If you wish to have your child at home, you must find a doctor or midwife who is willing to attend you, although this is not common practice for the birth of a first child.

Hospitals

The facilities and standards of NHS hospitals can vary considerably from excellent to basic. NHS hospital accommodation is in wards of various sizes, e.g. 12 beds, some of which are mixed. Many NHS hospitals also have private rooms.

If you have a baby in England, you need to register the birth with the local Registrar of Births, Deaths and Marriages (contact your local council for details), although hospital births are usually registered by the hospital. After registration, you're given a form (FP58) which must be handed in to your doctor's surgery.

INSURANCE

Insurance for individuals is compulsory in England in the following instances: if you have a mortgage, your lender will insist you take out buildings insurance; and if you drive a car, you must have third party motor insurance.

Other optional but highly advisable insurance policies include health, car breakdown, life, travel, pet and household insurance.

Health Insurance

Anyone living or working in England who isn't eligible for free treatment under the NHS is strongly advised to take out a private health insurance policy. Private health insurance is available from non-profit provident associations (e.g. BUPA, 💻 www.bupa.co.uk, AXA PPP, 💻 www.axappphealthcare.co.uk, and WPA, 💻 www.wpa.org.uk), and various other sources, including general insurance companies, banks and building societies. Most health insurance policies usually include consultations with specialists; hospital accommodation (usually a private room); nursing care; operations or other treatment (e.g. physiotherapy, radiotherapy or chemotherapy); physicians', surgeons' and anaesthetists' fees; all medicines, X-rays and dressings while in hospital; home nursing care; and a daily cash allowance when hospitalised under the NHS.

You cannot normally take out private health care to cover or obtain treatment for an existing or previous medical condition (usually you must

wait two years), and there's normally a qualifying period of around three months before you can make any claims at all. There are maximum age limits for taking out health insurance with some insurers, e.g. 65 for BUPA, although age limits may be higher if you're willing to accept some restrictions.

Home Insurance

Home contents insurance, also called household insurance, is recommended for anyone who doesn't live in an empty house – a 2003 report commissioned by *The Sunday Times* found that actual crime figures (as opposed to government figures) showed that England suffers one of the highest burglary rates in the world. A basic home contents policy covers your belongings against the same sort of 'natural disasters' as buildings insurance. You can optionally insure against accidental damage and all risks. A basic policy may include replacement locks, garden contents and temporary accommodation, but these may be optional extras.

Premiums

Premiums depend largely on where you live and your insurer. All insurance companies assess the risk by location, based on your postcode. It's important to shop around for the lowest premiums, which vary considerably depending on the insurer. It can be advantageous to have your buildings and contents insurance with the same insurer, as this avoids disputes over which company should pay if a fire or flood affects your home **and** its contents.

Security

Most insurers offer no-claims discounts or reductions for homes with burglar alarms, high security locks, neighbourhood watch schemes and smoke detectors. In high-risk areas, good security is a condition of insurance. Beware of the small print in policies, particularly those regarding security, which insurers often use to avoid paying claims. If there are no signs of forced entry, e.g. a broken window, you may be unable to claim

Vehicle Breakdown Insurance

Breakdown insurance for cars and motorcycles, when travelling within the UK and in most European countries, is available from British motoring organisations such as the AA, Greenflag and the RAC.

for a theft. If you're planning to leave a property empty for a long period, e.g. a month or longer, you should inform your insurer.

Claims

If you need to make a claim, keep copies of all bills, documents and correspondence, and send letters by recorded or registered post. Don't accept the first offer made, as insurance companies often try to 'get away' with making a low settlement.

EDUCATION

State Education

The majority of children in England are educated in the state system, where education is free. Note that private schools, also known as independent and public schools in England, are fee-paying. The quality of state education in England varies considerably, and some schools are excellent while others are poor.

In recent years, the gulf between the good and bad schools has widened (in state and private schools). In the worst schools, pupils have low expectations, lack ambition and aren't pushed to do their best. There can be a huge difference in examination results between schools, even those in the same area. Good schools are said to be getting better, while bad schools are getting worse (in recent years, failing schools have been threatened with take-over 'hit' squads).

Demand for the best state schools is very high, and it isn't uncommon for parents to move house in order to ensure they live in the catchment area of a good school. This has made the situation worse – some state schools have such a bad reputation, no parents want to send their children to them – and the Government is planning to change the catchment area system to end this practice. See **School Inspections** and **School Performance** below for further information.

The organisation of the education system varies from area to area, but the stages are broadly as follows:

- **Primary:** children attend primary schools from the age of 5 to 11; or infant schools, from age 5 to 7, followed by junior schools from 7 to 11.

In 2006, only a quarter of pupils obtained good GCSE (exams taken at 16) results in the core subjects that many employers now regard as essential. After 11 years of compulsory schooling, less than half of pupils obtained five good GCSEs, when English and mathematics are included.

- **Secondary:** the secondary phase is delivered through comprehensive schools, which take pupils from the age of 11 to 16 or 19. In some areas, post-16 studies for secondary pupils are provided by sixth form colleges or tertiary colleges.

The most important aspects of state education in England are described below.

National curriculum

The national curriculum was established under the Education Reform Act 1988, with the aims of providing a broad and balanced education for all, and raising standards by setting targets and monitoring progress.

All primary and secondary schools in England are required to follow the national curriculum, which consists of eleven subjects which all children must study at school: art and design, design and technology, English, geography, information and communication technology, history, mathematics, a modern foreign language, physical education (PE) and science. English, mathematics and science are termed 'core' subjects, and are compulsory up to GCSE level.

Key stages

Schooling is divided into four 'key stages', which help parents know what their children are learning at various ages. Parents receive a report containing the results of the exams, known as Standard Assessment Tests (SATs), held at the end of each key stage (at ages 7, 11, 14 and 16), based on national attainment targets. For further information contact the Qualification and Curriculum Authority, 83 Piccadilly, London W11 8QA (☎ 020 7509 5556, 💻 www.qca.org.uk)

> **'He shows great originality, which must be curbed at all cost.'**
>
> Peter Ustinov's school report

Examinations

The main examinations, known as the General Certificate of Secondary Education (GCSEs), are usually taken at 16, and pupils take a number of GCSEs (usually at least five) in individual subjects. Grades are awarded from A* (the highest) to E.

The General Certificate of Advanced (A) level is usually taken after a further two years of study. Passes in A-Level are the basis for entry to further education, and are recognised by all British and European universities and American colleges.

Education and Inspections Bill

In 2006, the Government passed the Education and Inspections Bill, which brings in several important changes for state schools. Key points of the bill include:

- Schools in England may set up independent 'trusts', with more control over admissions and budget;
- Parents can ask their local council to help them choose a school;
- Nutritional standards are applied to school meals;
- Local councils can offer free meals to all if they wish;
- Schools have the duty to ensure all children achieve their potential;
- All staff in schools have the power to discipline misbehaving pupils, both in and out of school;
- Detention can be imposed on weekends.

> **'Grammar schools are public schools without the sodomy.'**
>
> Tony Parsons (English writer)

School Inspections

The national government body, Ofsted, inspects all state schools in England at least every three years, which leads to a published report. The inspection report includes an overall judgement on the effectiveness of the school, and also indicates what a school should do to improve. Schools are expected to use Ofsted's recommendations as a basis for making any necessary improvements as quickly as possible – if they don't, a new head and staff can be imposed by Ofsted, or the school could even be closed.

School Performance

Every year the Department for Education and Skills (💻 www.dfes.gov.uk) publishes performance tables on the achievement and attainment of all schools. These tables provide a guide to how well a school is doing, as they list National Curriculum test results for each school in England, and show how they compare with other schools.

Most schools produce a prospectus for parents with detailed information about the school (some are also available online).

Miscellaneous

The following are some aspects of state education in England that you may find surprising:

- **Holidays:** The longest school holiday is during the summer, and lasts for about five weeks from mid-July to early September. Most schools also have a two week holiday at Christmas and Easter, and one week's half term break each term. Pupils also have days off on training days for staff.
- **Homework:** Homework isn't common in primary state schools, although all secondary schools set homework.
- **School day:** The school day is usually from 8.45am to 3.30pm.
- **Streaming:** Most schools tend to group pupils according to their ability from the age of 13 (a practice known as 'streaming'), in subjects such as English, Maths, Languages and Science.
- **Uniform:** Most schools require pupils to wear a school uniform. Uniforms vary from informal polo shirts and sweatshirts in the school colours to more formal blazers and ties. Uniform is also worn for sports.

Educating Your Child at Home

Most parents send their child to school, but you have the right to educate a child at home in England. As a parent, you must ensure your child receives a full-time education from the age of five. Local authorities carry out checks on parents who are educating their children at home to ensure that they're receiving a suitable education. If the local authority believes that a child isn't receiving the correct education, it has the power to serve a school attendance order, meaning the child must attend a school. Many local authorities have information on their websites about educating a child at home.

Illiteracy

Illiteracy is a problem in England, and is exacerbated by thousands of migrant families who don't speak English, or where English isn't spoken at home. Despite the officially 99 per cent literacy, it has been estimated that 20 per cent of adults in England have severe problems with basic literacy and numeracy. To put this into perspective, it has been calculated that one in three adults cannot work out the area of a room, while one in five would be unable to find a plumber in the Yellow Pages telephone directory. One report claimed that adults in England have poorer literacy and numeracy skills than those in every other European country, apart from Poland and Ireland.

Universities

Applications

Universities don't accept applications from individuals, and if you're planning to go to university in England, you need to apply via the central University and Colleges Admissions Services (UCAS), PO Box 28, Cheltenham GL52 3LZ (☎ 0870-112 2211, 💻 www.ucas.co.uk). UCAS publishes a handbook with over 100,000 entries, listing all universities, colleges and courses. Applicants can apply by post or online for a maximum of six courses (which may be at six different universities), for which there's a fee of around £15. UCAS processes your application, which is forwarded to the universities of your choice who then contact you individually. You should make your application in the autumn of the year before you plan to start your course, e.g. the autumn of 2007 for courses starting in October 2008.

Important Aspects

- Many English students go to universities quite a distance from their homes;
- Degree subjects last three or four years;
- Students may study a main subject plus one or two subsidiary subjects, and specialise in their main subject for the first one or two years.
- Many students choose a course combining a year spent working in industry or commerce, or living abroad with their studies, which is known as a 'sandwich course' and lasts four years.
- The most common degrees awarded are a Bachelor of Arts (BA) and a Bachelor of Science (BSc). Bachelors' degrees are given a classification, the

Cambridge University

> **'The exquisite art of idleness, one of the most important things that any university can teach.'**
>
> Oscar Wilde (Irish writer & wit)

highest of which is an 'honours' degree; awarded when the course includes extra detail in the main subject. The highest pass is a first-class degree, which is quite rare. Second-class degrees classified as 2:1 (very good) and 2:2 (average) are usual, while a third-class degree is poor. The lowest classification is a 'pass'.

- Tuition fees for UK and European Union (EU) students are set by the Government. In 2007, the tuition fees for UK and EU students were £3,070.
- The university academic year runs from September/October to June/July, and is divided into three terms of eight to ten weeks.

COUNCIL SERVICES

Refuse collection

Local councils provide households with bins for refuse (rubbish/ garbage), known as 'wheelie bins'. Household waste is usually collected on the same day each week by your local council (phone your local council or visit their website to find out which day). You should place your bin outside your house (many councils require bins to be placed on the pavement or the roadside) on collection day. Some collections are first thing in the morning so it's advisable to put your bin out the evening before.

Recycling

Most councils provide door-to-door recycling facilities for paper and glass. Some authorities also recycle cardboard and plastic and provide green bins for food waste. Many supermarkets also have recycling areas in their car parks, where you can dispose of glass, paper and sometimes unwanted clothes.

Other Rubbish

Most councils offer a free annual collection of up to five large household items, e.g. televisions, computers, fridges and furniture. You can also request further collections throughout the year, although there's a small charge

> **'And God said, "Let there be light"; and there was light, but the Electricity Board said he would have to wait until Thursday to be connected. And God saw the light and it was good; he saw the quarterly bill and that was not good.'**
>
> Spike Milligan (English comedian)

(usually around £5). Councils also collect garden waste, although you may have to pay for the plastic disposal bags. Some shops and charities offer recycling points for mobile phones. Councils publish leaflets containing information about the disposal of rubbish.

UTILITIES

Electricity

Supply

The electricity supply in England is 240 volts (V) AC, with a frequency of 50 hertz. This is suitable for all electrical equipment with a rated power consumption of up to 3,000 watts. Power cuts are rare in most parts of England, although some areas experience more than their fair share. Electricity companies only pay compensation for power cuts lasting longer than 24 hours.

Plugs & Lightbulbs

Modern English plugs have three rectangular pins and are unique, therefore, irrespective of the country you're from, you'll need to change all your plugs or use adaptors. English lightbulbs are the bayonet type (not the Edison type with a screw fitting), although you can buy adaptors.

Gas

Mains gas is available in all but the remotest areas of England. Using gas is the cheapest method of central heating and water heating – estimated to be much cheaper than other fuels. The emergency free telephone number to call if you suspect a gas leak is ☎ 0800-111999.

Electricity and Gas Bills

Electricity and gas companies usually levy a standing quarterly charge for supplying the service, reading meters and billing, which is added to your actual or estimated consumption. VAT at 5 per cent is applicable to all domestic bills.

Water

Ten private regional water companies provide water and sewerage services in England. Unlike gas and electric companies,

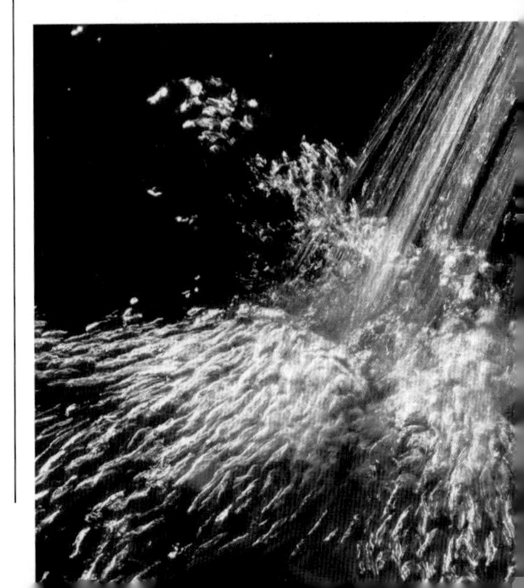

where you can choose your supplier, water companies have a monopoly in their area. Only 10 per cent of households have water meters, and these are billed for the actual water used, plus a standing charge. In all other households, water and sewerage rates are based on the rateable value of a property.

English tap water is usually good quality and many people drink it from the tap, although you may prefer to buy bottled water if you don't like the taste of chlorine.

Supply

Because of a shortage of reservoirs, especially in southern England, many areas experience an acute water shortage during prolonged periods (about a week) without rain, resulting in bans on the use of hosepipes and car washing. There's currently little water conservation in England.

> **'The itemised telephone bill ranks up there with suspender belts, Sky Sports channels and *Loaded* magazine as inventions women could do without.'**
>
> Maeve Haran (English author)

Telephone & Internet

Nearly all homes in England have a fixed-line telephone, and mobile phone use is among the highest in the world. Around half of households are connected to the internet, most with broadband connection. There are numerous providers: for information, contact your local telecoms advisory service (see your local telephone directory) or the Telecommunications Users' Association (☎ 0870-220 2071).

Installation

If you move into accommodation without a telephone line, e.g. a new property, you must request a line from one of the providers.

Making Calls

When dialling a number within your own exchange area, dial the number only. When dialling anywhere else, you must dial the area code before the subscriber's number. When calling a UK number from overseas, you must dial the international access code used in the country from which you're calling (e.g. 00), followed by the UK's international code (44), then the area code **without** the first 0.

Payphones are operated by BT (the largest company) and NWP Communications, and accept credit cards and coins. Emergency 999

calls are free from any payphone, many of which now provide internet access.

Mobile Phones

Mobile phone network providers include Vodafone, T-mobile, Orange, O2, and 3G. Details about areas of coverage are available on websites such as Price Runner (💻 www.pricerunner.co.uk).

Before buying a mobile phone, shop around and compare telephone prices and features; installation and connection charges; rental charges; and, most importantly, charge rates. One way to do this is via Buy (💻 www.buy.co.uk), which provides a mobile phone tariff calculator.

> **'I've often wondered how businessmen used to cope before mobile phones were invented. How did they tell their wives they were on the train?'**
>
> Pete McCarthy (travel writer)

Directory enquiries

Calls to BT national directory enquiries (☎ 118 500) cost 30p per minute, billed by the second, with an additional 25p standing charge per call. BT international directory enquiries cost £1.50 per minute, billed in seconds, with a £1.50 minimum charge. Use of the website service (💻 www.118500.com) is free. You can also access the free BT directory service on the BT website (💻 www.bt.com), and other companies such as 118 (☎ 118 118, 💻 www.118.com) or 192 (💻 www.192.com).

Internet Security

Bogus emails claiming to be from your bank and asking for confidential information such as your account numbers and passwords are rife in England. To avoid internet fraud, banks recommend you do the following:

- **Never give personal or financial information by email to anyone.**
- **Never click on links included in emails claiming to be from your bank.**
- **Beware of bogus emails and remember banks NEVER ask for confidential details by email.**
- **Keep your anti-virus programme regularly updated; experts recommend daily updating.**
- **Only use confidential information (unknown to others) for your user name, password and identify number when using the bank's secure website.**

Internet

There are a number of internet providers, including AOL (💻 www.aol.co.uk), BT (💻 www.bt.com) and Tiscali (💻 www.tiscali.co.uk). To help you choose, a number of sites offer news and advice on the various providers and provide feedback from people who have used the various services (e.g. 💻 www.thinkbroadband.com).

STAYING INFORMED

Television

Watching television (TV), referred to colloquially as the 'box' or 'telly', is England's most popular pastime. The British Broadcasting Company (BBC) – also known as 'Auntie' and the 'Beeb' – began daily radio broadcasts in 1922 and television broadcasts in 1929. The BBC is funded by a compulsory licence fee (see below), and is one of the few TV companies in the world without commercial advertising. Commercial TV, financed by advertising, began in 1955 with the launch of ITV, and there are now several companies offering hundreds of channels via digital terrestrial, satellite or cable TV, including:

- BBC TV – operates BBC1, BBC2, BBC3, BBC4 and digital services including BBC News 24;
- ITV – major commercial network, organised around regional franchises;
- Channel 4 – commercially funded but publicly owned national station;
- Five – national commercial channel;
- Independent Television News (ITN) – supplier of news to ITV and Channel 4;
- British Sky Broadcasting (BSkyB) – operator of digital satellite platform, Sky, the provider of film, entertainment channels and news channel Sky News;
- Virgin Media – a new, currently cable-only operator, which has set itself up to be a major competitor to Sky.

All broadcasters now provide digital broadcasts, and the analogue signal is expected to be switched off by 2012.

'Television is the first truly democratic culture – the first culture available to everybody, and entirely governed by what the people want. The most terrifying thing is what people want.'

Clive Barnes (Irish musician)

Licence

All homeowners with a TV must pay an annual TV licence, £135.50 for colour and £44.00 for black and white. TV licences must be renewed annually, and can be purchased from TV Licensing, Bristol BS98 1TL (☎ 0870-241 6468, 💻 www.tvlicensing.co.uk). The licence fee covers any number of TVs owned by the licence holder and his family at his main home.

Quality

British TV is widely recognised as the best in the world, although the quality of programmes varies from terrible to excellent. Home-grown TV companies produce around 75 per cent of all programmes, most of which are excellent. The competition to buy foreign, mostly American and Australian, programmes and exclusive rights to sporting events is fierce.

Programmes

The English love soap operas – dramas which chronicle the day-to-day lives of ordinary folk – of which the most popular include *Coronation Street*, a Manchester-based drama about the inhabitants of the eponymous street, and *Eastenders*, which follows a bunch of Cockneys in the capital. In recent years, reality and celebrity TV has become a national obsession, and there are programmes on everything from celebrity ice-dancing to wife swaps.

Satellite TV

You must buy a receiver and pay a monthly subscription to receive BSkyB (💻 www.sky.com) or Sky stations, with the exception of Sky News, which isn't scrambled. Subscribers receive a coded 'smart' card which is inserted in the decoder to activate it.

Radio

Radio reception is excellent in most parts of the country. In addition to the FM or VHF stereo wave band, medium wave (MW or AM) and long wave (LW) bands are in wide use throughout the UK. Shortwave (SW) band is useful for receiving foreign radio stations. There's no radio licence in the UK. The main radio stations are:

- BBC Radio - national services include Radio 1, targeted at younger listeners; Radio 2, a music station targeted at older listeners; Radio 3, classical music; Radio 4, general programmes and current affairs; Five Live, news and sport; and BBC Six, music. There's no advertising on BBC radio stations, whose programmes are among the best quality and the most popular;

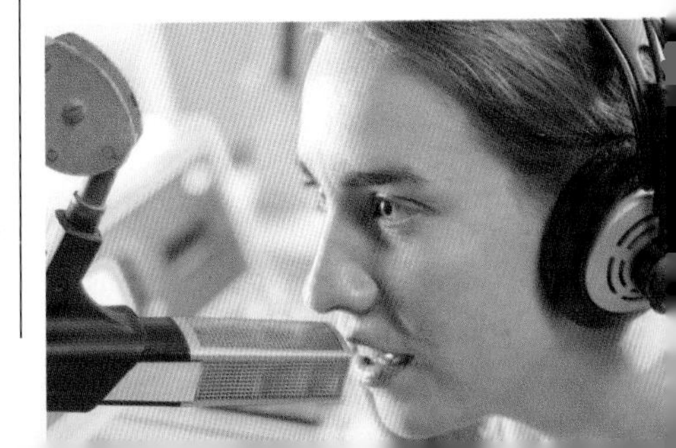

> **'I am amazed at radio DJs today. I am firmly convinced that AM stands for Absolute Moron. I will not begin to tell you what FM stands for.'**
>
> Jasper Carrott (English comedian)

- BBC Asian Network - for Asian communities in the UK;
- BBC World Service (see below);
- Virgin Radio - national commercial pop and rock station;
- Talk Sport - national commercial sports station;
- Classic FM - national commercial classical music station.

World Service

The BBC World Service broadcasts worldwide, in English and around 37 other languages, for over 770 hours a week. Although mainly intended for listeners outside the UK, the BBC World Service can be received in most parts of England. It aims to provide unbiased news, project British opinion, and reflect British life, culture, and developments in science and industry. For programme and frequency information ☎ 020-7240 3456 or visit 💻 www.bbc.co.uk/worldservice.

Commercial Radio

Commercial radio is hugely popular in England, and most large towns can now receive at least five commercial stations, with over ten in London. Stations provide a comprehensive service of local news and information, music and other entertainment, education, consumer advice, traffic information and local events, and provide listeners with the chance to air their views, often through phone-in programmes. Advertising on commercial radio is limited to nine minutes an hour.

Numb. 873

The London Gazette.

Published by Authority.

From Monday March 30. to Thursday April 2. 1674.

Warsaw, March 13.

THe Queen who hath been very ill, begins at present to recover, so that we doubt not but she is past all danger. The Senators and other chief of the Nobility are gone to the Convention at *Lublin*, which is held there, in order to the providing for the payment of the Army, and the directing several Military matters. The Crown General *Sobietski* is at present there, and under pretence of consulting about affairs relating to the Army, several private Conferences are there held concerning the Election of a new King; we every day more and more apprehend that great disorders will attend this Election, for that the Great Men of the Kingdom are very much divided in their opinions, as well as in their Interests; the Candidates are the Prince of *Transylvania*, the Prince of *Denmark*, Prince *Charles* of *Lorrain*, and Prince *Ragotski*; each of these by their Agents here, carry on their pretences with great earnestness, but as yet we cannot judge who is likeliest to succeed. Here is arrived the Count of *Zerstal* a Danish Gentleman, and though he remains here incognito without taking any Character upon him; yet it is not doubted, but he is sent hither by the King of *Denmark* to advance the Interests of his Brother. The Envoy of the Elector of *Brandenburgh* is likewise here incognito. From the *Ukraine* we have advice, that the Forces of *Muscovy*, have invested *Czechrim*, and in it have shut up *Dorosensko*.

Naples, March 13. On Wednesday last the Troops, designed for *Catalonia*, embarked on the Vessels that were provided for their Transportation. Our Viceroy continues the Levies in this Kingdom. The Prince *de Piombino*, General of the Galleys of this Kingdom, is arrived here from *Madrid*. The Dutch Capers we told you in our last, were come in here, having sold their two Prizes, are sailed again to cruise.

Genoua, March 18. On Tuesday last dyed here Signior [illegible], one of the Procurators of this Republick, being very much lamented by all people. The Prince of *Monaco* is gone hence on his way to *France*, he intending to accompany his most Christian Majesty in the Campagne this Summer. From *Milan* they write, that they had advice there, That the 13 Cantons being Assembled at *Baden*, had resolved, not to permit any Levies to be made within their Territories, for any Prince whatsoever, which the Spaniards are much offended at, who think that they only ought to have that Liberty.

Vienna, March 18. The Count *de Montecuculi* having excused himself from returning to the Imperial Army on the *Rhyne* by reason of his constant indisposition, accompanied with a great Age; the Emperor has appointed the Count *de Souches* to succeed him, and has accordingly sent him orders forthwith to repair to *Egra* in *Bohemia*, in order to the Rendezvous of the Troops, which are to march towards the *Rhine* for the reinforcement of the Army there. The Count of *Caplieres*, Governor of *Tyrol*, is made Commissary General of the Army.

Cologne, March 30. On Monday last the Duke of *Bournonville* received an Express from the Count *de Caprara*, who Commands the Imperial Troops, that are sent to the assistance of the Elector Palatine, which advised him, that 800 French horse having been sent out under the Command of the Marquis *de Beauvise*, first Brigadier to the Marquis *de Vaubrun*, to surprise some Imperial and Saxon Troops, who had their Quarters between *Spire* and *Manheim*, had at first the advantage, and had certainly executed their designe, but that the Count *de Caprara* upon notice thereof, came presently to their assistance with five Troops of Horse and as many Companies of Foot, and having rallied his own Men, fell upon the French with so good success, that above 100 were killed upon the place, and about 200 taken prisoners, the Marquis *de Beauvise* their Captain being likewise dangerously wounded. The French Ambassadors here have advice from the Court of *France*, that His Majesty of *Great Britain* had offered his Mediation to the most Christian King, and to the Queen of *Spain*, in order to the procuring a Peace between the two Crowns, and that it was thought his Majesty would accept thereof. The Dutch Ambassadors gave this week another Memorial to the Mediators of *Sweden*, in which they renew their instances for the obtaining Passports for the Ministers of the Duke of *Lorrain*, to come hither to assist as Principals at the Treaty; though it seems wholly broken up, by the detention of the Prince of *Furstenburgh*. Our Letters from *Worms* tell us, that great numbers of French Troops descend daily from *Alsatia* and *Lorrain*, towards *Landaw*, where are likewise arrived several Pieces of Artillery in order to some Siege, which gives great jealousie to the neighboring places, as *Spire*, *Newstadt* and *Frankendal*. The same Letters add, That the French assemble their Troops in *Lorrain* with design to march into the Palatinate, and give the Imperialists Battel. To morrow the Dutch Ambassadors Treat the English Ambassadors at Dinner. Great endeavors are still used for the releasement of the Prince of *Furstenbergh*, not without some likelihood of success.

Ostend, April 5. It is reported here, that Orders are come from *Brussels*, that, so soon as the French begin to approach these parts, the two great Dykes near this Town shall be cut through, and the Sea let in to overflow all the Countrey between this place, *Bruges* and *Sluys*, by which means these places will be secured, though a great many people ruined. Yesterday came in here two Capers with four pretended Prizes, being all Danes and Hamburgers, bound from *Burdeaux* to *Dunkirk*.

Brussels, April 3. On Wednesday last we received advice from *Leeuwe*, that two thousand French Horse and Dragoons had two days before appeared within sight of that place, which put the Garrison into a great Allarm, and occasioned the doubling of their Guards, and the manning their Counterscarp; that from thence the French marched towards *Harem*, *Diest*, and *Montegue*, forcing Contribution from all those Quarters, and

The Press

The English are avid newspaper readers, and there are newspapers to match all shades of political opinion. The most popular newspapers are the so-called tabloids, also known as the 'gutter press', who specialise in sensationalism – expect to find little 'hard news' in these, but plenty of celebrities, sex and breasts. The main newspapers are:

> **'The life of a journalist is poor, nasty, brutish and short. So is his style.'**
> Stella Gibbons (English novelist & journalist)

- *Daily Express* – daily, tabloid (right-wing).
- *Daily Mail* – daily, tabloid (right-wing).
- *The Daily Telegraph* – broadsheet (right-wing).
- *Financial Times* - daily, business broadsheet.
- *Guardian* - daily, former broadsheet (left-wing).
- *Independent* - daily, former broadsheet (liberal/left-wing).
- *The Mirror* - daily tabloid (left-wing).
- *The Sun* - daily tabloid (right-wing).
- *The Times* - daily, former broadsheet (right-wing).

BANKING

Banks offer a range of financial services including loans, mortgages and insurance. The major banks are: Barclays (💻 www.barclays.co.uk), HSBC (💻 www.hsbc.co.uk), Lloyds TSB (💻 www.lloydstsb.co.uk) and the National Westminster (💻 www.natwest.com). There's a strong public dislike (even hatred) towards the High Street banks in England, most of which provide a poor service and overcharge (rob) their customers.

- **Opening a bank account:** You need proof of identity, plus proof of address in the form of a utility bill. Foreign residents may be asked to provide a reference from their employer or a foreign bank. With a current account, you receive a cheque book and a cash card.
- **Cheques:** Cheques usually have two parallel lines printed across the face of the cheque, making them more secure as they can only be paid into a bank account and not cashed at a bank. Cheques usually take three to five days to clear.
- **Bank charges:** Most banks and building societies have a long list of service charges, and all make charges for 'bounced' cheques (cheques without funds), and going overdrawn without having an agreed overdraft. You can avoid charges by shopping around.

- **Bank managers:** You are unlikely to form a personal relationship with your bank manager, unless you deposit a great deal of money!
- **Cash machines:** All banks have ATMs or cash machines outside and/or inside their branch offices. Most ATMs are free to use.
- **Transferring money:** It can take up to four days to transfer money from one account to another, or to make a credit card payment online.
- **Credit card payments:** You can choose how much of your credit card bill you pay each month; the minimum amount is stated on your monthly bill. You can make payments online, at your bank, by post or by telephone.
- **Opening hours:** Normal bank opening hours are from 9 or 9.30am until 4 or 5pm, Mondays to Fridays, and many also open on Saturdays.

You should avoid fee-charging cash machines like the plague, as they charge you up to £1.75 for the privilege of withdrawing your money. Not surprisingly, they are popular with banks, and there are now thousands located throughout the country, particularly in poor areas where there are few banks.

- **Payment by debit and credit card:** Paying for goods and services by debit or credit card is by far the most popular means of payment in England, and cards are accepted almost everywhere. A 'chip and pin' system operates in most establishments – you slot your card into the machine, and key in your personal identity number (PIN).
- **Queues:** To avoid queues, visit your bank outside peak times, which are first thing in the morning, lunchtimes and Saturdays.

TAXES

Council Tax

Council tax is a local tax levied by councils on residents, to pay for services such as education, police, waste disposal and roads. Each council sets its own tax rate, and the amount payable depends on the value of your home, as rated by your local council (not necessarily the market value). The tax is payable in a lump sum or in ten instalments a year, from April to January. Full council tax assumes that two adults are living permanently in a property, and if there's only one adult, the rate is reduced by 25 per cent. There are other reductions for second homes, under 18's, the unemployed, students and the disabled. Council tax is generally higher in urban areas, and has spiralled in the last few years, and now represents a substantial expense for many households.

> **'I'm as poor as a church mouse, that's just had an enormous tax bill on the very day his wife ran off with another mouse, taking all the cheese.'**
>
> Rowan Atkinson,
> *Blackadder* (English comedy TV series)

Income Tax

Income Tax is a tax on personal revenue, although not all of your income is taxable. Everyone who's resident in England for tax purposes has a 'personal allowance', which is the amount of taxable income you're allowed to earn or receive each year, tax-free. In 2007-08, this allowance was £5,225. After your tax-free allowance, and any deductible allowances and reliefs have been taken into account, the amount of tax you pay is calculated using different tax rates and a series of tax bands. The basic rate of income tax will be 20p from April 2008 (reduced from 22p in 2007). The top-rate income tax threshold will be £43,000 from April 2009.

Taxable income includes:

- earnings from employment – most employers deduct income

tax directly from employees' wages under the system known as Pay As You Earn (PAYE);
- earnings from self-employment;
- most pensions income (state, company and personal pensions);
- interest on most savings;
- income from shares (dividends);
- rental income;
- income paid to you from a trust.

National Insurance

All employed people aged over 16 with earnings above a certain threshold, pay contributions to National Insurance (NI), the English social security system, to build up their entitlement to certain social security benefits, including a state pension. Once you reach state retirement age, you stop paying NI contributions. When you first start work in England, you should apply for an NI number, to ensure that your contributions are recorded on your account. For information, contact the National Insurance registration helpline (☎ 0845-915 7006, 💻 www.hmrc.gov.uk/nic).

Other Taxes

You may have to pay tax when you buy or sell things or give them away, for example:

- Capital Gains Tax if you sell or give away assets;
- Stamp Duty when you buy property or shares;
- Inheritance Tax on your estate when you die, including some gifts made up to seven years beforehand (so you need to plan when you're going to die carefully).

Tax on Goods & Services

Taxes are levied on certain goods and services, the main taxes being Value Added Tax (VAT – see below), fuel duty on petrol, excise duty on alcohol and tobacco and general betting duty.

VAT is payable on most goods and services and is normally included in the advertised price. There are two rates: standard rate (17.5 per cent), levied on most goods and services; and a reduced rate (5 per cent) levied on items such as children's car seats and domestic fuel. Some goods, e.g. food, books, newspapers and magazines, children's clothes and equipment for disabled people, are exempt from VAT.

COST OF LIVING

The cost of living in England is among the highest in the world, with high rates of tax on everything

from petrol to tobacco and alcohol to cars. British consumers pay more for food and most consumer goods than people in most other major countries, and, while direct taxes (e.g. income tax) are relatively low, indirect taxes are high. Most people in 'middle' England reckon that life is becoming more expensive, and the rapid rise in property prices and rents in recent years has meant that many families now pay between 30 and 50 per cent of their income in mortgage repayments or rent. However, salaries are also high, therefore you need to balance the cost of living against your income.

According to the annual cost of living survey conducted by Mercer Human Resources Consulting in 2006, London was the fifth most-expensive city in the world and the most expensive city in Europe. Only Moscow, Seoul, Tokyo and Hong Kong were more expensive than London, which was more expensive than Geneva, Copenhagen, New York City, Milan, Paris, Dublin, Sydney and Rome. No other UK city was ranked in the top 50.

London also didn't rank highly in the 2007 Mercer 'Quality of

Living' survey, languishing in a lowly 39th place, behind cities such as Vancouver, Auckland, Sydney, Wellington, Toronto, Melbourne, Ottawa, Perth, Montreal, Dublin, Honolulu, San Francisco, Adelaide, Brisbane, Paris and Boston, in the top 50 cities in the world. It was, however, ranked ahead of Washington DC, Chicago, Portland, New York City, Seattle Lexington, Pittsburgh and Winston Salem (all US cities). No other UK city was ranked in the top 50.

The UK's inflation rate is based on the Retail Price Index (RPI), which gives an indication of how prices have risen over the past year. The prices of around 600 'indicator' consumer items (excluding property) are collected on a single day in the middle of the month (a total of around 130,000 prices are collected for the 600 items in the RPI basket). The inflation rate in April 2007 was 2.8 per cent.

What is more important to most people than the cost of living and the quality of living is their **standard of living**, i.e. how much you will earn and what it will buy. On the plus side, the UK's standard of living has soared in recent years and, compared with most other European Union countries, British workers take home a larger proportion of their pay after tax and social security. However, the gap between rich and poor is vast, and growing, and is the largest since records began in 1886. There's also a considerable difference in the standard of living between the wealthy south of England, and the north of England, Scotland and Northern Ireland. While state pensioners are unable to afford basic comforts such as a healthy diet, a car and an annual holiday, many families have never been better off, and more and more people can afford to go on spending sprees, buying holiday homes, cruises, yachts, power boats, luxury cars and private aircraft.

It's difficult to calculate an average cost of living, as it depends on each individual's particular circumstances and lifestyle. What is important to most people is how much money they can save (or spend) each month. Your food bill naturally depends on what you eat, and is usually higher than in North America, and similar to most other Western European countries. However, even in the most expensive areas (i.e. London), the cost of living needn't be astronomical. If you shop wisely, compare prices (e.g. using the internet) and services before buying, and don't live too extravagantly, you may be pleasantly surprised at how little you can live on.

4.

BREAKING THE ICE

One of the best ways of getting round culture shock, and feeling part of life in England, is meeting and getting to know English people. Making friends in a new country is never easy, and the fact that the English are fairly private people only makes it harder. This chapter offers information and advice on important aspects of English society, such as how to behave in social situations, topics to steer clear of in conversation, expatriate communities, and dealing with confrontation.

'The more the English dislike you, the more polite they are.'

Rabbi Lionel Blue (British reform Rabbi)

COMMUNITY LIFE

You may be struck by the reserve of the English at first – in some areas, especially big cities like London, people tend to shy away from eye contact and talking to strangers. Try not to be put off by this and as soon as you move into your home, make an effort to become part of your new community. If possible, shop in local stores and use local amenities, as receiving a greeting from neighbours or a local shopkeeper makes you feel less alienated. However, the onus is on you to take the initiative, because you may find few English people make the effort if you don't.

Neighbours

When it comes to your neighbours, the chances are they won't immediately drop by or invite you to their home for a cup of tea. As an outsider, it may be left to you to make the first move. Shortly after you arrive, visit your neighbours' homes and introduce yourself (although, if you live next to Buckingham Palace, HM The Queen might not appreciate you dropping in unannounced). However, whether your relationships with your English neighbours blossom into real friendships, or never progress beyond a casual chat over the garden fence or a passing nod in the street, is likely to depend on factors such as your age and where in the country you live.

A 2005 survey found that residents of London and the north-east of England were least likely to become friendly with people living next door, and that the retired were most likely to be good friends with their neighbours, while young people didn't tend to socialise as much with people living nearby. In general, most English people like to feel part of their local community and usually chat to their neighbours in passing. If you want to start a conversation with your neighbour (or any other English person for that matter!) a comment on the weather is bound to get a response.

Love Thy Neighbour

It's a good idea to try to get on with your neighbour as much as possible – not only is it unpleasant to be on bad terms with those in your immediate vicinity, you never know when you will need to turn to a neighbour in a crisis or emergency. One way of smoothing the way to a good relationship is to be aware of the potential pitfalls.

> **Not so neighbourly**
>
> **Sometimes next door can become a nightmare, as it did for two north London neighbours, who spent ten years and more than £150,000 fighting a legal battle over a few inches of land, and for two men who died after separate arguments involving disputed hedges.**

There are many reasons why neighbours fall out, but the most common causes of disputes between neighbours in England centre on issues such as excessive noise, access to a neighbour's land for repairs, shared amenities or boundaries, fences and walls. The following is a brief guide to the rules and regulations:

Burglar alarms: Many households have burglar alarms, some of which go off for no reason and aren't switched off. If this is the case, phone the police or local authorities – if the alarm has been sounding non-stop for 20 minutes or intermittently for an hour, and is causing a noise nuisance, they may enter the house or business premises and silence it.

Dealing with noisy neighbours: If you have a problem with noisy neighbours, approach them first and politely ask them to keep the noise down. If there's no improvement, contact your local council. Councils can measure noise levels, and officers can visit the perpetrators to warn them that they face potential action if they don't reduce the noise, and have the power to seize noise-making equipment.

Fences and walls: Planning permission isn't usually needed before putting up a fence or wall, provided it isn't taller than two metres (6.6ft), or one metre (3.3ft) if next to a highway.

Hedges: Hedges can be a thorny issue in England – campaigners estimate there are about 100,000 ongoing disputes in Britain over high hedges, but a loophole in legislation has so far left local authorities powerless to help. If your neighbour's hedge is tall and blocks out light, you can prune the roots or branches. However, you shouldn't try to reduce the height of a hedge without first getting advice from a solicitor, especially as some hedgerows are protected by law. Hedgeline (☎ 024-7638 8822 – only the English could have a Hedgeline!) and local councils provide advice about hedge problems.

Parking space: Unless there are local parking restrictions giving a right to a particular space, you have no automatic right to a parking space on your road. However, you do have a right of access to your drive. If there is a shared drive, then each owner has a right of access and neither may block the drive.

Trees: If a neighbour's tree hangs over an adjoining property, you can ask them to trim it back. If this is not done, you have the right to trim the tree back to your boundary line, although any branches or fruit removed belong to the tree's owner, and should be returned. Councils have powers to deal with trees on private property that are in a dangerous condition.

Dealing with a dispute

It is never a good idea to get into a dispute with a neighbour, but sometime it's unavoidable. If you have a problem it's advisable to keep a record of what is said and done by whom, and to gather evidence in case the dispute escalates.

- Talk to your neighbour. Make notes about your complaint, so that you don't forget any of the things you want to say.
- Write a letter to your neighbour, outlining your concerns. This can also later be shown to the authorities to prove you have tried to tackle the problem.
- Record incidents in a daily log.
- Go to your local authority, but if they cannot help (or won't) you may have to take private legal action.

If you have had a legal dispute with a neighbour, you must disclose this when selling, and if it's a serious ongoing problem, it could affect your chances of achieving a good price or even selling at all.

- Ask the Citizens' Advice Bureau and a solicitor for guidance.

ROLE OF MEN & WOMEN IN SOCIETY

The traditional family stereotypes of the husband as the breadwinner and the woman as the homemaker are largely unreflective of modern English life. Many English women resume their working careers after having children, and expect their partners to take an equal share in childcare and housework. And, in a complete reversal of traditional roles, a growing number of men are choosing to be house-husbands, while the woman returns to work full-time.

The traditional family unit is also no longer deeply rooted – almost half of marriages end in divorce, and there are a high percentage of one-parent families and 'step families' (families whose children are from previous marriages). An increasing number of couples choose to live together without getting married (one of the main factors in the decrease in the number of marriages – see below), and co-habiting couples have similar rights to married couples, e.g. the right to make financial claims against one another if they split up.

> **Marriage**
>
> **The English are increasingly reluctant to 'tie the knot'. Statistics show that marriage is well and truly on the wane in England – in 2005 there were 244,710 marriages, the lowest level since 1896. The average age for a first marriage in England is now 31.7 for men and 29.5 for women, four years older than in 1991.**

Men

Overall, English men are still the highest earners, especially as many women choose to return to work part-time after they have children. For the English male, spare time usually revolves around sport – sometimes taking part but more often watching – particular favourites include football, rugby, cricket, snooker, darts and boxing; but there are few sporting contests that an English man doesn't enjoy, especially when he has a beer in his hand.

Women

Equal opportunities have achieved great things in England, and English women are among the most emancipated in the world. However, some disparities still exist between men and women in the workplace

– in the private sector, a woman doing the same job as a man is often paid less, and the number of women at the top of their professions in male-dominated sectors, such as politics, finance and the judiciary remain unrepresentative.

Homosexuals

Homosexual (and lesbian) couples in England enjoy the same rights as heterosexual couples, such as equal rights in financial matters such as inheritance, pensions provision, life assurance and maintenance where children are involved. Immigration and nationality rules also take account of civil partners when assessing someone's right to stay in the UK. Homosexual relationships in England are officially called a 'civil union' or 'civil partnership'; the first civil partnerships in England took place in December 2005, and a year later over 14,000 homosexual couples had 'tied the knot' in England.

The biggest homosexual communities in England are to be found in Brighton, Manchester and London, home to Europe's largest gay and lesbian population. Manchester has its own gay village, and boasts one of the biggest gay and lesbian arts scenes, 'Queerupnorth', which takes place each May.

Singles

There's an active singles scene in towns and cities, but many single English people, in common with those in many other countries, complain that it's difficult to meet other singles. Internet dating is increasingly popular, and there are also singles clubs in many cities and large towns.

Sexual Attitudes

Contrary to popular perception, the English aren't straight-laced about sex. In fact the nation has surprisingly liberal attitudes to sex and marriage. This is the country that features a topless woman on page 3 of the nation's favourite tabloid newspaper (*The Sun*, which has over 3m readers) every day, many of whom have become famous simply by having huge knockers. And the statistics speak for themselves: the percentage of unmarried women in England who

'I don't find English men sexy. They're all queer or kinky. The last Pom I went to bed with said to me, "Let's pretend you're dead".'

Germaine Greer (Australian writer & broadcaster)

are sexually active is around 90 per cent, and approximately one in four babies are now born 'out of wedlock' (to unmarried parents).

MEETING PEOPLE

Meeting people in England isn't usually a problem, as most English are friendly, although they aren't always the easiest of people to get to know well, and you may need to persevere before you penetrate their famous reserve. There are, however, a number of ways you can meet and socialise with English people:

After Work

Many English colleagues go to the pub after work, especially on Fridays, and this is a good way to get to know people informally. Even if you aren't a big drinker (pubs also sell non-alcoholic drinks), it's a good idea to show willing if you're invited along.

Expatriate Networks

Most places in England have expatriate networks whose activities often include social events, clubs and classes. Look in the local expatriate press for details or contact your local embassy or consulate.

Local Clubs

Find out about clubs and societies (councils and local newspapers are good sources of information), and join one or two as soon as possible after your arrival. You should also consider joining a local sports club, such as tennis or golf, which are ideal places to meet people and keep fit at the same time.

School or Childcare Facilities

School playgrounds and kindergartens, at the start or end of the school day, provide a ready-made place for contact with other parents. Look on the school notice board for news about forthcoming events and meetings. Most schools have parents' associations, which are worth joining and always welcome offers of help.

Arranging Meetings

If the onus is on you to arrange a meeting point, you should choose a local pub. It's unusual to invite someone to your home until you know them well, and don't suggest meeting at someone else's home unless they offer. If you're a single woman, always arrange to meet somewhere you know there will be other people, and tell someone where you are going.

Paying

If you meet people in a pub, it's customary to pay for drinks in rounds, where each person takes his or her turn to buy drinks for the whole group. If you're with a big group, buying a round is expensive, therefore someone may suggest having a 'kitty' or 'whip round', where everyone contributes a set amount, usually around £10, which is then used to buy drinks for everyone.

> **'On the Continent, people have good food; in England, people have good table manners.'**
>
> George Mikes (Hungarian born author & humourist)

INVITATIONS

Receiving Invitations

If you're invited to someone's home, you should consider this a compliment, as many English people don't invite people to their homes until they know them reasonably well. Invitations usually extend to your partner or spouse, but if your host isn't aware you have a partner, it's acceptable to ask for him or her to be included. If you have children, you shouldn't include them unless your host specifically mentions it.

Guests are normally expected to be punctual. Dinner invitations often state the time as 7.30pm for 8pm, which means you should arrive at 7.30pm for drinks, and dinner will be served (usually promptly) at 8pm. Anyone who arrives very late or worse still, not at all, can expect to be excluded from future guest lists (unless you have a very good reason, such as a fatal accident).

Most English people are informal, and there are no strict rules on etiquette. However, if you're going to be moving in formal circles, there are two invaluable guides: *Debrett's New Guide to Etiquette and Modern Manners* (John Morgan, Headline), sets out the customary way of doing things, and *Debrett's Correct Form* explains the correct forms of address, in speech and writing.

Dress Code

What to wear to someone's house depends on the occasion, and who else is going to be there. Dressing smart-casual is a safe bet for most occasions, but if you aren't sure, it's wise to ask in advance what you're expected to wear.

The Meal

Most English hosts serve a starter, main course and dessert at a dinner party. Lunch is usually a more casual affair, with perhaps just a main

> **Vegetarian Guests**
>
> Vegetarians are common in England, and many people are happy to provide alternatives for them and are sensitive to their requirements, i.e. not simply removing bits of meat from a dish and expecting this to be acceptable! If you're a vegetarian, you should inform your host when you accept an invitation. If you're providing the meal, ask your guests whether they are vegetarians or whether there's anything they cannot eat.

course and dessert. You should keep your hands above the table at all times and, in common with many countries, cutlery is used from the outside inwards, e.g. the cutlery on the extreme left and right is for the first course.

Gifts

If you're invited to dinner, it's customary to take a small present of flowers, such as a plant, chocolates or a bottle of wine (see **Alcohol Etiquette** below).When choosing flowers, avoid carnations (they signify bad luck for some people and for others they're closely associated with the cheap, wilted bunches sold at petrol stations!) and chrysanthemums (associated with cemeteries). If you stay with someone as a guest for a few days, it's customary to give your host or hostess a small gift when you leave.

Alcohol Etiquette

As a Guest

If you've never been to your host's home before, it's best to bring a bottle of good-quality wine. If you know your host fairly well, it's acceptable to ask what they like or what they're cooking, so you can choose something appropriate. You should aim to spend between £6 and £10 – i.e. not too cheap and not too expensive (although no wine is too expensive for a good dinner party). During the meal, if your wine glass is empty, you should only ask for a top-up if you know your hosts well. Otherwise, you should wait to be served.

> **'I only take a drink on two occasions – when I'm thirsty and when I'm not.'**
>
> Brendan Behan (Irish poet & author)

When Entertaining

As far as aperitifs go, some English people like to be offered spirits such as gin, vodka and whisky. However, if you're not a spirits drinker, it's acceptable to offer only wine. You should also offer a selection of non-alcoholic drinks (such as fruit juices or cordials) for those who are driving.

If your guests have brought wine, it's traditional to serve it, especially if they indicate that they're looking forward to trying it! However, if they bring an un-chilled bottle of Champagne or white wine, it's acceptable to save it for another occasion. Equally, if your guests have brought a dubious-looking bottle of wine, tactfully leave it to one side, unless they suggest that you open it (**you** don't have to drink it).

At an informal dinner, it's acceptable to serve just one type of wine, although you might like to offer a choice of red or white. When you want to get rid of guests at the end of the evening, stop serving alcohol and suggest coffee or tea, which will convey the message that it's time to go home.

Out for dinner

If you go out for dinner with friends and are choosing wine, it's best to point out a few wines in different price brackets and offer your friends the choice. If you don't like a wine someone else has ordered, it's advisable not to complain, but to bring out your newly-found British 'stiff upper lip' and make the best of it – most wines taste better after a glass or two anyway! However, if a wine tastes musty or stale, then there may be something wrong with it, and you're perfectly within your rights to ask for another bottle or choose something else.

RESPECTING PRIVACY

The English reserve and love of privacy is well known – the fact that most people live in houses rather than flats, is an indication that the nation loves having its own front door, and the seclusion from the outside world that this symbolises ('an Englishman's home is his castle'). It's wise not to ask an English person about private or family matters – unless they volunteer this information. And it's best not to share personal information about yourself – many English would be embarrassed by this – unless you're with a good friend.

However, no matter how highly they guard their own privacy, the English love gossip and scandal, and have an insatiable appetite for the 'inside information' on the private lives of 'celebrities'. The tabloid newspapers routinely feature celebrities' private lives, and there are a number of celebrity magazines, such as *Hello*, *OK!* and *Now*, which are among the most popular weeklies.

TABOOS

The English are generally relaxed and accommodating with foreigners' *faux pas* and most will easily forgive your mistakes, but certain subjects are taboo and social blunders are best avoided. Below is a short guide to areas where you need to tread carefully.

Conversation

It goes without saying that when getting to know new people of any nationality, it's important to keep the conversation limited to neutral topics so that you don't make anyone feel uncomfortable or give offence. Every country has its taboos, and England is no different, which naturally change as societies change; some topics that were once taboo in England, such as homosexuality, are now discussed openly. Subjects that you should avoid include:

- **Immigration** – many people have polarised views on immigration and asylum.
- **Personal wealth** – unlike other countries, such as the US, asking someone how much they earn or how much money they have in the bank is considered rude, even if you know them well. It's also considered bad taste to talk about your own wealth, or how much certain items cost. On the other hand, house prices provide hours of conversation in England!
- **Religion** – as in many European countries, religion is a personal matter in England, and it's best to make no references to any religion or beliefs. If you're asked about your own religion, keep your reply neutral and, if possible, non-committal. Be aware that there's growing hostility to some religions in England, in particular Islam.

- **Sexual references** – unless you know your hosts well, steer clear of any sexual references or innuendos as this may cause embarrassment.

Dress

The English are world famous for their lack of dress sense, and this, coupled with the fact that almost anything goes (England is, after all, the home of many 'alternative' fashion trends such as punk, grunge and gothic), means it's difficult to make a clothing *faux pas*. In general, the English favour casual wear, with smart-casual for formal occasions. Some foreigners (particularly if you're from France, Italy or Spain) might find that, on occasion, they're over-dressed.

EXPATRIATE COMMUNITY

If you move to an area which is popular with your fellow countrymen, the lack of cultural and language barriers will make socialising much easier. Many large cities and towns have well-established expat networks, and fitting into these is often straight forward. But, beware of becoming too dependent on expatriate society. Try to extend your contacts further afield, and make an effort to meet the locals too – getting to know English people will add variety and interest to your social life, and open new doors to you.

According to the Office of National Statistics (2004), around 1 in 12 (4.9m) of the UK's population were born overseas. Around 50 per cent of immigrants are aged between 25 and 44.

Advantages of Expat Communities:

- It's easier to fit in with people of your own nationality.
- You get the chance to relax and speak your own language.
- It's a means of letting off steam after the stress of culture shock.

Disadvantages of Expat Communities:

- Spending too much time with expats may mean you don't accept your move as definite.
- Time spent with other expats could be spent integrating with English people.

- Many expatriate groups are little more than an excuse to complain about everything English – this may accentuate your own negative feelings towards England and won't help you settle.
- Expat groups tend to be a varied bunch of people, perhaps not necessarily those you would mix with in your home country – and you may find yourself socialising with people you don't actually like.

CONFRONTATION

Stoicism is an essential part of the English character, and part of being stoical is putting up with things without complaining. Add to this the fact that the English go out of their way to avoid making a fuss, and it isn't surprising to discover that they usually actively avoid confrontation. If an English person doesn't agree with something, his way of showing this may be to stay silent, which can be confusing for foreigners, particularly Americans, who are more used to vocal disagreement.

Confrontations do occur, however, and there are numerous incidents of arguments that turn into physical fights, often with serious consequences. So-called 'road rage' (confrontation between drivers) is also common. As far as possible, it's best to remain calm and avoid confrontation with an English person – you will achieve little or nothing and you'll be at a cultural and possibly linguistic disadvantage. In the workplace, avoid arguing with your colleagues as you may earn yourself the unwelcome reputation as a difficult foreigner.

Bizarre By-laws

- **All British males over the age of 14 are required to carry out two hours of longbow practice a week, supervised by local clergy.**
- **London Hackney Carriages (taxis) must carry a bale of hay and a sack of oats.**
- **Any person found breaking an egg at the sharp end will be sentenced to 24 hours in the village stocks.**
- **It's illegal for a lady to eat chocolates on a public conveyance (but if you're a slut it's okay).**

DEALING WITH OFFICIALS

The Police

If you're stopped by the police for any reason, be polite. There's little point in being obstructive or argumentative and it may make things worse for you. (On the other hand, if you're apologetic and subservient, you may get off with just a warning.) If you think you've been stopped or fined illegally, you can make a complaint at the police station afterwards.

Civil Servants

Civil servants hold the key to many aspects of life in England, such as your work permit and tax affairs.

'Civil servants – no longer servants, no longer civil.'

Winston Churchill (former British Prime

In your dealings with civil servants you should be polite and calm and always thank them for their help.

Teachers

Most teachers are approachable and prepared to meet parents out of school hours, particularly if you're concerned about any aspect of your child's welfare. All schools hold parents evenings at least once or twice a year, when you have the opportunity to meet your child's teachers and discuss his or her academic progress.

Tower Bridge, London

5. LANGUAGE BARRIER

Being able to communicate with the English and knowing what to do and say when you meet them are priorities when you move to England, especially when you first arrive. Not being able to speak English is the biggest barrier to integration. Learning to speak a foreign language is never easy and full of potential pitfalls – all expats have stories to tell of when they said 'the wrong thing', often with embarrassing consequences.

> 'English is a simple yet hard language. It consists entirely of foreign words pronounced wrongly.'
>
> Kurt Tucholsky (German journalist & satirist)

Even if English is your mother tongue, you probably won't understand everything people in England say. Many people use a wide range of colourful colloquial expressions, idioms and slang words in their everyday speech, which may be unfamiliar to other English speakers. Some forms of slang, such as Cockney rhyming slang, are often incomprehensible to the uninitiated. People from different areas of the country speak with markedly different accents, and sometimes use dialect that bears little resemblance to Standard English. You may struggle to understand people who speak with strong accents and who use a lot of dialect; you're not alone, as many English people from other areas of the country have a similar problem! Added to which, is the seemingly endless stream of new words and phrases brought into English by films, soap operas and TV shows; teenage slang, new technology and pop music all provide an endless supply of new words and phrases.

To help keep your collection of language anecdotes as small as possible, this chapter offers tips on learning English; a brief history of the English language; a guide to regional dialects and accents; explanations of body and sign language; forms of address and greetings; and telephone and letter etiquette.

LEARNING ENGLISH

Relocation and culture shock experts generally agree that one of the best ways of settling into a foreign country is to learn the language as soon as possible. Even a basic knowledge of a few key phrases when you arrive will help you feel more in control (or less out of control) in everyday situations. Expats with no language knowledge tend to feel vulnerable, as all they can do is nod and gesture – some people also feel a strong sense of ridicule when they have no tools of verbal expression.

> **'How amazing that the language of a few thousand savages living on a fog-encrusted island in the North Sea should become the language of the world.'**
>
> Norman St.John-Stevas (British politician)

Know Before You Go

To give yourself the best chance, you should start learning English well in advance of your departure – if you can, allow yourself six months. Don't believe anyone who claims that the best way to learn a language is to arrive in the country and immerse yourself in it. While this is a good way of improving your language knowledge, experts generally agree that this is the worst way to learn a language from scratch – not only are you under stress from the logistics of your relocation, but you're also prone to picking up errors that will be difficult to eradicate later. It's far better to gain a grounding in the basics before you leave, and, in any case, knowing how to ask for things and understanding something of what is being said will make settling in easier.

To give yourself the best possible chance when you arrive in England, you should make your language learning as intensive as possible. Specialist language schools are available in large cities in most countries, and the British Council (the official British cultural representative abroad) offers language classes, and opportunities to experience British culture at first hand, in over 100 countries around the world (💻 www.britishcouncil.org).

> **There are now more speakers of English as a foreign language than mother-tongue speakers: around 600m proficient non-native speakers, as opposed to about 400m native speakers. In addition, there are some 90m speakers of English as a second language.**

Once in England

When you arrive in England, make sure that you commit yourself to some sort of learning method as soon as possible, preferably within the first week. There are literally thousands of language schools

throughout the country, with English courses to suit all levels and budgets.

When looking at schools, choose one that's a member of Arels-Felco Ltd., the association of recognised English language-teaching establishments in the UK. Members must follow the association's regulations and code of conduct, which include high academic standards and rules governing the welfare of students. Arels-Felco publishes an annual directory of members containing details of all courses, obtainable from Arels-Felco, 2 Pontypool Place, Valentine Place, London SE1 8QF (☎ 020-7242 3136). The British Council publishes *The Green List*, a listing of accredited schools, available only online (💻 www.britishcouncil.org).

THE ENGLISH LANGUAGE

A Brief History

English has several linguistic influences (detailed below) and their legacy means English has an extensive vocabulary, much larger than the Germanic languages or the Romance language family to which French, Italian and Spanish belong. Indeed, language experts believe that English probably has more words than most comparable world languages.

Old English

Celtic was England's native language until Germanic settlers arrived in the 5th century. Natives and settlers evolved a dialect that shared much of its grammar and basic vocabulary with Dutch and German; and this form of the language, spoken in England until around 1100, is known as Anglo-Saxon or Old English.

> **Old Norse**
>
> **The legacy of Old Norse is still evident in the north-east dialect spoken today:**
>
> ***bairn*** **- child (from the Old Norse, modern Swedish, modern Danish barn)**
>
> ***bait*** **- snack, food eaten at work (from the Old Norse *beit*)**

Old Norse

The Vikings' presence in England between 787AD and 1042, also left an enduring linguistic stamp on the language. The Vikings spoke Old Norse – the ancestor of the modern Scandinavian languages (the word 'Viking' is Old Norse for 'pirate raid') – and this language has greatly influenced the English vernacular. Common words such as 'get', 'take', 'give', both' and 'same' come from Old Norse, as do pronouns like 'they', 'them' and 'their'.

Over 1,500 place names in England, particularly in Yorkshire and Lincolnshire, have Scandinavian origins: the 'by' in places like Rugby and Wetherby

ı8th of December, and left it the Monday
ollowing. The General refuſed me a ſight o
he library, and the Cook the neceſſary food
erhaps I outſtaid their liking. I return (t
ıſe a faſhionable expreſſion) more penetrate
with cold, than the civility of the inhabitants
nore ſtuffed with compliments than with
ood; and when I ſee two ſwaggering Capu-
hins, with their paunches as full as their
wallets, I cannot help thinking of the Scrip-
ure phraſe, " He hath filled the *hungry* with
good things, and the *rich* he hath ſent empty

means 'farm' or 'town' in Old Norse; the 'thorpe' in Scunthorpe and Linthorpe means 'village'; and the 'thwaite' in Braithwaite means 'isolated area'.

Norman Conquest

Following the Norman Conquest in 1066, the English language was influenced by Norman French, which became the language of the ruling class for a considerable period; while Latin became the language of scholarship and of the Church. A vast number of French and Latin words entered the English language during this period and the Latin alphabet was also adopted.

Dialects & Regional Variations

Many English people feel a strong connection with their home town, and retain great pride and affection for the area where they grew up. Accent, dialect and language are an intrinsic part of shaping a person's identity, and the way that many people speak instantly identifies them as coming from a particular place. An accent is also much more than a geographical pointer – it brands your social class as effectively as if you had the words written on your forehead. The higher up the social ladder you are, the less likely it is that you will speak with a regional accent, and the upper classes generally speak 'The Queen's English' (or 'Oxford English') or 'received pronunciation', meaning it's difficult to gauge whether they come from a country estate in Surrey, a farm in the West Country or a mining village in Northumberland. On the other hand, many working class people speak with broad regional accents, immediately revealing which part of the country they come from. (See also **Appendix D**.)

The accepted authority on British English, the online Oxford English Dictionary (OED), is updated every three months with at least 1,000 new and revised entries.

Regional Dialects

Linguists believe that regional variations in accent, language and dialect have been a constant presence in English from the time of the 5th century Western Germanic settlers, whose speech was accented according to which part of the North Sea coast they had hailed from; these dialectical differences were transplanted into English. The distinct north-east dialects arose because the Old Norse-speaking Vikings colonised this region for much longer, leaving a lasting linguistic imprint.

However, the biggest factor behind the regional differences in

> **'I was criticised for swearing on television. The word I used was 'bloody', which, where I come from in Yorkshire, is practically the only surviving adjective.'**
>
> Maureen Lipman (actress & comedienne)

speech and dialect, is probably that, like every other language, English is a porous mass that is constantly evolving to absorb changes in society, lifestyles, business, culture and technology. Often, new permutations of language are created locally in certain regions, and while some areas might then adopt these new forms, others won't.

Traditional dialects are most commonly found in northern and western urban areas and in remote rural locations. These dialects are significantly different from Standard English and are difficult for outsiders to understand. It isn't easy to map out precise dialectical areas in England, as they don't tend to fall into neat divisions such as counties. For example, someone from east Yorkshire speaks very differently from someone from north Yorkshire, who might well share a similar accent and dialect with people living in the neighbouring county of Durham. The following are the main accents found in England (from south to north):

- **Home Counties:** A large part of southern England, including Berkshire, Buckinghamshire, Hampshire, Hertfordshire and Sussex, is known as the Home Counties, and they share a similar pronunciation and dialect.
- **'Estuary English'**: a regional accent usually spoken in Essex and Kent. A particular feature of the accent is the 'th' sound which is changed to an 'f' or a 'v', for example: 'fanks' – thanks, 'bruvver' – brother. Glottal stops – the omittance of the middle 't' or the end 't' of a word – are also prevalent, for example: 'sui' – suit; 'ligh-er' - lighter. Estuary English is commonly heard on soap operas, TV shows and from the mouths of pop stars and footballers.
- **The West:** in the area stretching from Cornwall to Herefordshire, speakers pronounce a longer 'r', e.g. 'cart' becomes 'carrt' and 'farm' 'farrm'.
- **The East:** in the counties of Northamptonshire,

Cambridgeshire, East Anglia and Essex, the 'r' is not pronounced in many words.

- **The North:** In the north, dialects have pronunciations such as 'wrang' and 'lang' rather than 'wrong' and 'long', and 'blinnd' or 'finnd' rather than 'blind' and 'find'. In the area including Lancashire, Staffordshire, Cheshire and neighbouring areas, older dialects pronounce 'land' as 'lond' and 'hand' as 'hond'.

Cockney Rhyming Slang

Cockney rhyming slang originated in London around a century ago, and linguistics believe it was invented for use as a code for those engaged in illegal activities to keep the police in the dark. Cockney rhyming slang is a form of idiomatic speech in which a particular word is replaced with a phrase of two or three words that rhymes with it. Its humorous nature appealed to people outside the criminal world and the slang gradually propagated, even washing up as far away as the shores of the US and Australia with English immigrants. (See also **Appendix D**.)

Cockney Pearly Kings and Queens

> **Rhyming Cockney slang**
>
> **'Would you Adam and Eve it? My china plate's about to get cash and carried so we all went down the battle cruiser. Anyway, he had one too many kitchen sinks and got lord and mastered. Next thing I know my china plate's had a left and right with the ginger pops and ended up in the jug and pail!'**
>
> **Translation: 'Would you believe it? My mate's about to get married so we all went down to the boozer (pub). Anyway, he had one too many drinks and got plastered (very drunk). Next thing I know my mate has had a fight with the cops (police) and ended up in jail!'**

Regional & Minority Languages

England has two officially recognised minority languages, under the European Charter for Regional or Minority languages, Cornish and British Sign Language. Romany and Yiddish are also spoken.

Cornish

The original Cornish language dates from the 9th century, and at the time of the Norman Conquest there were an estimated 40,000 Cornish speakers. By 1800, this form of Cornish had almost died out; but a new strain of the language, Modern Cornish, evolved, with elements of grammar and pronunciation from original Cornish and English words such as 'telephone' and 'television'. The 20th century saw a resurgence of Cornish, with some speakers reverting to a form of original Cornish, known as Unified Cornish.

Cornish Words:

beach	*treth*
Cornwall	Kernow
lighthouse	*golowji*
mountain	*menydh*
restaurant	*boesti*
tree	*gwydhenn*

In 1988, a breakaway faction created yet another new strand, Common Cornish. Each version has its own spellings, and tries to avoid using English words by coining new vocabulary.

British Sign Language

British Sign Language (BSL), recognised by the government as a full, independent language, is the visual language of the UK's deaf community. BSL is unrelated to English, and is an expressive language with a full grammar based on space and timing. Statistics from the British Deaf Association suggest up to 250,000 people use BSL daily.

Romany and Yiddish

The Roma people (gypsies), who arrived in Britain in late medieval times, spoke a tongue called Romany, which originated in northern India and was historically related to Punjabi and Gujarati. A type of Romany, known as Anglo-

What does this mean?

Romany, still survives today in the form of Romany words spoken with English grammar and English pronunciation. Romany has donated a number of words to English, including 'cushti/cushty' meaning 'good' or 'brilliant'.

In the early 20th century, a high concentration of Yiddish speakers lived in the East End of London, and today there are still a number of speakers in England. Yiddish words in English include 'chutzpah' (extreme impudence), 'shlep' (to drag an object), 'shtum' (quiet) and 'bagel' (ring-shaped bread roll).

Colloquialisms & Idioms

English is particularly rich in idioms (phrases with a special meaning, where literal translation makes no sense), which form one of the most difficult aspects of the English language for foreigners. For example, 'to turn up' means to arrive or to find (something), but the idiom: 'a turn up for the books' means to be pleasantly surprised by something that has happened. Idioms refer to

> **'American is the language in which people say what they mean, as Italian is the language in which they say what they feel. English is the language in which what a character means or feels has to be deduced from what he or she says, which may be quite the opposite.'**
>
> John Mortimer (English writer & dramatist)

a variety of topics such as weather, colours, food, furniture, animals, language, games and sports, and English speech is richly idiomatic – you may often find there's an idiom in every other sentence! A good guide to English idioms is *The Oxford Dictionary of Idioms* (Oxford Paperback Reference). Some examples are:

- 'Frankenstein foods' – genetically modified foods (from Bram Stoker's *Dracula*);
- 'An Orwellian future' – a dystopian world of dehumanised beings (from George Orwell's *1984*);
- 'To be a scrooge/ Scrooge-like' – to be mean (from Charles Dickens' *A Christmas Carol*);
- 'To grin/smile like a Cheshire Cat' – to grin widely from ear to ear (from Lewis Carroll's *Alice in Wonderland*);
- 'An Aladdin's cave' – a treasure trove (from *Aladdin*).

English has a range of expressions that reference other languages. These sometimes have derogatory meanings – especially when they relate to France and the French!

- 'Pardon/excuse my French' – excuse my bad language (used humorously);
- 'French letters' – contraceptives;
- 'To take French leave' – to leave without first getting permission;
- 'It's all Greek to me' – I can't understand a word of it;
- 'When in Rome, do as the Romans do' – follow the manners and customs of the country you're in.

> **Hamlet** (William Shakespeare)
>
> **To be or not to be, that is the question:**
> **Whether 'tis nobler in the mind to suffer**
> **The slings and arrows of outrageous fortune**
> **Or to take arms against a sea of troubles,**
> **And by opposing end them?**

Shakespeare

No book on English culture would be complete without a reference (or two) to the greatest exponent of the English language, William Shakespeare (1564-1616), also the country's greatest playwright. Shakespeare, also known as the Bard, is thought to have written about 37 plays and over 150 sonnets; works which are now seminal texts. So enduring is Shakespeare's contribution to English that expressions he coined are common currency to this day. There are 29,066 different words in Shakespeare's plays and he coined around 2,000 words and invented many well-known idioms and phrases, including:

Shakespearian Phrases

'a foregone conclusion' (from *Othello*)

'a laughing stock' (*The Merry Wives of Windsor*)

'All that glisters is not gold.' (*The Merchant of Venice*)

'at one fell swoop' (*Macbeth*)

'bloody minded' (*Henry VI*)

'cold comfort' (*The Taming of the Shrew*)

'eaten out of house and home' (*Henry V*, Part 2)

'fair play' (*The Tempest*)

'green-eyed monster' (*Othello*)

'in stitches' (*Twelfth Night*)

'I will wear my heart upon my sleeve' (*Othello*)

'love is blind' (*The Merchant of Venice*).

'tower of strength' (*Richard III*)

FOREIGN LANGUAGES

There are around 350 languages spoken in England – a survey of London school children in 2000, found that over 300 languages were spoken in the city's schools alone – with the most widely used being Bengali/Sylheti, Turkish, Somali, Urdu, Greek, Portuguese, Chinese, Gujarati, Punjabi and Polish. In the vast majority of large English towns and cities, particularly London, you will hear many languages spoken as many migrants predominantly use their mother tongue on a day-to-day basis, and some have only a smattering of English.

Radio and TV programmes in England are broadcast in over 30 languages, e.g. Sky offers a wide range of foreign language channels; the BBC provides news in 33 languages on its website, and its World Service broadcasts programmes in a variety of languages (see 💻 www.bbc.co.uk/worldservice); and there are a number of Asian radio stations, including the BBC's Asian Network

(💻 www.bbc.co.uk/asiannetwork) and Sunrise Radio in London.

SLANG & SWEARING

Like all languages, English has a rich vocabulary of slang and swear words, the usage of which depends on the company you're in and the context. But, unless your English is proficient it's best to avoid using them – usually only native speakers know when it's appropriate to use them and which one to use. All too often foreigners make terrible *faux pas* by swearing in the wrong situation, wrongly or too harshly. It's important to know what's being said, however, and two useful guides to English slang are *The Oxford Dictionary of Modern Slang* (Oxford Paperback Reference) and *The Little Book of Essential English Swear Words* by S. Ferris (Summersdale Publishers).

BODY LANGUAGE & GESTURES

Body language plays a key role in communication, especially at a subconscious level; an awareness of the impact your body language is having on an English person makes a big difference to how successfully you communicate with them.

Eye Contact

Eye contact is an important part of establishing a rapport, especially when communicating with English people, who do not often make physical contact when speaking. Failing to make eye contact is associated with being dishonest or having something to hide. However, it's considered rude to stare at someone if you aren't talking to them.

Personal Space & Physical Contact

Many English people jealously protect their personal space and dislike anyone invading it. If possible (it never is on public transport in London!), keep at least an arm's length between you and other people, especially if you're in a queue or holding a conversation.

English people seldom touch each other when speaking, and may be embarrassed or uncomfortable if they feel that someone is standing too close or being too familiar. Touching someone to get their attention, or accidentally touching someone without saying 'excuse me' or 'sorry', is considered impolite.

Gestures

The English don't generally use gestures to express themselves – during a conversation between two English people, the only thing that moves is likely to be their mouths; hands and arms are kept firmly down. Pointing your finger (unless you're giving directions) is considered rude and should be avoided. There are certain gestures, however, that are commonly used (listed below), although it's best not to imitate them unless you're proficient in English – you might make the wrong gesture or be misinterpreted.

- Moving your shoulders up and down once: 'I don't know' or 'maybe';
- Nodding your head up and down: 'yes';
- Shaking your head from side to side: 'no';
- Pointing your thumb up with your other fingers closed: 'good' or agreement;
- Making a v-sign with your first and second fingers with your palm outwards: 'victory' or 'peace';
- Making a v-sign with your first and second fingers with your palm inwards: one of the most insulting signs!
- Winking one eye: 'it's a joke' or 'I'm lying'.

GREETINGS & MANNERS

Formal Greetings

When you're introduced to an English person in a formal setting, you should shake hands and say "Nice (or 'pleased') to meet you". In more formal circles, the phrase "How do you do?" is used, and surprisingly, the correct reply to this is "How do you do?". Handshakes should be firm (but not hand-crushing), with a lighter touch between men and women. When asked "How are you?", the correct response is "I'm fine, thank you, and you?", although many English now use the American reply – "I'm good". When you take your leave of someone you've met for the first time, it's polite to say "Nice to meet you".

Formal greetings are "Good morning", usually used before noon or 1pm, "Good afternoon", used after lunch and before 5 or 6pm, and "Good evening", used after 5 or 6pm. "Good night" is only used when you say goodbye, and never as a greeting. The English rarely use "Good day" as a greeting.

Informal Greetings

Informal greetings are "Hi" or "Hello" or "Morning", "Afternoon"

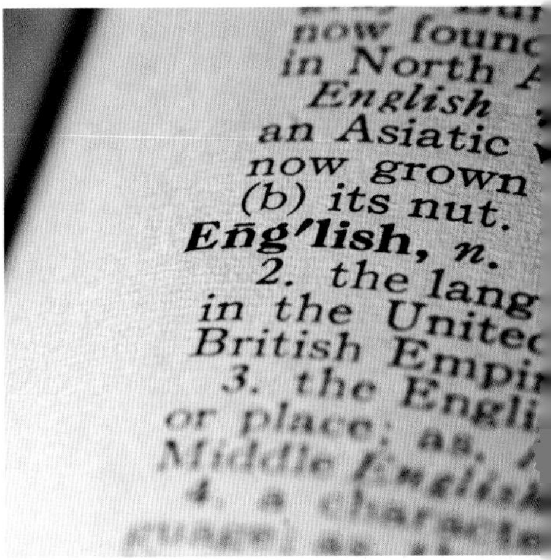

> **'A kiss on the cheek is sufficient greeting. After all, we are not French generals.'**
>
> Lady Diana Cooper (British socialite & actress)

or "Evening" (the word 'good' is dropped in informal situations). The common response to an informal "How are you?" is "Fine, thanks" or "Fine, cheers". In informal situations, English people often use "cheers" instead of "thank you", and "cheers" can also be used as an informal 'goodbye'. If you want to introduce yourself to someone, the usual practice is to extend your hand for a handshake and say, "Hello, I'm Liz" or "My name's Liz".

Most English people greet each other with a handshake, or simply wave to one another, although it's now increasingly common for men to kiss (more a peck) women friends on one or both cheeks in the continental fashion. Women friends and family generally kiss and hug each other when they meet. Men shake hands, and may pat each other on the back gently at the same time. English men don't generally hug or kiss one another unless they're from a culture where this is common practice (or they're gay).

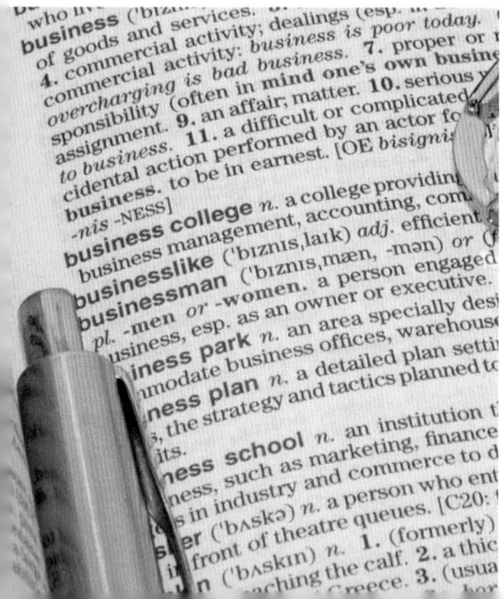

Forms of Address

Formal Address

In formal situations, English people are generally introduced by their title (Mr, Mrs, Miss or Ms), their first name and surname, e.g. Mr David Jones. When you address them, you should use their title plus their surname, e.g. Mr Jones. It's considered rude to call someone by their first name unless they have specifically asked you to do so. Other titles are also important, e.g. Doctor (Dr) and Reverend (Rev), and you're expected to use the title when you address someone formally, e.g. Dr Smith.

Informal Address

The English use first names for informal address. As a rough guide, when you're introduced to someone, it's best to follow the cue of the person doing the introducing, i.e. if someone is introduced as Bob, you can usually call him Bob. However, you should avoid calling someone by a shortened name or nickname unless they ask you to. For example, if you're introduced to a Michael, don't shorten his name to Mick or Mike unless he says something like "Please call me Mike".

In 2006, the most popular babies' names in England were Olivia for girls and Jack for boys. Jack has been the most popular boys' name for 12 years.

Children

When addressing children, the English use first names and only tend to kiss children who are relatives or whom they know very well. Children usually address adults they're familiar with by their first name, or if they're a relative, as 'Uncle Simon' or 'Aunty Sarah'. Children are expected to address adults they don't know by their title and surname, e.g. Mrs Mitchell; at school, children address their teachers by their title and surname, never by their first name.

TELEPHONE, LETTERS & EMAIL

Many English, particularly the younger generations, prefer modern means of communication, such as email and mobile phone text messages (texting), to the more traditional letter and faxes. Many English workers now spend as least as much time communicating by email as they do by telephone, and it's common practice for colleagues in adjacent offices to email each other, rather than speak face-to-face. In common with many other countries, mobile phone use has skyrocketed in England, and the vast majority of adults use or own one (or a number).

According to the Mobile Data Association (MDA), some 214 million text messages were sent in England on New Year's Day 2007, up from 165 million in 2006 and 133 million in 2005.

Telephone

Telephone communication is the most formal, particularly by mobile. When you answer the telephone, you should say "Hello?". Some English people recite their telephone number when they answer the phone, although this is becoming increasingly rare. Businesses often say the name of the company, followed by "Good morning/afternoon" and the name of the person speaking, and "How may I help you?".

Letters

Starting

Formal letters: If you don't know the person's name, you should start 'Dear Sir/Madam'. If you do know the name, you should use the title and surname, e.g. Dear Mr Brown. If you aren't sure of a woman's title (e.g. Mrs, Miss or Ms), use 'Ms'.

Informal letters: If you're on first-name terms with the person you're writing to, you should use

> **Date**
>
> **The date is written under your address on the right-hand side of the page, and should follow the format, day/month/year. It's now common to write the date as 18 August 2007, rather than 18th August 2007 and you may come across an all-digit date, e.g. 18/8/07.**

'Dear' plus their first name, e.g. 'Dear Paul'.

It's acceptable to put a comma or colon (:) after the name.

Addresses

You should write your address in the top, right-hand corner of the page, as follows:

Number and street name
Town
County
Postcode

If it's a formal letter, you write the name and address of the recipient under your address but on the left-hand side of the page. Don't use commas in the address.

Contents

Formal letters should start with 'I am writing to you to ...' followed by a brief explanation of the letter's content or purpose, or 'Thank you for your letter dated 11 March', if you're replying to a letter.

Signing Off

Formal letters: If you started the letter with 'Dear Sir/Madam', you should end the letter 'Yours faithfully'. If you used the name of the person at the start of the letter, end with 'Yours sincerely'. If you know the recipient, appropriate endings include 'Best wishes' and 'Kind regards'.

Informal letters: There are many endings from 'Yours truly' and "From' (both more formal) to 'Love from' and 'Lots of love' (usually reserved for close friends and relatives).

Email

English people usually use a less formal style when writing emails, even when writing business emails. The use of a person's first name is common in emails, and many business emails begin simply by using the person's first name, rather than with 'Dear'. Colleagues or business acquaintances will often start with 'Hi' or 'Morning' when emailing each other, but this is best to be avoided when emailing people you don't know, or people in positions of authority. If you're contacting someone in another organisation, you should start with 'Dear' followed by the person's title and surname. Most people use the endings 'Regards' or 'Best Wishes' for business emails.

POETRY

England has a long tradition of poetry writing and has produced a wealth of world-famous poets – far too many to mention here One of the most popular English writers, in both prose and verse, in the late 19th and early 20th centuries was Rudyard Kipling, whose poem *If* is reproduced below.

If (Rudyard Kipling, 1865-1936)

If you can keep your head when all about you
Are losing theirs and blaming it on you;
If you can trust yourself when all men doubt you,
But make allowance for their doubting too:
If you can wait and not be tired by waiting,
Or, being lied about, don't deal in lies,
Or being hated don't give way to hating,
And yet don't look too good, nor talk too wise;

If you can dream – and not make dreams your master;
If you can think – and not make thoughts your aim,
If you can meet with Triumph and Disaster
And treat those two impostors just the same:.
If you can bear to hear the truth you've spoken
Twisted by knaves to make a trap for fools,
Or watch the things you gave your life to, broken,
And stoop and build'em up with worn-out tools;

If you can make one heap of all your winnings
And risk it on one turn of pitch-and-toss,
And lose, and start again at your beginnings,
And never breathe a word about your loss:
If you can force your heart and nerve and sinew
To serve your turn long after they are gone,
And so hold on when there is nothing in you
Except the Will which says to them: "Hold on!"

If you can talk with crowds and keep your virtue,
Or walk with Kings – nor lose the common touch,
If neither foes nor loving friends can hurt you,
If all men count with you, but none too much:
If you can fill the unforgiving minute
With sixty seconds' worth of distance run,
Yours is the Earth and everything that's in it,
And – which is more – you'll be a Man, my son!

Cornish tin mine

6.

THE ENGLISH AT WORK

One of the most common mistakes foreigners make when coming to England to work or start a business is to assume that they can continue working in the same way that they did in their home country, particularly if they had a successful business there. Many newcomers underestimate the difference in business culture between the English and southern Europeans and Americans, for example. Working in England usually involves a fairly steep learning curve for a foreigner – professionally, linguistically and culturally.

'Work is the curse of the drinking classes.'

Oscar Wilde (Irish writer and wit)

This chapter contains information about the cultural differences you can expect to experience when working for or with the English, setting up a business in England and business etiquette.

WORK ETHIC

The English have a strong work ethic and work some of the longest hours in Europe. Many people don't take a proper lunch break – having a quick sandwich at your desk is common – and many people commute long distances to and from their place of work. Not surprisingly, the average English worker has high stress levels.

On the positive side, many companies, particularly in the public sector, have now introduced measures aimed at helping employees achieve a 'work-life balance', including 'flexi-time' and term-time working for parents. Some progressive private-sector firms even offer one or two annual paid 'duvet days' (stay at home days).

The English work culture has radically changed since the '70s, when people generally had a 'job for life', to a culture where it isn't uncommon for employees to change jobs every two years. The shift away from the comfortable 'feet under the table' culture began in the '80s, when new legislation reduced the power of the trade unions and

Many English admit that work often takes precedence over family and leisure time. A survey of English managers found that a third worked every weekend, half never saw their children during the week, and one in ten said they never had time to eat lunch.

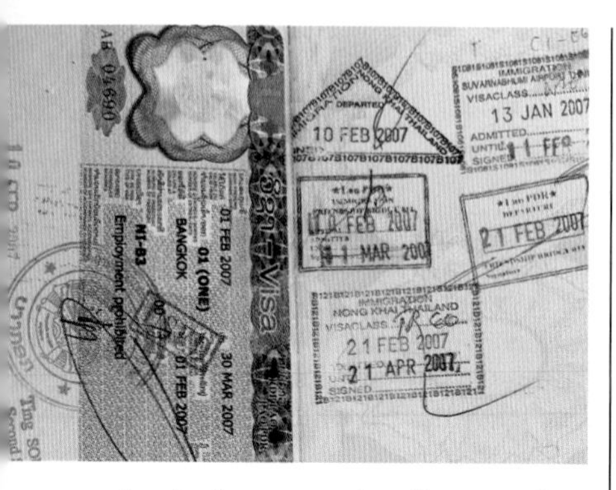

privatised many nationally-owned services (who are major employers) such as telecommunications, electricity, gas and water. When these services entered private hands, steps were immediately taken to cut costs by reducing the number of employees.

Most English people have an innate respect for rules and regulations, and like structure, are set in their habits and can be resistant to change. Most are also respectful of their superiors, polite, and dutifully comply with work regulations.

PERMITS & PAPERWORK

If they cannot recruit anyone from within the EEA, employers are permitted to recruit people from outside the EEA for a specific job in a specific location. Note, however, that a work permit doesn't allow you to enter or remain in England, therefore you also need to apply for a visa to remain in the UK. For information about work permits, visit the Home Office website (🖳 www.workingintheuk.gov.uk).

'I am deeply indebted to my lack of shorthand and typing. It probably saved me from a lifetime of hard work.'

Patrick Campbell (British journalist)

FINDING A JOB

England has a strong economy and relatively low unemployment, and finding work is usually straightforward, although it's advisable to start your search before you arrive in England.

Speaking English

You need a good command of English for most jobs, with the exception of low-paid work such as cleaning or manual labour. You will also need a good command of English to understand your contract and rights as an employee.

Qualifications

All EU qualifications are recognised in England, as are many non-EU qualifications. If your future employment depends on your qualifications, you should contact UK NARIC (🖳 www.naric.org.uk), which is the body responsible for assessing qualifications obtained outside the UK. They provide a Standard Evaluation Service with a 'letter of comparability', which lists the equivalent UK qualification of an overseas qualification.

Employment Agencies

Government

The Government-run recruitment agency is called Jobcentre Plus (☎ 0845-6060 234, 🖳 www.

jobcentreplus.gov.uk) and there are centres in most English towns, where vacancies are advertised for a wide variety of jobs. You can visit any centre to look at vacancies, and staff will help with interview practice and preparing CVs.

Private

There are many recruitment agencies in England, although not all are reputable. Look for a well-established agency and ask around for recommendations. Some recruiters are aimed at specific sectors, such as accountancy or health. Major agencies include: Adecco (www.adecco.co.uk), Hays (www.hays.com) and Reed (www.reed.co.uk).

> **'You should always believe what you read in the newspapers, for that makes them more interesting.'**
>
> Rose Macaulay (English novelist)

Newspapers & Publications

Newspapers are an excellent source of information, and most national and local newspapers have weekly job sections. For example, *The Guardian* advertises media, marketing and public relations jobs on Mondays, and vacancies in the health and social care sectors on Wednesdays; *The Times*, *Financial Times*, *Telegraph* and *Independent* advertise general appointments on Thursdays; and *The Times Educational Supplement* (published on Fridays) advertises education and teaching vacancies. Newspaper websites have jobs sections – *The Guardian* (www.guardian.co.uk/jobs) is particularly comprehensive, with links to application forms and the relevant companies' websites.

Local newspapers also advertise jobs once a week, but more senior (and therefore better-paid) vacancies tend to be advertised in national and industry publications rather than local papers. There are specialist and trade magazines for certain professions, e.g. accountants and engineers.

Curriculum Vitae

There's no universally recognised format for a curriculum vitae (CV) or résumé, but when writing one, you should ensure that you:

- Tailor the contents to the job you're applying for, listing experience, skills and qualifications relevant to the job;
- Start with your personal details – full name, date of birth, nationality and contact details;
- Follow with professional qualifications and educational

Make sure your CV explains clearly and concisely what you have to offer and remember good presentation is vital – employers have to sort through hundreds of CVs and any that are poorly written or have spelling mistakes are rejected straight away.

history (in reverse order) and list the grades and passes obtained;

- Present your career history in reverse chronological order, starting with your most recent position;
- Include at least two referees (see **References** below), but ask their permission first;
- Limit your CV to two sides of an A4 sheet. Using bullet points rather than full sentences can minimise the word count.

Selection Process

The standard selection process for jobs in England is through interviews, usually one, but candidates for senior positions are often interviewed at least twice. Some companies require you to attend an assessment centre with other candidates, and the selection process may take place over a few days.

Some companies like candidates to undergo tests before an interview to help determine their aptitude for the position, which may take the form of multiple-choice questionnaires or specific tasks relevant to the position, for example, drafting a letter. For certain jobs, a pre-employment medical examination is also required.

References

English employers generally ask for references; usually two, but sometimes three. Your first reference should be provided by your current or most recent employer, and the second may be a character reference (i.e. provided by someone who knows you well), although some companies request that all references be from past employers. If you're a school leaver or student, a reference may be required from a tutor at your last educational institution.

In England, an employer isn't legally obliged to provide an employee with a written reference, although it's unusual for companies to refuse. Prospective employers

usually contact your previous employer directly, in writing or by telephone for a reference.

Salary

Your salary is stated in your contract of employment, where salary reviews, overtime rates, piece and bonus rates, planned increases and cost of living rises may also be included. You generally receive an itemised pay statement or wage slip with your salary.

Salary Payments

Salaries are generally paid directly into your bank account each month. The date varies, and some people are paid in the middle of the month and others at the beginning or end. Some lower paid workers or those in temporary employment (known as 'temps') are paid weekly.

Salary Reviews

Salaries are generally reviewed annually. In the private sector, annual increases are negotiated by individual employers, independent pay review boards or, if the majority of employees are union members, by unions (which is called collective bargaining). In the public sector, pay increases are automatically agreed with unions, and are on a set pay scale. A percentage of your annual salary increase compensates for a rise in the cost of living, although some employees, particularly in the public sector, may receive pay rises below the annual rate of inflation.

> **'People say I wasted my money. I say 90 per cent went on women, fast cars and booze. The rest I wasted.'**
>
> George Best (Northern Irish footballer)

Pensions

Under English employment law, all companies with five or more staff must provide pension schemes. Many people also pay into separate or additional personal pension schemes.

Discrimination

Racial and sexual discrimination is prohibited in the workplace in England, and two major laws passed in 2003 did much to reduce it. In theory, this means that anyone who meets the employment criteria should get the job, although in practice this isn't always the case. If you think you have been the victim of discrimination you should contact the Equal Opportunities Commission (36 Broadway, London SW1H 0BH (☎ 020-7222 1110, 💻 www.eoc.org.uk).

Retirement

Your employment conditions may be valid only until the generally recognised British retirement age, which is currently 60 for women and 65 for men, but will be 65 for everyone from 10th April 2010. If you wish to continue working after you've reached retirement age, you may need to negotiate a new contract of employment, and if your employer has a compulsory retirement age, he isn't required to give you notice. However, it's illegal to have a lower compulsory retirement age for women than men or vice versa.

CONTRACTS

Under English law, a contract of employment (also known as a 'statement of terms and conditions' or an 'offer letter') exists as soon as an employee proves his acceptance of an employer's terms and conditions of employment, e.g. by signing a contract and starting work, after which the employer and employee are bound by the terms offered and agreed. A written contract of employment usually contains all the terms and conditions agreed between the employer and employee, and no distinction is made between full-time and part-time workers with regard to rights in the workplace.

'The difference between a supermarket trolley and a non-executive director is that, while both hold a vast quantity of food and drink, only the trolley has a mind of its own.'

T.P. Blenkin (English businessman)

STARTING OR BUYING A BUSINESS

There are no restrictions for EEA nationals who wish to set up a business in the UK or work as self-employed. However, there are strict controls and rules for non-EEA nationals.

A New Business

If you're a non-EEA national and wish to set up a new business in England, you must apply to the Home Office. You will need to provide evidence that you have sufficient funds to establish the business, which must create at least two new full-time jobs for people already settled in England.

An Existing Business

If you're a non-EEA national planning to take over or join as a

partner or director in an existing business, you must make an application to the Home Office, and provide a written statement of the terms on which you will join or take over the concern. These include audited accounts for the business for previous years, and evidence that your services and investment will lead to an overall increase in employment, and create at least two new full-time jobs for people already settled in England.

Further information about setting up a business in England can be found on the Foreign and Commonwealth Office website (💻 www.fco.gov.uk).

WORKING FROM HOME

Working from home saves you money on rental costs and commuting, but you must ensure that the tenancy agreement, mortgage agreement or title deeds of your home don't place any restrictions on business use. You may also need planning permission from your local council. The following are also important considerations:

BUSINESS RATES

Business rates are payable to local councils on most business premises. If you plan to both live and work on the premises, you may have to pay business rates and council tax.

Insurance

Depending on the business and how you trade, you're required by law to take out certain types of insurance, such as:

- **Employer's liability insurance**: Compulsory if you have employees. This insurance provides cover for claims made by employees who are injured or become ill as a result of their employment.
- **Health and accident insurance**: This pays a regular income or lump sum if you're unable to work due to an accident or sickness.
- **Premises and contents insurance**: You must have insurance for the premises you work from and for its contents, even if you work from home and already have household insurance. This is because most household insurance only covers residential use.

- **Public liability insurance**: This provides cover against claims by members of the public who are injured or have property damaged as a result of carelessness at work by you or your employees.
- **Vehicles insurance**: Vehicles used for business purposes must be specifically insured for this, even if they're already insured for private use.

Further information about working from home is available from local councils and the government's Small Business Service (☎ 0845-600 9006 – 8am-8pm, Monday to Friday, 💻 www-businesslink.gov.uk).

> **'Make lots of money. Enjoy the work. Operate within the law. Choose any two of the three.'**
>
> Jack Dee (English comedian)

BLACK ECONOMY

The black economy operates at all levels in England, among both employers and workers – paying in cash, declaring a percentage of your income rather than all of it, invoicing for half a job but charging for all of it, employing unregistered workers, etc. You may even find yourself part of the black economy unwittingly. If possible, however, you should avoid it, as it's highly illegal, and if you accept illegal employment you have no rights and are entitled to no benefits – and can be deported!

WORKING WOMEN

Whilst women are equal in the eyes of English employment law, there's no doubt that the glass ceiling is still an obstacle for many women, particularly in male-dominated sectors such as banking and finance. Research carried out by the Equal Opportunities Commission (EOC) found that women working full-time earn some 20 per cent less than men, and that women hold fewer than 10 per cent of the top positions in stock market companies, the police, the judiciary and trades unions. Even when they're retired, it doesn't get any better for women – retired women have, on average, just over half the income of retired men.

On the positive side, however, there are now more women at

> In 2007, the Equal Opportunities Commission claimed that unless there was a dramatic change in recruitment and promotion, it would take another 200 years to achieve an equal number of women in Parliament, 60 years to win parity in the financial sector, and 40 years to reach equality among the judiciary.

the top of their professions and this trend is expected to increase. In general, women are free to wear whatever they wish to work (within reason!) and are treated equally and with respect by their male colleagues. As a general rule, English women don't expect or tolerate sexist comments about their appearance or dress. Nonetheless, this isn't the case everywhere, especially in male-dominated industries; there have been several cases of high-flying businesswomen taking their employers to an industrial tribunal, after being driven from their jobs by sexism or discrimination.

Maternity Pay

You're entitled to statutory maternity pay (SMP) under English law, provided you meet certain conditions: you must have worked for the same employer for 26 weeks continuously, prior to the 15th week before your baby is due, and your average weekly earnings must be at least the national insurance lower earnings limit. SMP is paid for up to 39 weeks as the following rates: 90 per cent of your average gross weekly earnings for the first six weeks, and 90 per cent of your

gross weekly earnings or £108.85 a week (whichever is lower) for the remaining weeks.

BUSINESS ETIQUETTE

Business Cards

When meeting new people, it's traditional to shake hands and exchange business cards. The English tend to quickly look at the card and then put it away in their wallet.

Business Gifts

Giving

Exchanging business gifts isn't usually expected in England. The main exception to this rule is at Christmas, when many companies give gifts, ranging from chocolates to a bottle of whisky or a case of wine. In some sectors such as finance and banking, gifts may be more extravagant.

If you give business gifts, the most appropriate are consumable items, for example a bottle of wine or a hamper of food. Be careful not to make your gifts too extravagant – a more expensive item is likely

A 2006 study found that the traditional 60-minute lunch break in England has shrunk to an average of 20 minutes. A knock-on effect of these snatched breaks is that the English spend more money than any other European country on food eaten on the move (an average of £229 a year), compared, for example, with just £56 a year in Spain.

to be perceived as over-generous, and might even be construed as bribery. **You should not offer cash payments as gifts.**

People working in the public sector aren't generally allowed to accept gifts – or there's a strict cap on the value of any gifts received. Some professional bodies also impose similar restrictions on their members regarding the acceptance of gifts.

Receiving

If you receive a gift, it's polite to open the present as soon as you receive it, and in front of the person who gave it to you.

Business Hours

Offices usually work from 8 or 9am to 4.30 or 5.30pm, Mondays to Fridays, although it's common for senior staff to work much longer hours. Lunch is usually an hour taken between noon and 2pm, although many people take a much shorter lunch break.

Business Lunches

Extended business lunches are rare in England. If you're invited to a business lunch, this is usually from noon onwards and is generally over by around 2pm.

Dress

You should dress smartly for meetings. Men wear suits and ties, and are usually close-shaved with conservative haircuts; women wear business suits or smart trousers, skirts and tops. Personal hygiene and a well-groomed appearance are important. Many companies have 'dress down Fridays', when employees are permitted to wear smart casual clothes (which may not include jeans), i.e. no suit or tie for men.

Greetings

Formal

When you first meet business people it's customary to shake hands. Typical greetings are "Hello/good morning/afternoon", "nice/good to meet you", or the more old-fashioned "How do you do?" (this greeting is rarely used by younger people).

The English place great importance on good manners, which should be borne in mind when doing business. They don't respond well to arrogance or over-familiarity, and it's best to be polite but reserved, at least initially. Always remember to say 'please' and 'thank you', as these aren't simply implied in English (as they are in some other languages). Most English people use first names in a business context, but check before assuming this is the preferred form of communication.

Informal

English colleagues generally greet each other with 'hello' or 'good morning' and don't shake hands with colleagues each day, as is the custom in some other European countries. Conversations at work are likely to be restricted to 'safe' subjects such as sport, usually football, leisure time, popular entertainment – often the previous evening's TV – travel, and holidays. Don't be surprised if your colleagues seem to keep themselves to themselves, especially at first. This isn't a personal slight, but because the English don't rush into making friendships, and you'll probably find that your relationships blossom in time.

'Three things in life are certain: death, taxes and more meetings.'

Simon Jenkins (British newspaper columnist)

Meetings

It's usual to exchange pleasantries at the start of a meeting. Business meetings are generally disciplined and follow a strict agenda. It's considered rude to answer your mobile phone during a business meeting (unless you're a senior manager), or to get up and leave before a meeting is finished.

Negotiating

As a general rule, the English don't react well to pushiness or the hard sell. Negotiations tend to be friendly and relaxed, and you may well find that people use jokes and humour to lighten the mood in a business setting. If you're trying to sell products or services, you should try to adopt a similar, understated style.

Timekeeping

Being on time for an appointment is essential when doing business with the English, but just as you should ensure that you aren't late,

> **'I always arrive late at the office, but I make up for it by leaving early.'**
>
> Charles Lamb (English essayist)

you should also try not to arrive too early. If you're unavoidably held up, you should phone to explain what has happened.

Although the English expect visitors to be punctual, this does not necessarily mean that your meeting will start on time. Don't be surprised if you have to wait 15 minutes or more for a meeting to start, and it may well run over its allotted time.

EMPLOYING PEOPLE

Under English employment law, if you take someone on to work in your home, for example, a cleaner or a nanny, you may be legally classed as their employer. If this is the case, you have certain obligations, such as deducting Income Tax and National Insurance contributions from their wages through the Pay As You Earn (PAYE) scheme.

The rules for establishing someone's employment status, i.e. whether they are employed or self-employed, are complicated, and it's best to obtain official advice from the HM Revenue & Customs New Employer Helpline (☎ 0845-6070 143 – 8am-8pm, Mondays to Fridays; 8am-5pm, Saturdays and Sundays).

TRADE UNIONS

As a nation, England has become much less unionised, and nowadays fewer than a third of the workforce belongs to a trade union. There are nevertheless unions representing most professional sectors. The Trade Union Congress (TUC) is the national organisation for English trade unions; to find out which union is best to join for your profession, visit the TUC's website (💻 www.tuc.org.uk – go to 'unions'). The TUC also operate a 'Know Your Rights' telephone line (☎ 0870-600 4882 – 8am-10pm), where you can request information leaflets about employment rights and other issues.

WORKING HOURS

The European Union's working time directive covers most workers in England, and entitles them to:

- four weeks' paid holiday a year;
- a break when the working day is over six hours;
- a period of 11 hours each day when no work is done;

- a period of 24 hours without work every seven days;
- a ceiling of 48 hours on the maximum average working week;
- a ceiling of an average of eight hours' night work in every 24 hours;
- free health assessment for night workers.

Flexible Working Options

A number of English companies offer flexible working arrangements to help employees achieve a better work-life balance, including:

- part-time work;
- flexible hours – employees can choose their start and finish times, or work longer hours on some days so they can take more time off;
- term-time working for parents of school-age children;
- job-sharing – two people share a single full-time job (jobs are advertised as 'job shares').

Full-time workers in England work an average of 44 hours a week, over 25 per cent work over 48 hours a week – two-thirds of the workforce are unaware of the 48-hour limit.

Holidays

Your annual holiday entitlement usually depends on your profession, position and employer, and your individual contract of employment. Under EU rules, employees are

allowed four weeks paid holiday a year and the average holiday allowance for English employees is 23 days a year.

Holiday entitlement is calculated on a pro rata basis per completed calendar month of service, if you don't work a full year. Usually, all holiday entitlement must be taken within the holiday year in which it's earned, although some companies allow employees to carry holidays over to the next year.

Before starting a new job, check that any planned holidays will be approved by your new employer. This is particularly important if they fall within your probationary period, usually the first three months, when holidays aren't generally permitted.

Holidays may normally be taken only with the prior permission of your manager or boss, and in many companies must be booked up to one year in advance. Most companies allow unpaid leave in

> **'It is wonderful when a calculation is made, how little the mind is actually employed in the discharge of any profession.'**
>
> Samuel Johnson (poet & critic of English literature)

exceptional circumstances only, such as when all your holiday entitlement has been used up. If you resign your position or are given notice, most employers will pay you in lieu of any outstanding holidays, although this isn't an entitlement, and you may be obliged to take the holiday at your employer's convenience.

The Government proposes to increase the current statutory minimum holiday entitlement from four weeks to 5.6 weeks (a maximum of 28 days) to include bank holidays in holiday entitlement. This means that the holiday entitlement for someone working a five-day week will rise from 20 to 28 days.

Christmas

It's becoming increasingly popular for English workers to take two weeks' holiday during Christmas and New Year, and many companies now insist that this end-of-year break is mandatory, and forms part of the national holiday entitlement; apart from Christmas, Boxing and New Year's Days, which are official public holidays.

Easter

Good Friday and Easter Monday are bank holidays in England, and many people like to go away for a long weekend.

Public Holidays

Compared with many other European countries, the UK has few public or national holidays – normally referred to as bank holidays, as they're days when banks are officially closed – all of which (apart from religious holidays) fall on Mondays. Schools, businesses and many shops are also closed on public holidays. The only national religious holidays are Christmas and Easter.

Bank Holidays

HOLIDAY	Date/Month
New Year's Day	1st January
Good Friday	March or April
Easter Monday	March or April
May Bank Holiday	First Monday in May
Spring Bank Holiday	Last Monday in May
Summer Bank Holiday	Last Monday in August
Christmas Day	25th December
Boxing Day	26th December

7.
ON THE MOVE

The good news about English public transport is that you can get a train or a bus to almost anywhere, and that most cities and large towns have a good integrated public transport service. The bad news is that it's among the most expensive in the world and your journey may take a good deal longer than you envisaged. Public transport has a poor reputation – ask any English person their opinion about public transport, and they will almost certainly launch into a rant about sky-high prices, overcrowding, endless engineering works, frequent delays and cancellations, and seasonal chaos caused by a sprinkling of snow or falling leaves. Crime can also be a problem when using public transport, particularly late at night.

> 'Everywhere in life is somewhere else and you get there in a car.'
>
> E.B. White (American author & humourist)

On the motoring front, the good news is that driving standards are generally excellent and the road network is good; the bad news is that many roads are frequently gridlocked and fuel costs are amongst the highest in Europe – and positively eye-watering compared to North America.

As a consequence of the unreliability and high cost of public transport, Britain is becoming more like the US every day, where the car has complete hegemony over public transport. If you live in a major city, it isn't always essential to own a car, but if you live in the country or a city suburb off the main rail and bus routes, it's usually mandatory to own a car.

Disability awareness in reasonable in the UK and improving. There's reserved parking for the disabled in towns and cities, cars with hand controls can be hired, taxis are available that accommodate wheelchairs, and most buses and trains are equipped to cater for travellers with disabilities.

To help you get around England safely and cost effectively, this chapter contains useful tips about motoring, road rules, driving etiquette and using public transport.

DRIVING

English Drivers

In general, the English have a reputation for being good drivers and most are reasonably considerate, e.g. drivers usually give way to cars waiting to enter the flow of traffic or change lanes. English drivers generally obey roads rules, with the exception of parking and speed limits, which are routinely

ignored – foreigners are frequently surprised at how fast English people drive (often up to 50 per cent above the legal speed limit). Another surprising aspect is that many drivers are reluctant to use their lights in poor visibility, or don't even switch them on when it's completely dark at night.

English Roads

The English road network runs to around 4,850mi (7,760km) and the standard of roads is generally good, but the constant heavy volume of traffic means that some main roads and motorways are in poor condition – traffic bulletins often refer to traffic jams caused by the 'sheer volume of traffic'! Poor road design and substandard workmanship also add to the problems – some suburban roads are full of potholes, and roads in all areas are often badly repaired after being excavated by utility companies and local councils. Not surprisingly, road repairs cost the English taxpayer millions of pounds each year.

Road Rage

Although most English drivers are mild-mannered, road rage, when drivers lose their temper and attack or drive into other motorists, is becoming more common. Triggers for road rage include tailgating, headlight flashing, obscene gestures, obstruction and verbal abuse.

Weather Conditions

Don't underestimate the English weather, particularly in winter when snow, ice, fog, wind and heavy rain cause havoc, and driving conditions can deteriorate quickly anywhere. In winter it gets dark at around 4pm, which, when combined with heavy rain, can be like driving in fog. When road conditions are poor, you should allow two or three times as long to reach your destination.

Local radio stations and BBC Radio Five Live feature constantly updated traffic bulletins.

Motorways

Motorways ('M' roads) have two or three lanes in each direction. Motorway travel is generally fast, although it's often slowed to a crawl by road works and contra-flows (two-way traffic occupying a single carriageway). On three-lane motorways, relatively few motorists use the left-hand (slowest) lane, which in effect reduces the

> **Motorway Driving**
>
> Motorways bring out the worst in English drivers: common faults include poor lane discipline, overtaking on the inside, driving too fast in poor conditions (e.g. fog and heavy rain), and failing to keep a safe distance from the vehicle in front.

motorway to two lanes. The sides of motorways are often marked with a white line with a ribbed surface, which warns you through tyre sound and vibration when you drive too close to the edge of the road.

SOS telephones are situated along motorways – arrows on marker posts at the roadside indicate the direction of the nearest telephone. The hard shoulder (left-hand side of the road) is for emergencies only – stopping here is dangerous and many fatal accidents involve vehicles parked on the hard shoulder.

Minor Roads

Some 'B' roads, minor roads and country lanes are single track. Take extra care when driving on these, particularly as many locals – who know the roads and may drive fast – tend to assume there's nothing coming and take up most of the road.

Toll Roads

England has just a few toll roads (the English don't take kindly to paying to drive on a road), which include the following:

- **Dartford Crossing:** part of the M25, the bridge (going south) and tunnel (going north) cross the Thames in the east of London; the toll is £1;
- **M6 toll road:** the toll for the 27mi (43km) route is £2 and avoids the congestion around Birmingham;
- **Severn Bridge:** cars crossing from Wales into England pay £4.80 to cross the bridge. Travel in the opposite direction is free (it's assumed that nobody could possibly want to stay in Wales for long).

Roadside Parking

One of the biggest problems when driving in towns and most residential areas is the huge number of cars parked on the roadside. Drivers often have to stop because one side of the road is partially or completely blocked, making a two-way road effectively into a one-way street.

Road Rules

Before you take to the road, read *The Highway Code*, available from bookshops and British motoring organisations, priced £1.99. The most important feature of driving in England is that **you drive on**

> 'I found a way to make my wife drive more carefully. I told her that if she has an accident, the newspapers will print her age.'
>
> Jan Murray (American comedian & actor)

the left. If you aren't used to this, take extra care when pulling out of junctions, one-way streets and at roundabouts. The road rules and tips below are designed to help you adjust to driving in England.

Bus & Taxi Lanes

Bus lanes are indicated by road markings, and signs indicate the period of operation – usually during rush hours only (although some lanes are in 24-hour use), and which vehicles are permitted to use them. Don't drive in lanes reserved for buses and taxis, unless it's necessary to avoid a stationary vehicle or obstruction. Bus drivers get irate if you drive in their lane and you can be fined for doing so.

Drinking & Driving

An average of 3,000 people in England are killed or seriously injured each year in accidents involving drinking and driving, and drink-driving offences are taken **very** seriously. You're no longer considered fit to drive when your blood/alcohol concentration exceeds 80mg of alcohol per 100ml of blood. Penalties for exceeding the limit are a maximum of six months' imprisonment, a fine of up to £5,000 and a minimum 12 months driving ban. An endorsement for a drink-driving offence remains on a driving licence for 11 years.

Alcohol-related offences are particularly prevalent among young men aged 17-29. Campaigns usually feature shocking images, and are targeted at young males to highlight the risks and consequences of drink-driving.

Hazard Warning Lights

Hazard warning lights are used to warn other drivers of an obstruction, e.g. an accident or traffic jam on a motorway.

> **It's illegal to use a hand-held phone whilst driving, for which the penalty is a fine of £60 and three penalty points on your licence.**

Lane Markings

White lines are used to indicate traffic lanes in England, and roads

may also have studs to indicate lines (and the edges of roads) at night, called cat's eyes. The lines down the centre of roads and at the edge of traffic lanes have the following meanings:

- a single broken line indicates that overtaking is permitted in both directions;
- a double line with a broken line on your side of the road means that overtaking is permitted in your direction;
- a single or two solid lines indicates no overtaking in either direction;
- a solid line to the left of the centre line, i.e. on your side of the road, means that overtaking is prohibited in your direction.

If you drive a left-hand drive car, take extra care when overtaking (the most dangerous manoeuvre in motoring) and when turning right. It's wise to have a special overtaking mirror fitted to your car.

Cat's eyes (invented in the UK in 1933) are used to indicate lanes and the edges of roads at night. They comprise two pairs of reflective glass spheres set into a rubber dome, which reflect a vehicle's lights at night. They come in various colours, depending on their use, as follows:

- white cat's eyes are used for the centre of a road, lane markings and traffic islands;
- red cat's eyes are placed along the hard shoulder of a motorway;

- orange cat's eyes are placed along the edge of the central reservation;
- green cat's eyes denote joining or leaving slip roads at junctions, e.g. on a motorway;
- blue cat's eyes are used for police slip roads.

Pedestrian Crossings

The English take pedestrian crossings very seriously (unlike motorists in many other countries). Always approach pedestrian crossings with caution, and don't park or overtake another vehicle on the approach to a crossing, marked by a double line of studs or zigzag lines. Pedestrians have the legal right of way once they've stepped on to a crossing without traffic lights and you **MUST** stop for them. Motorists who don't stop are liable to heavy penalties. At pelican crossings – a pedestrian crossing with lights – a flashing amber light follows a red light to warn you to give way to pedestrians.

Not that one (Lincolnshire)

Priority

There's no priority to the right (or left) on English roads. At crossroads and junctions, there's an octagonal 'Stop' sign (and a solid white line on the road) or a triangular 'Give Way' sign (with a broken white line on the road), where a secondary road meets a major road. 'Stop' or 'Give Way' may also be painted on the road surface. You must stop completely at a 'Stop' sign, even if there's no traffic approaching. At a 'Give Way' sign you aren't required to stop, but must give priority to traffic on the major road.

Roundabouts

The English like roundabouts and you will come across them everywhere. Traffic flows clockwise round roundabouts and vehicles already on the roundabout (coming from your right) have priority over those entering it. Some roundabouts have a filter lane, reserved for traffic turning left. When on a roundabout, you should signal as you approach the exit you wish to take. Some large roundabouts have traffic lights, which may be in operation only during peak traffic times (indicated by a 'part-time signals' sign). There are also mini roundabouts, indicated by a circular blue sign with arrows in a clockwise circle (see box).

Speed Limits

The following speed limits are in force throughout the UK, unless otherwise indicated by a sign:

- Motorways and dual-carriageways: 70mph (113kph)
- Unrestricted single carriageway roads: 60mph (97kph)
- Built-up areas (towns): 30mph (48kph)

Speed limits are always marked in miles per hour. Speed cameras (both fixed and mobile) are in widespread use throughout the country. The UK has more speed cameras than any country in the world.

> **'Speed cameras are fatuous instruments of oppression designed to exercise power and subservience purely for its own sake.'**
>
> Auberon Waugh (English writer)

Speed Ramps

There are a number of road-calming (a euphemism for 'enraging') measures in operation in the UK, the most common of which are 'speed bumps' or 'sleeping policemen' and one-way chicanes (where the road is narrowed to allow just one vehicle to pass, and priority is given to one way or the other). Speed bumps are common in residential areas, near schools, on private roads, in university grounds and in car parks. They're designed to slow traffic where there's a danger to pedestrians, and are usually indicated by warning signs; if you don't slow down when crossing them, you risk damaging your car or even turning it over (which has led to fatalities).

Seat belts are compulsory and must be worn by all passengers.

Traffic Lights

The sequence of traffic lights in England is red, red/amber, green, amber and back to red. Red/amber is an indication that you should get ready to go, but you mustn't move off until the light changes to green. Amber means stop at the stop line. You may proceed only if the amber light appears after you have crossed the stop line or if stopping could cause an accident. A green filter light, shown in addition to the full lamp signals, means that you may drive in the direction shown by the arrow, irrespective of other lights showing. Be warned that there are cameras at many traffic lights, to detect motorists who drive through red lights.

Traffic Police

Police usually only stop motorists if they've committed a traffic offence. If you're stopped and don't believe that you have committed an offence and wish to contest it in a court of law, don't accept a fixed penalty notice, but ask for a full charge to be brought against you. You aren't required by law to carry your vehicle papers in England when motoring, but the police may ask to see the following:

- driving licence (British if held)
- vehicle registration document (log book)
- test certificate (MOT)
- insurance certificate (or an international motor insurance certificate, if you drive a foreign-registered car)

If you don't have your papers with you when you're stopped by the police, you must take them in person to a police station (of your choice), usually within seven days.

Speed camera

The Points System

As well as fines and prison sentences, a penalty points system is also in operation for driving offences, whereby points are added to a driving licence when a driver commits an offence. If you accumulate 12 or more penalty points within a three-year period, you're automatically disqualified from driving for a minimum period of six months. For every offence that carries penalty points, a court has the discretionary power to order the licence holder to be disqualified, usually for a period of between a week and a few months.

Central London Congestion Charge

In an effort to improve the traffic flow in central London (and make money to invest in public transport), a 'congestion charge' was introduced in February 2003, which has been very successful. Most vehicles must pay £8 per day to enter an area originally roughly bounded by the railway stations of Marylebone, Euston, St Pancras, King's Cross, Fenchurch Street and Victoria. This was extended in February 2007 (see map) and now covers a much wider area.

Congestion Charge road marking

The area is marked by signs showing a white C in a red circle (see photo), and you can pay on the spot or in advance of your journey.

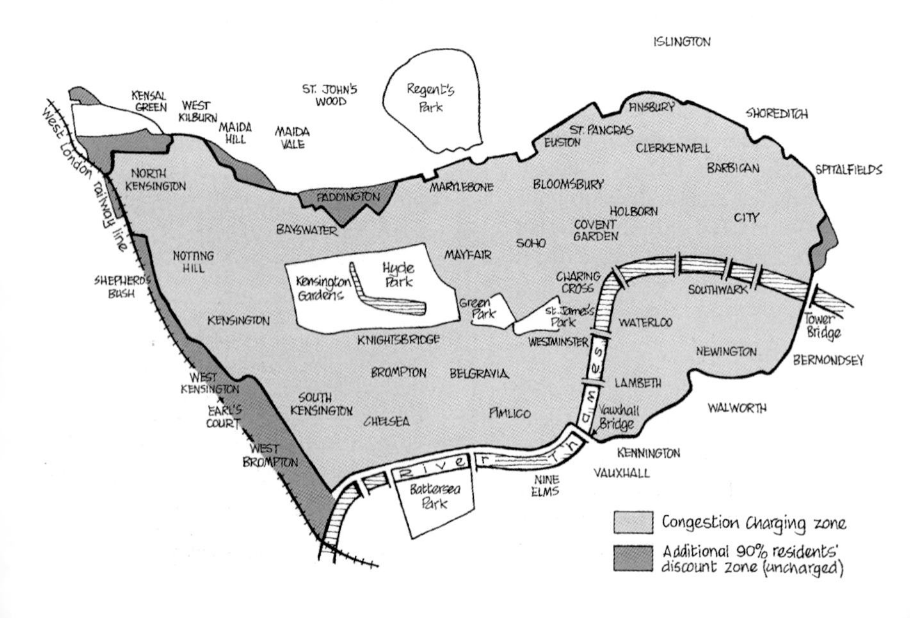

CCTV cameras check whether vehicles remain in the charging area for longer than the period paid for, in which case owners are liable to a fine. Certain vehicles and drivers are exempt from the congestion charge, including the disabled, residents who live in the charging area, vehicles using 'alternative' fuel (including electrically-powered vehicles) and vehicles with nine or more seats.

For further information, see the Congestion Charge website (💻 www.cclondon.com).

Motorcyclists

Motorcycling is popular in the UK, both as a means of transport and as a leisure pursuit. In general, laws that apply to cars also apply to motorcycles, but there are some that specifically apply to motorcyclists:

- A moped (a motorcycle with an engine not exceeding 50cc) can be ridden at the age of 16 with a provisional motorcycle licence. The maximum speed limit for a moped is 30mph (50kph).
- A full motorcycle licence can be obtained at the age of 17 after passing a test.
- British standard (or equivalent) approved crash helmets are compulsory for both riders and passengers.
- It's illegal for motorcyclists with a provisional licence to carry a pillion passenger (unless the pillion passenger holds a full motorcycle licence). To carry a pillion passenger, a motorcycle must be fitted with a dual seat and foot-rests.
- You must use dipped headlights at all times.
- You must have valid third party insurance.
- You cannot ride a motorcycle over 250cc until you've held a full motorcycle licence for two years.

Parking

Parking in most cities and towns is often a problem, particularly on-street parking, and most roads without parking meters or bays have restricted or prohibited parking.

> **'To park your car for an hour in Soho (London) costs more than the minimum wage. There are people working in McDonalds in Soho, who can look out of their window and see parking meters earning more than they do.'**
>
> Simon Evans (English comedian)

On-road Parking

On-road parking & waiting restrictions are indicated by single or double yellow or red lines at the edge of roads, usually accompanied by a sign indicating when parking is prohibited, e.g. 'Mon-Sat 8am-6.30pm' or 'At any time'. If there are no days indicated on the sign, restrictions are in force every day, including public holidays and Sundays. Yellow signs indicate a continuous waiting prohibition, and also detail times when parking is illegal. Blue signs indicate limited waiting periods. In general, a single yellow line means that parking is prohibited during the hours of 8am and 6.30pm, and double yellow lines indicate no parking at any time.

Double red lines indicate a red route, where you aren't permitted to stop between 8am and 7pm (or as indicated by a sign), Mondays to Fridays, except for loading.

Car Parks

In most towns, there are public and private off-road car parks, indicated by a sign showing a white 'P' on a blue background. Parking in public car parks and at meters is often free on Sundays and public holidays.

In many areas there are 'park and ride' parking areas (usually situated on the outskirts of a city or large town), where parking and/or public transport into the local town or city may be free (particularly at Christmas).

Fines

Fines for illegal parking vary from a fixed penalty ticket of £30 for parking illegally on a yellow line, to a £60 fixed penalty and three points on your driving licence for parking in a dangerous place, or on the zigzag lines near a pedestrian crossing. Penalties for non-payment, or overstaying your time in a permitted parking area (e.g. at a parking meter or in a pay-and-display area), are set by local councils.

CYCLING

If you cycle around England, it's a good idea to stick to the quieter 'B' roads and country lanes rather than the congested 'A' roads. Some English cities and large towns have designated cycle lanes on certain roads. It's illegal to cycle on pavements and in most public parks, and off-road cyclists must stick to bridleways and byways designated for their use.

It's advisable to wear a helmet and reflective clothes at all times, and at night you must wear a rear reflector and have front and back lights on your bike. Child passengers must ride in a special child's seat.

PUBLIC TRANSPORT

Public transport in England varies from region to region and town to town, and at its best is good, although it's invariably expensive. In fact, the UK has Europe's most expensive public transport, particularly trains, and probably the most expensive in the world. The really bad news is that, apart from costing an arm and a leg, it's also very unreliable, particularly rail services. Some areas and towns are poorly served, and services are often infrequent, unreliable or cancelled altogether.

The major cities usually have an integrated public transport system, where the same ticket is valid on buses, suburban trains and underground (metro), as applicable, fares being calculated on a zone system. Bus and rail services in most areas are severely curtailed on Sundays, public holidays and, in some cases, also even on Saturdays (often due to the ubiquitous 'engineering works').

Personal Safety

In general, most major towns and cities in England, including London, are safe places to walk and use public transport, without fear of harassment or assault. However, some cities have 'no-go' zones – ask locals or the police where these are and avoid them. You should take care at night, particularly if you're unfamiliar with an area; single women should take extra care. If there's no public transport at night, you should take a **licensed** cab to your destination.

> **Excuses, Excuses**
>
> **The excuses made by train companies for delays and overcrowding include the following:**
>
> **'After a horrific four hour journey where I had to stand from Newcastle to London, the conductor apologised, claiming that the overcrowding was caused by too many passengers.' (passenger)**
>
> **'We are sorry to announce the cancellation of the 8.16 to Bedford. This is due to slippery rain.' (BBC Online)**
>
> **'Rush hour commuters delayed for up to half an hour were astonished to be told their trains had been held up because the sun was too bright.' (*London Evening Standard*)**
>
> **'It was the wrong kind of snow.' Terry Worrall (British Rail)**

> **'The only way of catching a train I ever discovered is to miss the train before.'**
>
> G. K. Chesterton (English writer)

Trains

Once the pride and joy of the British, the UK rail network has paid the price for privatisation and a long-term lack of investment. Punctuality

is disrupted by ongoing track repairs and speed restrictions, and the press continually publishes horror stories regarding delays and other problems. However, some mainline rail routes, especially to and from London, have fast and frequent rail services – Manchester, for example, is just two and a quarter hours from London by train. On the other hand, cross-country travel is time-consuming and few routes are direct, meaning you must usually make a number of connections.

Numerous rail companies operate in England with a bewildering selection of fares, routes and services. It's advisable to use National Rail Enquiries (☎ 08457-484950, 💻 www.nationalrail.co.uk), which provides a centralised information service for all train services in the UK.

Prices

The train ticket price system is complicated, and often seems to follow no logic; for example, for reasons known only to the rail companies, it's often cheaper to travel from the north of England to London, rather than vice-versa.

As a general rule, tickets are cheaper if you book well in advance – tickets bought on the spot are often considerably more expensive – and avoid travelling on Fridays. Most rail companies offer special deals on tickets, with huge savings on normal prices. Like airline travel, trains now offer a limited number of discounted tickets per journey, and these usually sell out quickly (e.g. at least one month before travel), although you can sometimes get good deals a week or two in advance. If you don't plan to make any changes to your ticket, and don't mind travelling during restricted hours (e.g. after 9am and not between 3.30 to 6.30pm). it's also cheaper. The Trainline website (💻 www.trainline.co.uk) provides an online booking service, including reductions and special offers.

Several discount passes are available, including the Young Person's Railcard (£20) for full-time students and those aged between 16 and 25, and the Senior Railcard for the over 60s (£20), both of which give a third off most fares. A Family Railcard (£20) entitles up to four adults to a one-third discount, and up to four children to a 60 per cent

Paying thousands of pounds a year for a season ticket doesn't guarantee you a seat, even if you buy a first class ticket. Many rush-hour passengers are forced to stand for the whole of a journey, which may be an hour or more.

reduction. Passes are available from most stations.

Split-ticketing is a popular way of reducing the cost of rail travel, which involves buying two tickets for the same journey. For example, for the journey between Manchester and London, instead of buying a Manchester-London ticket, you buy a ticket from Manchester to a station en route, e.g. Stoke-on-Trent, and another ticket from Stoke-on-Trent to London. Providing the tickets are for the same train, you don't have to leave the train when it arrives at Stoke-on-Trent. Buying two tickets often works out cheaper than a single fare, particularly if you're travelling at peak times.

Buying Tickets

You can buy tickets up to three months in advance using online booking systems such as Trainline (🖳 www.trainline.co.uk), which offers online booking services for all train companies, and from train company websites. You can also buy tickets at any station, but if you board a train without a ticket (which isn't illegal) you must pay the full fare, either to a ticket inspector on the train or at your destination.

Seat Reservations

Reservations are available on long-distance trains and can usually be made from about two months in advance of the day of travel, up to around two hours before the train departs from its start point; or, for early morning trains, up to 4pm the previous evening. However, this doesn't apply to commuter trains, where it's often impossible to find a seat, and paying thousands of pounds for an annual season ticket **doesn't** guarantee you a seat.

> **'Nothing is so uninteresting to look at as clouds from the inside.'**
>
> Richard Gordon (British author)

A seat reservation is usually included in the ticket price, and the seat and carriage numbers are stated on the ticket. If a seat reservation isn't included, it's advisable to book a seat as most trains are usually full, especially at peak times, and it isn't always possible to get a seat without a reservation. At weekends and on public holidays, many long-distance services allow passengers to upgrade a ticket by buying a first-class supplement, which is worth buying if you have a long journey.

Comprehensive information about train travel in England can be found on Seat 61 (🖳 www.seat61.com).

Air Travel

Most major towns and cities have an airport, many of which handle both international and domestic flights. London has five international airports and is served by most major international airlines. Domestic air travel is popular, particularly for long distances.

Airports

Most airports have a reasonable selection of amenities, including shops and restaurants, although the food is usually mediocre at best and expensive. Car hire is usually available, and most airports have public transport services to the nearest town or city (a wide number of destinations are served from major airports). All airports ban smoking.

Fares

The huge competition for customers means it's possible to buy promotional flights for as little as £10 one way, although taxes and charges may be extra (and can add quite a bit). Most people book tickets online – in fact, it's the only way to book tickets with budget airlines such as Easyjet and Ryanair – but you can also usually book tickets directly with airlines, online agents and through High Street travel agents.

'The trouble with many rail passengers is that they think the railways are being run for their benefit.'

Jeremy Clarkson (TV presenter & author)

Coaches

Numerous companies operate coach (bus) services between large towns and cities, as well as connecting services to smaller towns and villages. In some cases, coach travel is the most direct way of getting around and, unlike trains, you always get a seat! Coaches are built to high standards with double-glazing, air-conditioning and toilets.

National Express (☎ 08705-808080, 💻 www.nationalexpress.co.uk) is the country's largest coach company, and operates throughout Britain with express services between many major towns and cities.

GETTING AROUND IN LONDON

London has a generally excellent public transport network with integrated bus, train and underground services. For general information, contact Transport for London's 24-hour Travel Information Service (☎ 020 7222 1234, 💻 www.tfl.gov.uk).

Taxis

Taxis in London are known as 'black cabs' (traditionally, they

> **The Knowledge**
>
> **Unlike taxi drivers in most other countries, London cabbies must undergo extensive training regarding London's streets and landmarks called 'the knowledge, which takes an average of two to three years to pass. This means that a black cab driver will usually know exactly where you want to go without referring to a map or using a Satnav system.**

were all black, but many now carry advertising and are painted in a multitude of colours) and like red buses, are an iconic symbol of the city. There are usually plenty of cabs available – they're for hire when the yellow sign on the roof is lit – and to hail one you just put your arm out. Many taxi drivers, known as 'cabbies', are chatty and love to regale passengers with their views on everything from football to politics.

Fares

London cabs are expensive, with fares starting at £2.20 with further costs depending on the tariff. Tariff 1 is from 6am to 8pm, Monday to Friday and public holidays, when a journey of 1 mile costs £4.20 to £6.20 (depending on traffic) and a journey of 2 miles £6.60 to £9.40. There are no additional charges for extra passengers or luggage. Tips are discretionary but many passengers round the fare up to the nearest pound. Many London cabs accept payment by credit or debit card.

Minicabs

Minicabs are generally cheaper competitors of black cabs, but you cannot hail a minicab on the street and must book one by phone. Minicab fares aren't metered, therefore it's essential to agree the fare before starting a journey.

There are numerous minicab operators in London, including specialist operators such as Ladycabs (☎ 020-7254 3501), with women drivers, and a good option for women travelling alone at night, and Freedom Cars (☎ 020 7734 1313), who cater for the gay and lesbian market.

London Underground

The London Underground, known as 'the Tube', is usually the best way of getting around London, particularly during rush hours. Greater London is served by 12 lines, along with the Docklands Light Railway and an urban rail network. Services – delays and disruptions permitting – are usually good. Travel on weekends is often disrupted by engineering works, when whole lines may be shut down, and sometimes travel between stations is by bus. Few tube

stations offer access for disabled passengers.

Fares

Travelcards and Oyster cards offer the best fare options. Travelcards are available for one, two or three consecutive days' travel. Oyster cards are electronic passes, which you press against a reader when entering and exiting the electronic gates to a station. Cards can be purchased and topped up at tube stations or online (💻 https://sales.oystercard.com).

If you're discovered by an inspector without a valid ticket, which includes travelling in a zone that your ticket doesn't cover, you're liable to an on-the-spot fine of £20.

Buses

Buses are a quick and convenient way to travel around London (the city has some 17,000 bus stops), and offer plenty of sightseeing opportunities en route. All buses are wheelchair accessible. Night buses are prefixed with the letter 'N' and come on duty before the tube shuts down, although services are infrequent and buses stop only on request.

Commuting

According to 2006 figures, the average English commuter spends 139 hours a year travelling to and from work (Londoners spend 225 hours a year). Between 1991 and 2001, the number of people commuting over 50km (31mi) increased by 30 per cent.

Riverboat Services

Thames boat services are popular with visitors, and there are frequent services up and down the river, although they aren't a viable service for most commuters. A Riverboat Services Guide is available from Transport for London (💻 www.tfl.gov.uk).

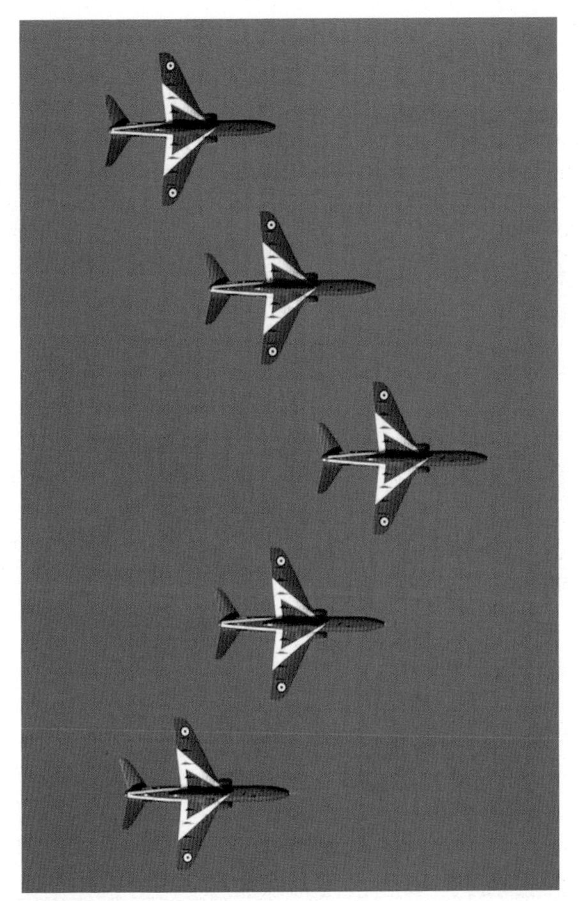

Red Arrows, RAF acrobatic team

Padstow, Cornwall

8.

THE ENGLISH AT PLAY

Becoming socially adept in a different culture is perhaps the most difficult obstacle to 'fitting in' abroad. It's also the area where you're most likely to make mistakes. To help you avoid social gaffes, this chapter contains information about social customs, dress code, dining, and leisure and sports activities.

'Clothes make the man. Naked people have little or no influence in society.'

Mark Twain (American writer)

DRESS CODE

Your appearance and, most of all, how others see you is generally of less importance in England than in other European countries, although much depends on the circles you move in and whether you're trying to make a good impression, e.g. on a prospective boss or a member of the opposite sex. Most people will take you as they find you and expect you to do likewise. On the other hand, the English have become much more fashion conscious in recent years and the urban young are at the cutting edge of fashion.

Smart casual wear is the order of the day in most situations, and smart trousers, a shirt with a collar, shoes (rather than flip flops or trainers) and maybe a jacket is an acceptable outfit almost anywhere for men, and a dress or skirt and blouse for women. However, if you're invited to a special social occasion, you should inquire about the appropriate dress beforehand.

Women

Unlike many of their European counterparts, English women don't feel it necessary to spend a lot of money on an outfit. Many prefer to buy in discount fashion shops such as Primark and TK Maxx and wear inexpensive clothing – a recent survey found that 55 per cent of women happily boast about the low price of their clothes.

In general terms, women in the north of England tend to dress up more than their southern counterparts – and they don't let the English weather get in the way of a fabulous outfit. Spend a night in any northern town and you'll see scores of women in glamorous attire, towering heels and almost always no coat, even in the depths of winter. Southern women tend to take a more casual approach to dressing up, although this is by no means universal.

> **Cosmetic Surgery**
>
> **The English might not be spending their money on clothes, but personal appearance is another matter: the demand for cosmetic surgery in England has soared in recent years and it's estimated that there are around 70,000 cosmetic surgery operations and 50,000 non-surgical cosmetic procedures (e.g. Botox injections) performed annually.**

Men

English men have probably one of the worst reputations in Europe as poor dressers, and tales of English male tourists wearing no shirts, and sandals with socks are legendary. Jeans and T-shirts are the order of the day, with shorts being worn as soon as there is any glimpse of the sun or warmer weather. In general, Englishmen have little interest in fashion and style, although, despite their reputation for being a bit scruffy, a growing number now take their appearance seriously. Englishmen are more likely than women to buy designer clothes, although they lag behind most of their more suave European counterparts when it comes to grooming; the average Englishman spends around one-third less per year on personal care products, compared, for example, with the average Frenchman.

EATING

Meals

Meals aren't generally social occasions in England with the exception of those held on special occasions, e.g. Christmas and the midday meal on Sundays when relatives often get together.

The terms used for meals in England can be somewhat baffling to a foreigner. The first meal of the day is called 'breakfast' by everyone, but the midday meal is called 'lunch' in the south and 'dinner' in the north and west. The evening meal is known as 'tea' (like the nation's favourite drink) in the north and west (most children also call it 'tea'), but as 'dinner' in the south. So, if someone invites you to dinner, they could be talking about midday or they might be asking you to an evening meal! To add to the confusion, there are also different words for dessert – some people call it 'pudding', while other people use 'afters' or 'sweet' (or dessert).

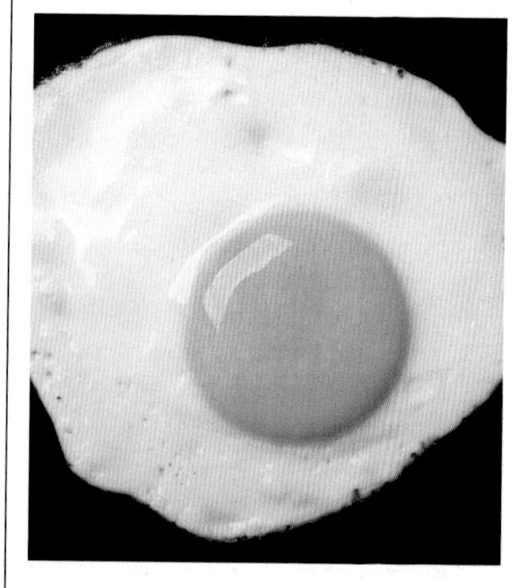

Breakfast

For many English people, breakfast usually consists of a rushed bowl of cereal or a piece of toast.

Commuters often buy breakfast en route or in their work canteen. Few people eat the famous 'full English breakfast' consisting of sausages, fried eggs, bread, tomato and bacon (popularly known as 'a heart attack on a plate'), except perhaps at weekends.

The word 'lunch' is believed to originate from the Spanish word *loncha*, meaning slice. This would have described a slice of meat served with beer or wine as a snack (similar to tapas).

Lunch

Lunch in England is usually eaten between noon and 2pm during the week; weekend lunches are generally later. Unlike many Europeans, very few English people go home for lunch during the working week. Indeed, it's becoming increasingly rare for workers to take a full hour's lunch break – many people tend to buy a sandwich or take a home-made lunch box, which they often eat at their desks. In general, lunch is more likely to be a snack rather than a full cooked meal, with the exception of Sundays, when many people have a large cooked meal.

Ready Meals

Pre-cooked meals that can be heated in the oven or microwave are known as 'ready meals' in England. The ready meals market has soared in recent years, and it's estimated that over three-quarters of English households now eat ready meals.

Afternoon Tea

Afternoon tea with sandwiches and cakes is a typically English tradition, although nowadays few families have afternoon tea. However, it's also available at cafes, tea rooms and hotels, and is a memorable, if expensive, experience at a 5-star hotel.

Dinner

Dinner (also confusingly called tea or supper) is eaten in the evening, although there's no standard time; some people eat as soon as they arrive home from work, usually around 6pm, while others eat later, at around 8 or even 9pm. The evening meal is usually cooked, and popular choices include meat and potato-based dishes such as 'shepherd's pie'; pasta dishes such as spaghetti bolognaise; or meat or fish in a sauce, served with rice or potatoes and other vegetables. Many families don't sit down together for an evening meal, especially during the week, and it's common for them to

eat the evening meal in front of the television.

Formal & Informal Dining

During your stay in England you will probably receive invitations to meals in both informal and formal settings. Knowing which cutlery to use, making the right conversation and knowing how to behave at the table will make you feel more comfortable and might make the difference between being invited again or not!

Conversation

What you talk about depends on the occasion and how well you know the host. As a general rule, it's best to let your host lead the conversation and do most of the talking. When you start a conversation, you should stick to neutral topics such as the weather – always a good bet with the English – and local news and events, leisure activities or holidays. Fellow guests are likely to ask you questions about your home country and your impressions of England; needless to say, it's wise to stick to the positive ones. You should avoid asking anyone personal questions, especially about money and how much they earn – and don't mention work unless someone else raises the subject.

> **'We must do lunch sometime' is the polite euphemism for 'I don't care if I never see you again.'**
>
> Marcus Hunt (author)

Formal Dining

Cutlery is placed on the right and left-hand sides of the place setting, and you use the implements from the outside in, i.e. the outermost cutlery is for the first course. Dessert cutlery is positioned above the place setting, the spoon being uppermost, with a dessert fork below. You should always use both a knife and fork if they're provided, and most food should be eaten using cutlery. The knife for buttering your roll is usually placed on the side plate. Items such as steak knives may only be provided if you order a steak – or steak is being served – and the same also applies to fish knives and forks.

Most English people eat with a knife and fork, rather than just a fork, as Americans do, even when eating a meal at home. Forks are held with the prongs facing down in the left hand and the knife in the right. When you have finished eating, you should place your knife and fork side by side in the middle of the plate.

Spoons

When eating soup, you should tip the bowl away from you and dip the spoon into the soup with a movement that directs it away from you rather than towards you. However, when eating breakfast cereal you should tip the bowl towards you. The golden rule when using a spoon is that savoury food is tipped away from you and sweet food towards you.

When to Start

It's polite to wait for everyone to be served (regardless of the formality of the occasion) before starting a meal. At formal meals you should wait for the host to start, unless he gives you permission to start beforehand.

Noises

As in most countries, coughing and blowing your nose loudly are considered rude at the table. If you need to cough, do it as discreetly as possible into your napkin and if you need to blow your nose, do so quietly. Burping at the table is considered very rude. If you absolutely have to, excuse yourself from the table or do it as discreetly as possible.

Seating

On formal occasions, guests are usually seated male-female, with the hosts at the ends of the table. It's polite to wait for the host to tell you where to sit and not to sit down until you're invited to do so. At large occasions such as weddings, cards with guests' names may be placed on tables. It's considered impolite to change places before or during the meal, but after dessert guests are free to mingle and sit elsewhere.

Table Manners

You should eat with both hands above the table, use the napkin to wipe the corners of your mouth (and fingers) and keep your elbows off the table. When eating informally, however, many people often sit with their elbows on the table between courses.

> **'Etiquette is knowing how to yawn with your mouth closed.'**
>
> Herbert V. Prochnow (American banker & author)

Toasts

Making toasts is a popular tradition in England. On informal occasions, people clink their glasses together and say "Cheers!" On formal occasions, the host usually makes the first toast by getting to his feet, raising his glass and making his 'speech'. The correct response is to raise your glass.

Napkins

Although some English people use the term 'serviette', 'napkin' is

generally considered the correct form. Napkins should be placed across the lap rather than tucked into your clothing.

CAFES, RESTAURANTS & PUBS

Cafes & Restaurants

To paraphrase a well-known children's poem by Henry Wadsworth Longfellow, when the food in England is bad, it's very, very bad, and when it's good, it's very expensive indeed! But don't despair – contrary to popular myth, not all English food is grey, lumpy or watery. In fact, you can usually find at least one or two good and reasonably-priced restaurants in most towns. Large towns and cities also have a wide range of ethnic restaurants such as Chinese, Indian, Lebanese, Turkish, Greek and Thai. To ensure you choose a good restaurant, ask for recommendations or check the online reviews, e.g. 💻 www.restaurant-guide.com, www.squaremeal.co.uk and www.toptable.co.uk.

In general, eating out isn't cheap in England, and it's easy to pay £100 for two (including wine) for a mediocre meal in an average restaurant. However, if you look around, it's possible to find medium-priced restaurants where you can enjoy a good meal for two with a bottle of wine for around £50.

> **American-style coffee shops such as Starbucks have proliferated across the country in recent years, and serve a wide range of coffee, tea and snacks. Internet cafes are also common.**

Cheap Eats

Places to eat cheaply include ethnic restaurants; in-house cafes in department stores and museums, which serve reasonably priced meals throughout the day; pubs, where food is usually only served during fixed hours at lunchtime (e.g. 12-2pm) and in the evening (e.g. 7-9.30pm); and markets. In general, you should try to avoid motorway service stations and anywhere there's a 'captive' clientele, where food can be awful and over-priced.

General Points

- **Alcohol:** Most restaurants are licensed to serve alcohol, but it's usually expensive – many charge three to five times the shop price for branded wine, or offer cheap table wine in own-label bottles or carafes. 'Bring your own' (BYO) alcohol restaurants are rare. English cafes aren't licensed to sell alcohol.

- **Booking:** It's wise to book a table at restaurants. You can do this by telephone or in person, and it's polite to telephone if you wish to cancel a reservation.
- **Slow service:** If service is slow, you should politely tell the waiter that you are in a hurry. If a dish is going to take longer than around 15-30 minutes to prepare and serve, the waiter should tell you this when ordering.
- **Opening hours:** Opening times for restaurants are usually between 12pm and 3pm for lunch and 6pm and 10.30pm for dinner. Many cafes are open all day but close around 6pm in the evening.
- **Prices:** Restaurants and cafes are obliged by law to display their tariffs in a clearly visible place at the entrance. Service or cover charges must also be clearly stated and prices shown must be inclusive of VAT. If a restaurant attempts to include any charges that aren't listed on the menu, which is a common practice in tourist areas, you should refuse to pay.
- **Seating:** When you enter a restaurant, a waiter usually takes you to a table, but if there are several free tables you may be offered a choice. Some restaurants have a sign at the entrance asking you to wait for a waiter to show you to a table.
- **Water:** If you don't want to buy a bottle of mineral water, ask for a glass or jug of tap water, which should be provided free of charge.
- **Paying the bill:** When you're ready to pay the bill, you should attract the waiter's attention by catching his eye, beckoning to him or calling to him discretely (shouting for the waiter is bad manners). When you want to pay, you ask for the 'bill' rather than the 'check' or, if you can attract the waiter's eye from across the room (an impossible feat in many establishments, where it seems that staff are trained to look anywhere except at the customers), you can make the universal air-writing signal with

your hands. Few waiters will bring you the bill unprompted.

- **Tipping:** Many restaurant and hotel bills include a service charge (10 to 15 per cent), designed to reduce tipping (and increase profits). In spite of this, most English people still feel obliged to leave a tip, a practice which is encouraged or even expected in many establishments.

> **'It was my Uncle George who discovered that alcohol was a food well in advance of modern medical thought.'**
>
> P.G. Wodehouse (English comic writer)

Pubs

A pub (an abbreviation of 'public house') is a typical English drinking place, and almost every English town and village has a least one. They are a British tradition going back to Roman and Saxon times (drunkenness isn't a new phenomenon – the British have been sots for millennia), when inns were established to meet the needs of travellers. A pub is one of the most welcoming places in the UK (particularly on a freezing winter's night, when many have inviting open log fires), and represents the heart of local communities.

In rural areas, there are traditional country pubs, often in picture-postcard, beamed cottages, featuring hand-pumped ales, crackling fires and hearty home cooking. Elsewhere, you'll find a huge variety of drinking establishments, from quiet, homely places where families are welcomed, to loud, student-filled chain pubs with earth-shaking music and barely enough space to stand. Most pubs attract a particular crowd of regular drinkers, known as 'locals', and some don't care for outsiders invading their patch – you're likely to recognise this as soon as you enter! Pub owners, known as landlords, have the right to refuse to admit or serve a customer, and cannot by law serve anyone who's drunk.

Age Limits

The legal age for buying and consuming alcohol in a pub is 18. Children over 14 are admitted at the discretion of the landlord, and are also allowed in beer gardens, family rooms, pub restaurants and an increasing number of pub lounges.

Drinks

Pubs offer a vast range of beverages, including many draught beers (on tap) drawn from casks or kegs,

such as bitter, stout (e.g. Guinness), mild ales and continental lagers. Numerous bottled and canned beers are also available. Pubs stock wines and a good selection of spirits, and they also sell a variety of low-alcohol beers and a wide choice of non-alcoholic drinks.

Beer and lager are sold in half-pints or pints (568ml); wine is sold by the glass or bottle; and spirits in measures of one-sixth of a gill (24ml), which is a single measure. Non-alcoholic drinks are sold by the bottle or glass.

Entertainment

Many pubs provide entertainment, including the screening of major sporting events shown on large TV screens; quiz nights, when groups of contestants compete to answer the highest number of questions correctly; quiz machines, based on board games such as *Monopoly* and *Cluedo*; pool tables (similar to snooker); darts competitions; and live music/comedy shows, usually held once a week.

Food

Most pubs provide reasonably priced hot and cold food at lunchtimes and in the evenings. Lunch is usually served between noon to 2pm and evening meals from 7pm to 9.30pm.

Wine bars, most of which serve food, can be found in most cities and towns and have become increasingly popular in recent years.

Rounds

When a group of English people is in a pub they usually buy drinks in 'rounds', where each person takes his or her turn to buy drinks for everyone else in the group. This is known as 'buying a round' or 'getting a round in'. When you're drinking in a group, try not to drink faster than the others, as the person buying the next round usually waits until most people have finished their drink before buying more. You don't have to drink in every round, but you should always pay for a round when it's your turn.

Where there are large groups, a 'kitty' or 'whip round' may be made, where everyone puts the same amount of money into a fund which is used to buy drinks for everyone.

Drinking in rounds may mean that you drink more and spend more money than you wish to. If you only want to have one or two drinks and leave early, you should insist that you're excused from the round and buy your own drinks.

NIGHTLIFE

Most large towns and cities have a lively nightlife scene, including nightclubs and wine bars. Many people also go to pubs, where there's often entertainment. The following points apply to nightclubs:

- **Age:** Nightclubs are for those aged 18 or over and the doorman (usually called a 'bouncer') may ask you to show proof of your age in order to let you in.
- **Buying rounds & paying:** In most clubs, you order at the bar and pay when your drinks are served. In venues with waiter service, you pay when the waiter brings your drinks, rather than ask for the bill later.
- **Dress code:** Casual dress is the norm for most nightclubs, although some don't allow jeans, trainers or leather jackets (dress may be completely arbitrary). Women can usually get away with any outfit. Bouncers (99.9 per cent are men) tend to be stricter with male clubbers, and you might find that they don't like your trainers or T-shirt (or face) and refuse you entry.
- **Opening hours:** Clubs typically open between around 10pm-2pm, although some are open until 5am. Many people go to clubs at the traditional pub closing time of around 11pm.
- **Types of drinks & cost:** Clubs serve the same range of drinks as pubs, although prices can be astronomical and are usually two to four times as much as in pubs. Entrance fees vary considerably, and usually range from anywhere between £5 and £30.

FAMILY OCCASIONS

Birthdays

Most English people like to celebrate their birthdays, whether this is a drink in the pub with friends, a meal in a restaurant or a large party. 'Landmark' birthdays such as 18, 21, 30, 40 and 50 are often celebrated with a big party for friends and family.

> **'It will be a traditional Christmas, with presents, crackers, door slamming and people bursting into tears, but without the dead thing in the middle. We're vegetarians.'**
>
> Victoria Wood (English actress & comedienne)

Christmas & New Year

Christmas is a major event in the English calendar and preparation starts as early as August in England, when department stores display Christmas cards and decorations. Christmas shopping (for presents and food) is important – the media announces the countdown to Christmas with a running tally of the number of 'shopping days' left until 25th December. During the last few weeks before Christmas and particularly during the last week, shops are extremely crowded.

The English celebrate Christmas on 25th December, when most spend the day with family or friends, eating, drinking and opening presents, before settling down in front of the TV or playing board games. The Queen's Speech is broadcast at 3pm, when she makes her annual address to the nation and the Commonwealth, although its popularity is waning. Traditional Christmas fare is roast turkey and vegetables, and Christmas pudding, a heavy, steamed fruit confection, which is usually laced with brandy and *flambéed* before serving. The 26th December is a public holiday, known as 'Boxing Day'.

New Year

Most teenagers and young adults go to pubs and bars to celebrate New Year's Eve. Large cities have huge fireworks displays and most city centres are packed with revellers. The traditional gathering place in London is Trafalgar Square. The start of the New Year is signalled by the chimes of Big Ben.

July and August are the most popular months to get married in England. The average wedding costs around £16,000.

Weddings

Invitations

Wedding invitations are sent out at least a month before the event and you should reply as soon as possible.

Gifts

Many couples draw up a gift list with a department store such as John Lewis or the House of Fraser. Invitations often include details of how to access the guest list, and the

easiest (but most impersonal) way is online – you simply place your order, and the store delivers all the presents to the bride and groom. You can also go into the store and order from the list.

Dress

A wedding is an opportunity for people to dress up, and you'll certainly be expected to make an effort; if you're invited to a formal wedding, men are usually expected to wear a suit and tie. Some weddings request that men wear morning suits with top hats (usually hired), which will be indicated on the invitation, although this is usually only expected of the key players (best man) and family members. Women usually wear cocktail dresses with sumptuous matching accessories (including hats).

> **'Memorial services are the cocktail parties of the geriatric set.'**
> John Gielgud (English actor)

Funerals

Christian funerals are held several days after the death, usually at least a week, and sometimes as long as two weeks. English funerals are generally low-key sombre affairs, although this depends very much on the family's background and traditions. A funeral may be held in a church or at a crematorium, and there are sometimes readings (usually read by close friends or relatives) and music (often the

deceased's favourite song or piece of music).

Mourners have traditionally been expected to wear black with a black tie for men, although this is no longer obligatory and nowadays any sombre colours are acceptable. There's usually a family gathering after the burial or cremation (often one of the few times that a whole family will get together), when refreshments are served. It's traditional to send flowers or a wreath to the family, church or the funeral directors (as requested), although some families ask for donations to be made to a charity rather than flowers to be sent.

POPULAR CULTURE

The favourite leisure activities of the English are watching television (particularly sport), shopping, gardening, gambling, dining out, and watching and playing sport. Other popular leisure activities include visiting museums, art galleries, botanical gardens and stately homes; going to the cinema, musicals, opera and the theatre; and attending dance and popular music shows. The UK is renowned for its arts and cultural scene, and there are modern performing arts centres in all the main cities; and cinemas, concert halls, galleries and theatres also abound in the major towns and cities.

National and local newspapers publish cinema programmes and review the latest films. London's entertainment magazines *What's On* (mainstream, conservative) and *Time Out* (progressive, more for the younger reader) carry comprehensive reviews and details of all London's cinemas, theatres and shows, as does the *Evening Standard's* weekly *ES* magazine.

Major Events

The following is a list of some of England's most important social events (see also **Major Sporting Events** below).

Chelsea Flower Show

The prestigious Chelsea Flower Show (💻 www.rhs.org.uk/chelsea) blooms for a week in mid-May, hosted by the Royal Horticultural Society (RHS) and held in the grounds of Chelsea Royal Hospital. Tickets are expensive at almost £100 a day and difficult to obtain.

Crufts

Crufts (💻 www.crufts.org.uk), named after its founder Charles Cruft, is an annual international championship show for dogs, organised and hosted by the Kennel Club (UK) in March, and staged at the National Exhibition Centre (NEC) in Birmingham. It's the largest annual dog show in the world, lasting four days, and has been staged since 1886. The main competition is for the 'best in show' award, which is generally considered the highest award attainable by a dog and its owner.

Farnborough Air Show

The Farnborough International Air Show (💻 www.farnborough.com) is a seven-day international trade fair for the aerospace business which is held biennially (the next is scheduled for July 2008) at the Farnborough airfield in Hampshire. It has been held since 1948, and, along with the Paris Air Show, is one of the world's premier events for the aerospace industry, particularly for the announcement of new developments and orders.

Glastonbury Festival

The Glastonbury Festival of Contemporary Performing Arts (💻 www.glastonburyfestivals.co.uk), commonly abbreviated to the Glastonbury Festival or Glasto, is the largest greenfield

Chelsea Flower Show, London

> **'Opera is when a guy gets stabbed in the back and instead of bleeding, he sings.'**
> Ed Gardner
> (American comic actor & writer)

music and performing arts festival in the world. Best known for its contemporary music, it also features dance, comedy, theatre, circus, cabaret and many other arts. From small beginnings in 1970, the 2005 event included almost 400 live performances and was attended by around 150,000 people.

Glyndebourne Opera Festival

The Glyndebourne Opera Festival (💻 www.glyndebourne.com) is held during the summer in the stunning gardens at Glyndebourne, a 700-year-old country house near Lewes in Sussex. Opera-goers dressed in evening wear – black tie and evening gowns – picnic in the grounds while listening to world-class opera singers. A special train runs from London Victoria Station to Glyndebourne for the event.

Notting Hill Carnival, London

Last Night of the Proms

A Mecca for classical music lovers worldwide, the Proms season (a series of concerts) runs from mid-July to the second week in September, when the famous 'Last Night' takes place. The Proms are held in the Royal Albert Hall in

Land of Hope and Glory
(A.C. Benson, 1862-1925)

Dear Land of Hope, thy hope is crowned,
God make thee mightier yet!
On Sov'reign brows, beloved, renowned,
Once more thy crown is set.
Thine equal laws, by Freedom gained,
Have ruled thee well and long;
By Freedom gained, by Truth maintained,
Thine Empire shall be strong.

Land of Hope and Glory,
Mother of the Free,
How shall we extol thee,
Who are born of thee?
Wider still and wider
Shall thy bounds be set;
God, who made thee mighty,
Make thee mightier yet
God, who made thee mighty,
Make thee mightier yet.

Thy fame is ancient as the days,
As ocean large and wide:
A pride that dares, and heeds not praise,
A stern and silent pride:
Not that false joy that dreams content
With what our sires have won;
The blood a hero sire hath spent
Still nerves a hero son.

Kensington, London (💻 www.bbc.co.uk/proms).

Land of Hope and Glory (see below) is an English patriotic song written by poet and essayist Arthur Christopher Benson, set to the trio theme from Elgar's *Pomp and Circumstance March No. 1*. It's played on the Last Night of the Proms amid much flag-waving, and is also the English 'anthem' at the Commonwealth Games.

Notting Hill Carnival

The Notting Hill Carnival (💻 www.mynottinghill.co.uk) is an annual event (since 1959) in Notting Hill, London, held over two days during the August summer bank holiday weekend (the last weekend in August). It's organised by members of the UK's Caribbean population, and is the largest street festival in Europe, attracting up to 1.5m people.

Trooping the Colour

Trooping the Colour (💻 www.trooping-the-colour.co.uk) is a military pageant performed by regiments of the Commonwealth and the British army, first performed during the reign of Charles II in the 17th century; the colours of a regiment were used as a rallying point in battle, and were trooped in front of the soldiers every day to make sure that every man could recognise those of his own regiment.

This impressive display of pageantry is now held in June each year to celebrate the official Birthday of the Sovereign, and is performed by her personal troops, the Household Division, on Horse Guards Parade, London, with the Queen attending and taking the salute. The Queen now attends in a carriage, but until 1987 she took the salute on horseback (riding side-saddle), wearing the uniform of the regiment whose Colour was being trooped. The regiments take their turn for this honour in strict rotation.

Admission to most museums and art galleries in England is free, although a charge is usually made for 'special' exhibitions staged for a limited period only.

THE ARTS

Museums & Art Galleries

England has an impressive number and variety of museums and art galleries, which include some of the world's most important collections (the British have been looting and pillaging for centuries to fill them). London is home to England's most celebrated collections.

Leading museums and galleries are open seven days a week (including on public holidays) from around 10am to 5 or 6pm, Mondays to Saturdays, and 2 or 2.30pm to 6pm on Sundays. Opening times vary, so check in advance, particularly when planning to visit the smaller London and provincial museums and galleries, some of which open on only a few days a week. Many museums and galleries provide reductions for disabled people and some have wheelchair access.

In addition to the great national collections, there are also many excellent smaller museums, galleries and displays in stately homes and National Trust properties throughout the country, many of which are well worth a visit. Local councils publish free directories of local arts organisations, and information about special events and activities.

Cinema

There has been a cinema renaissance in the last few decades, following a decline in the '60s and '70s, when many cinemas were turned into shops, bingo halls and even places of worship. Today there are some 2,500 separate screens, and attendances have more than doubled in the last ten years alone. The mainstream cinema scene is dominated by the major chains such as MGM and Odeon. In the last decade, many multiplexes have been built (often in new out-of-town leisure and shopping complexes), each with ten or more screens; Dolby or THX surround sound; comfortable, extra-wide seats with ample leg-room; and air-conditioned auditoriums. Free parking, cafes, restaurants, bars and games rooms may also be provided.

Most cinemas offer reductions (usually half price or less) for children and pensioners, although you should check in advance, as

Film Classification

Classification	Age Restriction
U	None
PG	Parental guidance advised
12a	No one under 12 is admitted unless accompanied by an adult
15	No one under 15 is admitted
18	No one under 18 is admitted

some reductions apply only to certain performances. Many cinemas have a reduced price day, usually Mondays, when admittance for afternoon shows is cheaper. Many modern cinemas have facilities for the disabled.

All films on general release are given a classification by the British Board of Film Censors (see box) which denotes any age restrictions:

Children (or adults) who look younger than their years may be asked for proof of their age, e.g. a school identity card, student card or driving licence, for admittance to age-restricted performances.

Theatre, Opera & Ballet

The UK is world-renowned for the quality and variety of its theatre, opera and ballet companies, and London has the world's most vibrant theatre scene with over 150 commercial and subsidised venues, including around 50 in the West End. On average, between five and ten major productions open each week, and a much greater number when smaller and fringe venues are taken into account.

Major auditoriums include the Royal National Theatre (South Bank), the Barbican Centre, the Royal Opera House (Covent Garden), and the Royal Court Theatre. Performances include modern drama, classical plays, comedy, musicals, revue and variety, children's shows and pantomime, opera and operetta, ballet and dance. London's fringe theatre is lively and extensive, and provides an excellent training ground for new companies and playwrights. Many venues nationwide support youth theatres, and people of all ages who see themselves as budding Laurence Oliviers or Katherine Hepburns can audition for local amateur dramatics societies. The theatre is well patronised throughout the country, and is one of the delights of living in England, particularly if you live within easy reach of London.

Good theatre and musical entertainment isn't, however, confined to London, and many provincial towns also have acclaimed theatres, concert halls and arts centres that attract international stars (and seats cost only a fraction of London's West End prices). The arts are subsidised by the Arts Council which, among other things, funds a repertory company touring programme that ensures the arts reach areas without permanent theatres.

Opera, along with ballet, is patronised by only a small minority of the middle and upper classes. Ticket prices for performances at the Royal Opera House in Covent Garden partly explain why: a seat in the orchestra stalls costs around £150, while a seat offering a reasonable view costs in excess of £60. Dance performances in general tend to be less expensive than opera. In addition to classical ballet, dance companies are popular and numerous throughout England, specialising in everything from contemporary dance to traditional forms from all corners of the globe.

> **'You sound like someone who should be singing on a cruise ship. Halfway through your song, I wished the ship was sinking.'**
>
> Simon Cowell (judge on the TV programme, *Pop Idol*)

Free programmes covering London or provincial theatres are available from Tourist Information Centres, and a number of websites provide comprehensive information, such as the Official London Theatre guide (💻 www.officiallondontheatre.co.uk); you can sign up for a weekly email bulletin to keep up to date with what's on, and London Theatre (💻 www.londontheatre.co.uk). Many British newspapers contain reviews of London and provincial shows, particularly broadsheet daily and Sunday newspapers which have their own theatre critics.

Concerts

Classical concerts are staged regularly throughout the UK by British and international performers, and celebrated international festivals cover orchestral, choral, opera, jazz, folk, rock and world music. London's unrivalled concentration and variety of music venues, and its four major orchestras, the London Symphony Orchestra (LSO), the London Philharmonic Orchestra (LPO), the Royal Philharmonic Orchestra (RPO) and the Philharmonia, make it the music capital of the world. Acclaimed provincial orchestras include those in Birmingham, Manchester and Bournemouth, along with the BBC National Orchestra.

In addition to classical and choral music, just about every other kind of music is performed regularly somewhere in the UK. This includes brass and steel bands, country & western, folk, heavy metal, hip hop, house, jazz, indie, medieval, reggae, rock, rhythm and blues and soul, to mention just a selection. The UK is a world leader in the popular music industry, and London is the centre

of the action, with more 'gigs' in one night than most provincial cities stage in a month. These range from pub sessions to mega rock star concerts that fill Wembley stadium.

Many publications are dedicated to the popular music industry, most prominently the *New Musical Express;* classical music fans are catered for by *Classic FM, Classical Music, Gramophone,* and *Early Music Today* magazines.

Gardens, Stately Homes, Parks & Zoos

Lists of gardens, stately homes, castles, theme parks, zoos, botanical gardens and national parks are available from tourist offices or are to be found in any good guide book, and touring by car is the best way to see them. Most are open throughout the year, although many have reduced opening hours from October to March.

The National Trust (NT) is a privately-funded charitable organisation, and one of the UK's most respected institutions with 3.5m members. It looks after over 300 historic buildings and gardens, 50 industrial monuments and mills, and more than 600,000 acres (240,000ha) of countryside in England, Wales and Northern Ireland. Many gardens, landscaped

'I was flattered to have a rose named after me until I read the description in the catalogue: no good in a bed, but perfect up against a wall.'

Eleanor Roosevelt (American political leader & wife of President Franklin D. Roosevelt)

parks, and prehistoric and Roman sites, are also in its care. You can become a member from around £32.50 a year or £58.50 a year for a family (including all children aged under 18), which provides free access to all NT buildings and sites. For further information contact the National Trust (Membership Department, PO Box 39, Warrington WA5 7WD, ☎ 0870-458 4000, 💻 www.nationaltrust.org.uk). You can join online or on-the-spot at any National Trust property and have your entrance fee refunded.

English Heritage has broadly similar aims as the National Trust. Membership costs £34 a year for adults, which enables you to visit 400 English Heritage properties without further charge. You also receive a property guidebook, maps, an events diary, a quarterly magazine and free entry to special events. For information contact English Heritage (Customer Service Department, PO Box 569, Swindon SN2 2YP, ☎ 0870-333 1181, 💻 www.english-heritage.org.uk).

If you're a keen horticulturist, you may be interested in joining the Royal Horticultural Society (80 Vincent Square, London SW1P 2PE, ☎ 020-7834 4333, 💻 www.rhs.org.uk). Membership starts at £44 and entitles you to free entry to many beautiful gardens and a range of other benefits.

The UK has a number of internationally acclaimed zoos, including London and Whipsnade (50km/30mi north of London), but there are also others throughout England (e.g. Bristol, Chester and Manchester) plus a number of safari parks (e.g. Longleat) where animals roam free.

The country also has around 100 theme parks which are very popular (attracting over 100m visitors annually), and an excellent place for a special (i.e. expensive) day out for the children. The most popular include Alton Towers (Staffordshire), Pleasureland (Southport), Thorpe Park (Surrey), Chessington World of Adventures (Surrey), Pleasure Island (Lincolnshire) and Legoland (Windsor, Berkshire).

> **'I always read the last page of a book first so that if I die before I finish, I will know how it turned out.'**
>
> Nora Ephron (American film director/producer & novelist)

LIBRARIES

English public libraries are excellent and the best source of local and general information on almost any subject. They are found in even the smallest of towns, and many rural areas are served by travelling or mobile libraries, which usually visit once a week. Public libraries are operated by county and borough councils, and membership is free and available to anyone who lives, works or studies in England. To join, you need to show proof of identity and your current address; membership allows you to borrow up to ten books at a time for a period of three or four weeks.

In addition to lending books, local libraries also provide reference sections where you will find encyclopedias, dictionaries, trade directories, Stationery Office publications, atlases, maps, telephone directories and any number of other reference works. Many also have computers connected to the internet, which can be free of charge for up to two hours at a time. Most libraries keep copies of local and national newspapers and magazines in their reading rooms. Books in large type are available for those with poor eyesight, and 'talking books' (on CD) for blind and partially-sighted readers are also usually available.

SPORT

Sport is an integral part of England's culture and the favourite topic of conversation after the weather. The British are sports mad, although most people confine their interest to watching or gambling rather than taking part. The English are famous for their sense of fair play and playing by the rules – cheating is considered very bad form. It's both a unifying and divisive pastime and competition is fierce between rival teams and their fans.

Sports centres abound in all towns and cities and provide facilities for a wide range of sports. Among the most popular are football, rugby (union and league rules), cricket, athletics, fishing, snooker, horse racing, motor racing, golf, archery, hiking, cycling, squash, lawn bowls, badminton, tennis, swimming and skiing – a large number of which were British inventions. Most water (sailing, windsurfing, waterskiing, canoeing, yachting) and aerial sports (hang-gliding, parachuting, ballooning, gliding, light aircraft flying) also enjoy a keen following.

'It's not the winning or losing, it's the taking part that counts.' is a well-known saying in England, where many people seem to take it to heart, particularly the England football team.

Major Sporting Events

Listed below are some of England's premier sporting and social events – not surprisingly many involve horses and gambling.

Badminton Horse Trails

The Badminton Horse Trials (🖳 www.badminton-horse.co.uk) is a three-day event, one of only five elite international four star events in the world. It's staged annually (since 1948) in May in the park of Badminton House, the seat of the Duke of Beaufort in Gloucestershire. The cross country day (of the three-day event) attracts crowds of up to 250,000, which is the largest for any paid-entry sports event in the UK.

The Boat Race

The Boat Race (🖳 www.theboatrace.org) is an annual race for heavyweight eights between

> **The racing car in front is absolutely unique, except for the racing car behind, which is absolutely identical.'**
>
> Murray Walker (F1 motorsport commentator)

the boat clubs of Oxford and Cambridge universities. It takes place on the River Thames in spring, on Easter weekend, the Saturday after Good Friday, with 250,000 people watching the race live from the banks of the river, and millions more watching on TV. The first race was held in 1829 and it has been held annually since 1856. Members of both teams are traditionally known as blues, with Cambridge the light blues and Oxford the dark blues.

British Grand Prix

The British Grand Prix is a race in the calendar of the FIA Formula One World Championship and is currently held at the Silverstone Circuit (💻 www.silverstone.co.uk) near the village of Silverstone in Northamptonshire. It's one of the world's premier motor racing events, attracting 100,000 spectators.

Cheltenham Festival

The Cheltenham Festival (💻 www.cheltenham.co.uk/festival) is the most prestigious meeting in the National Hunt (steeplechase) racing calendar in the UK, with race prize money second only to the Grand National (see below). It takes place annually over four days in March at Cheltenham Racecourse in Cheltenham, Gloucestershire and usually coincides with St Patrick's Day, which makes it extremely popular with the Irish (who also enter their best steeplechase horses). There are 24 races in total, the highlights being the Champion Hurdle and the feature race, the Cheltenham Gold Cup.

Cowes Week

Cowes Week (known as Skandia Cowes Week since 1994 – 💻 www.skandiacowesweek.co.uk) is the longest-running regular regatta in the world, having started in 1826. The event is held on the Solent, the area of water between southern England and the Isle of Wight, and is run by Cowes Combined Clubs in the small town of Cowes on the Isle of Wight. It's held at the beginning of August, usually from the first Saturday after the last Tuesday in July, until the following Saturday. A typical Cowes week involves over 1,000 boats and 8,500 competitors and attracts over 50,000 visitors.

Epsom Derby

The first Epsom Derby (💻 www.epsomderby.co.uk) took place in 1780, and over two centuries later it remains one of England's top horse races, attracting pedigree horses and equally well-groomed visitors. The Derby race meeting takes place in early June over several days, including 'Derby Day', the Saturday when the Queen attends. Dress is usually smart casual, although if you're fortunate enough to obtain tickets for the royal stand you'll need to dress to the nines – morning coats and top hats are *de rigueur* for men, while the ladies are immaculately turned out in their best dresses and hats.

FA Cup Final

The Football Association Challenge Cup (💻 www.thefa.com), commonly known as the FA Cup, is the oldest and most famous football knockout competition in the world. The first competition was staged in 1871-72 when 15 teams took part – in 2007 almost 700 teams participated. It's staged at (the new) Wembley Stadium, which has 90,000 seats and was completely rebuilt between 2003 and 2007 with a retractable roof.

> **'Horse sense is something a horse has that prevents him betting on people.'**
> W.C. Fields (American comedian & actor)

Glorious Goodwood

Goodwood Racecourse (💻 www.goodwood.co.uk) is a horserace track five miles north of Chichester, Sussex, controlled by the family of the Duke of Richmond, whose seat is the nearby Goodwood House. It hosts the annual Glorious Goodwood meeting in July/August over five days, and is one of the highlights of the British flat racing calendar.

Grand National

The Grand National (💻 www.grandnational.org.uk) steeplechase is the most valuable National Hunt handicap horserace in the UK and the biggest betting race in the British racing calendar. It's held on a Saturday in early April at the Aintree Racecourse in Liverpool, (since 1836) and is run over 4.5mi (7.2km) – two circuits of the Aintree 'National' course and its daunting fences.

Henley Royal Regatta

The Henley Royal Regatta (💻 www.hrr.co.uk), first held in 1839, takes place in early July on the Thames at Henley, when hundreds of teams from all over the world compete during the week-long event. The place to be is in one the various competitors' enclosures, but for a more low-key regatta, you can picnic on the banks of the Thames.

London Marathon

London Marathon

The London marathon (💻 www.london-marathon.co.uk) was

inaugurated in 1981, when 20,000 people applied to run; since then applications have risen to over 100,000, of which 46,500 are accepted. Today, it's recognised as one of the world's premier marathon races, alongside the New York City marathon. Special places are allocated to charity runners, who dress in eccentric costumes and often finish hours behind the rest of the competitors – but make a lot of money for charity.

The Open

The Open Championship (www.opengolf.com) is the oldest of the four major championships in men's golf, first played in 1860, and the only major held outside the USA. It's administered by the Royal & Ancient, the governing body of golf outside the United States and Mexico, and has prize money of £4m, the largest of the four majors. It takes place every year on one of nine historic links golf courses in the UK, on the weekend of the third Friday in July, when players compete for the Claret Jug.

Royal Ascot

Royal Ascot week is held at the Ascot racecourse (www.ascot.co.uk) in Berkshire and is one of the most famous race meetings in the world, although it's more famous for the people who attend (and the

> **'The depressing thing about tennis is that no matter how good I get at it, I'll never be as good as a wall.'**
>
> Mitch Hedberg (American stand-up comic)

Andy Murray

women's outfits) than the racing. It takes place over four days in mid-June, from Tuesday to Friday. Ladies' Day (Thursday) gives female race-goers the chance to compete to wear the most extravagant (and expensive) hats.

Royal International Horse Show

When it began in 1907, the Royal International Horse Show (www.hickstead.co.uk/rihs.htm) was the highlight of the society season; today it's the highlight of the equestrian year, and takes place over five days in July at Hickstead, Sussex. Horses and riders from around the world compete for prestigious trophies, including the King George V Gold Cup, the Prince of Wales Cup (formerly the King Edward VII Gold Cup) and the Queen Elizabeth II Cup.

Wimbledon Tennis

Considered by many to be the seat of world tennis, the Wimbledon Tennis Tournament (💻 www.wimbledon.org) is one of the most popular sporting events in England in spite of the fact that it has been over 70 years since a Briton (Fred Perry, 1936) won the men's title, and 30 years (Virginia Wade, 1977) since a British woman won the title. Held during the first two weeks of July, Wimbledon is famous for its immaculate grass courts, the ruling that players must wear white, Pimms (an alcoholic drink), and strawberries and cream.

Centre Court and Number One Court host the top players, but if you want tickets you'll have to join the scores of avid tennis fans who camp outside overnight for the privilege. Alternatively, turn up early in the morning (and queue for a few hours), and you'll be able to buy a grounds admission ticket, which gives you access to all the outside courts, and, just as importantly, allows you to soak up the unique atmosphere.

> **'Some people believe football is a matter of life and death. I'm very disappointed with that attitude. I can assure you it is much, much more important than that.'**
>
> Bill Shankly (manager of Liverpool FC)

Football

You don't need to spend much time in England to realise that football (it's rarely called 'soccer') is the nation's passion and light years ahead of any other sport in popularity. Not only are football matches screened almost every day of the week, but match results, players' performances and teams' league positions are the subject of endless debate in almost every workplace, pub and meeting place. Top footballers are paid outrageous wages – many in excess of £100,000 a week – and their social lives fill pages of newspapers and magazines, which feature pictures of footballer's wives and girlfriends (collectively known as WAGs) flaunting the latest 'must have' fashion item.

Wembley Stadium

In the last decade, the price of tickets has increased by up to 200 per cent (along with players' wages), and it can now cost over £90 (£1 per minute) to see a category 'A' Premiership match, although the average is around £30. Even so, season tickets are almost impossible to obtain for the top teams such as Arsenal, Chelsea, Liverpool and Manchester United, and match tickets are also as rare as gold dust for the top matches. The good news is that you can watch numerous live games on Sky Sports TV.

There are many websites devoted to football, of which one of the best is the BBC's (💻 www.bbc.co.uk/football).

Football Leagues

All major cities in England have a professional or semi-professional football team, and most towns and villages have at least one amateur club. There are 92 professional clubs in England playing in four leagues: the Premiership (💻 www.premierleague.com), the Championship, League One and League Two. The Premiership consists of 20 clubs, and the lower divisions have 24 clubs each. There are also a number of non-League clubs who play in several divisions.

The English football season runs from early August to mid-May, with no mid-season winter break, as in many other European countries. At the end of the season, the three teams at the bottom of the Premiership League are relegated to the Championship and three Championship teams promoted in their place. The same process takes place in the Championship League and League One. In League 2, one team is relegated to the Conference (non-League) and one team promoted in its place. The Premiership League has created a chasm between the top clubs and those in the lower leagues. Relegation from the Premiership costs a club over £20 million in lost revenue from TV fees, sponsorship, advertising and ticket sales, and can precipitate the loss of a club's best players.

It's tempting to make comparisons between cricket and a minority sport played in North America called baseball. The nearest equivalent in England is rounders – a game played by girls.

Cricket

The real character and sporting traditions of the English are embodied in the game of cricket, a study of which provides a valuable insight into the character of the English. It's a game for gentlemen, embodying the great English traditions of fair play, honour and sportsmanship (except when played by Australians, who haven't the remotest concept of these things). Foreigners may have a bit of difficulty understanding what cricket is all about (see the box), but after a few decades, most get the hang of it. If you don't know the difference between a stump and a bail, an over and a wicket, you may as well skip this bit, as any attempt to explain would take around 100 pages, and almost certainly end in failure.

Imagine if you can, a baseball match that lasts up to five days with interminable breaks for breakfast, drinks, rain, streakers (naked runners), lunch, injuries, stray dogs, more rain, rest days, more drinks, tea, bad light, dinner, supper, and even more rain, and which always ends in a draw (if not abandoned due to rain) – and you will have a rough idea what it's all about. A cricket team consists of 11 players and a 12th man, who has the most important job of all – carrying the drinks tray. He's also sometimes called on to play when one of his team-mates collapses from frostbite or is overcome by excitement.

Like baseball, one team bats and the other team attempts to get them out (or committed to hospital) by hurling a ball at the batsman's head. The team in the field (not batting) stands around in set positions, with peculiar names such as gulley, slips, short leg, square leg, long leg, peg leg, cover point, third man (they made a film about him), mid-off, mid-on, and oddest of all – silly mid-off and silly mid-on. Only someone who's a few pence short of a pound stands directly in front of a batsman as he's about to hit a very hard ball

Cricket for Foreigners

'Cricket is quite simple. You have two sides... ours and theirs, one in the field and one out. Each man in the side that's in, goes out, and, when he's out, he comes in and the next man goes in until he's out. Then, when they have all been in and are all out, the side that's been in the field goes in and the side that's in goes out and tries to get out those coming in. Sometimes you get men still in and not out. Then when both sides have been in and out, including the not-outs, that's the end of the game... it's really very simple.' Anon

in your direction at around 100mph (160kph).

When the bowler strikes the wicket or the batsman with the ball, everyone shouts in unison "Howzat!" (very loudly, as the umpire is usually asleep, hard of hearing, short-sighted or all three). Cricketers play in a white uniform, and the only colourful things about the game are the ball (red) and the language used by the batsman (blue) when he's hit by the ball, or when the umpire gives him out leg before wicket (lbw) to a ball that didn't touch him, and in any case was a million miles away from the wicket. One of the unwritten rules of cricket is that the players (gentlemen) never argue with the umpire, no matter how short-sighted, biased and totally ignorant of the rules the idiot is.

Competitions

The first-class cricket season in England runs from April to September, when the main competition is for the County Championships, competed for by 18 county teams organised into two divisions. Matches are played over four days, after which many result in a draw, due to the vagaries of the English weather. County teams also compete in the ECB National Cricket League, where limited-over matches are played in one day, and one-day knockout competitions, the Twenty20 Cup and the Cheltenham & Gloucester Trophy (the final of which is played at Lord's, the home of English cricket).

In addition to the first-class County Championship, there's a Minor Counties Championship (Eastern and Western Divisions), a Second XI Championship and a multitude of local village, school, university, pub and women's teams, who compete at all levels throughout England. There's an England ladies cricket team (who have been doing well lately, but have a hard job getting misogynists to take them seriously) and the game is played at all levels by women and girls throughout the UK. For those who wish to play with a straighter bat or brush up on their googly technique, there are cricket schools and coaching courses in many areas.

Test Matches

Cricket is also played at international level (called test matches) by a number of Commonwealth countries, including Australia, India, New Zealand, Pakistan, South Africa, Sri Lanka, the West Indies and Zimbabwe. During the English cricket season, the England cricket team is usually engaged in one or two minor series of international matches (three tests) or a major series (five or six tests). If you think four days (county matches) is a long

'Look around the poker table. If you don't see a sucker, get up, because it must be you.'

Amarillo Slim (professional gambler)

time for a single match to last, a test match lasts five days, usually with a rest day after two or three days' play. One-day internationals are also played.

The England cricket team also conducts overseas tours during the English winter, when it plays a series of test matches. The old enemy (in cricketing terms) are the Aussies (Australians), with whom England compete every few years for the Ashes (see **Chapter 2**). A world cup knockout competition also takes place at regular intervals, which always seems to be won by the Australians.

The largest cricket website in the world is Wisden's (💻 www.cricinfo.com) and the England and Wales Cricket Board site (💻 www.edb.co.uk) is equally indispensable.

GAMBLING

Gambling is an extremely popular pastime, and England probably offers the widest range of ways to bet (lose) your money. The English will bet on anything, including the national lottery, football pools, horse and greyhound racing, bingo, casinos, names of royal babies or ships, public appointments, election results and who the Prime Minister will sack next (or who will resign) – you name it and someone will 'make a book' on it. Betting shops, also known as 'bookmakers' or 'bookies', are found in all towns, and accept bets on horse and greyhound racing (many betting shops have TVs screening races), other sports results, and almost any other predictions, from the names of royal or celebrity babies to whether there'll be a white Christmas (odds for this are increasingly high, and rising due to global warming).

Lottery-type gambling is also available in the form of the football pools, sweepstakes, the National Lottery (see below) and scratch cards. There are also bingo halls, casinos and slot machine (or amusement) arcades throughout the country.

National Lottery

National Lottery (💻 www.national-lottery.co.uk) tickets cost £1 each, and jackpots can reach as much as £20 million when 'rolled over' for a few weeks, i.e. no one wins the main prize, and the first prize pot goes forward to the next draw. You must be aged 16 or over to play. Tickets can be bought from any outlet displaying the National Lottery symbol (see box). There are two draws a week, on Wednesday and Saturday (the main draw) evenings, both of which are shown live on television.

The symbol for the National Lottery is a smiling hand with crossed fingers, but your chances of winning the jackpot are 1 in 14 million (you're more likely to get hit by lightning).

9. RETAIL THERAPY

Napoleon's famous remark that England was a 'nation of shopkeepers' is an historical marker of just how the country's shopping habits have changed. Today, independent shopkeepers are fighting a losing battle against powerful, multi-national conglomerates, and English high streets are now a succession of national chain stores, rather than specialist shops. In 2006, a group of MPs warned that small, independent retailers might vanish completely by 2015, but while MPs are forecasting a worst-case scenario, it's not all bad news for small shops: in some areas, communities are fighting back with campaigns to save independent retailers, and there's still demand for specialist shops that offer personal service, and stock products that can't easily be found in mainstream outlets.

> **'People who say money can't buy you happiness just don't know where to shop.'**
>
> Tara Palmer-Tomkinson (British model, socialite & one-time 'It girl')

While many people may miss old-fashioned greengrocers, bakeries, haberdasheries and fishmongers, there's no doubt that as a nation, the English love the all-purpose, sleek superstores and shopping centres that have mushroomed throughout the country. It's now possible to satisfy all your retail requirements without even going near an English town centre. The fact that the high street has become increasingly homogenous hasn't succeeded in putting off shoppers, with UK retail sales totalling more than the combined national economies of Portugal and Hungary. So, even if England is no longer a 'nation of shopkeepers', it's very definitely a nation of shoppers.

Shopping 'etiquette' in England may vary considerably from what you're used to, and this chapter provides information on aspects of shopping that are uniquely English, or that you may find surprising.

CUSTOMER SERVICE

Customer service in England is a hit and miss affair: some stores take customer service seriously, while in others, the shopper is more likely to thank the sales assistant than vice versa. Most department stores have

> **It's polite to exchange pleasantries with staff in shops, but expect to get more response from those in small shops. In some large stores and supermarkets, you may barely get a 'hello' from the cashier serving you.**

courteous, knowledgeable and well-trained staff, and supermarkets are also placing increasing importance on customer service. Elsewhere, expect to come across anything, from staff who can't do enough for you, to sullen individuals who act as though taking your money is a huge inconvenience to them. Don't expect staff to automatically approach you as you enter a shop; most sales assistants leave you to your own devices unless you ask them for help.

Gift-wrapping isn't a common practice in England, and shops usually only offer this service at certain times of the year, such as Christmas or Valentine's Day – and it isn't free.

OPENING HOURS

There are no hard and fast rules for opening hours in England. In smaller towns and villages, shops generally open between 9 and 9.30am and close around 5.30 or 6pm, Monday to Saturday. In larger towns and cities, shops often stay open until 7pm or 8pm. In smaller towns and villages, shops may close at lunchtime for an hour or two, and some stores close on Mondays. Thursday is traditionally 'late night' shopping, when many shops open until 8pm or later. Many large supermarkets are open 24-hour hours a day, every day.

Sundays & Public Holidays

Under the 1994 Sunday Trading Act, shops are permitted to open on any Sunday with the exception of Easter Sunday. Small shops under 280m2 (ca. 10,000ft2) may open all day, and larger shops can open for a maximum of six hours only, between 10am and 6pm.

Sunday shopping is now so popular that it has been dubbed the 'new religion'. The Catholic Church saw a 15 per cent decline in Sunday mass attendances between 1994 and 2002, although it maintained that there was no clear link to Sunday trading. The Church of England also announced it had seen a change over the past decade, with churchgoers now attending services during the week, instead of just the traditional Sunday service.

> **'The best shopping is done when it is unpremeditated. Virginia and Tony went out one Saturday morning to buy a reel of cotton and came back with a Bentley.'**
>
> Joyce Grenfell (English film & TV actress)

Many shops open on public holidays with the exception of Christmas Day.

BLACK MARKET

The buying and selling of goods and services illegally in England is known as the black market, so-called because these transactions take place 'in the dark' or out of sight of the law. Black market goods may be stolen or illegal, although most are counterfeit items which include DVDs, CDs, video games, watches, drugs (copies of prescription drugs), cigarettes, and copies of designer clothing and accessories (e.g. Gucci bags, Dior sunglasses and Rolex watches) – known as 'knock-offs'. Copies can be quite convincing and they fool many people, but a closer looks will reveal that they are just cheap rubbish.

It isn't unusual to be offered black market goods in pubs, markets, cafes or by street vendors. Black market goods are usually much cheaper than in the shops – a sure sign that they are fakes or stolen – although some can be very expensive because they're illegal, dangerous or difficult to get hold of, such as exotic or rare animals and birds (in which there's a huge trade). There are severe penalties for both buyers and sellers of black market goods. In some countries, such as Italy, you can be heavily fined if you're found with counterfeit goods, with fines running into thousands of euros.

The illegal reproduction of copyrighted material such as music, films and computer video games, known as piracy, is a booming business – in 2006, some 20 per cent of DVDs (48 million) sold in Britain were pirate copies.

QUEUING

Queuing is an English institution and is as carefully observed in shops as anywhere else. In any establishment where there's more than one person waiting to be served, people form a neat line behind each other. Turns are strictly observed and queue jumpers are frowned on. In some stores and supermarket counters you take a number from a dispenser and wait for it to be called.

SALES

Given the high cost of living, it isn't surprising that the English love a bargain, and sales are extremely popular. The largest sales take place

after Christmas, with some shops starting their sales on Boxing Day (26th December), although most begin around the 27th December and last for up to six weeks. The sales after Christmas are actually 'New Year' sales, which traditionally started on the 2nd January, but retailers have brought them forward over the years, originally to offset lower than expected sales over the Christmas period.

Sales also take place in the summer, usually beginning in July. It isn't unusual to find people camping outside shops overnight before the first day of the sales to make sure that they're first to grab the best bargains. Sales are a good time to stock up on otherwise expensive goods such as clothes, shoes and home furnishings, and there are some genuine bargains to be had.

TYPES OF SHOPS

Despite the threat from out-of-town shopping centres and giant supermarkets, specialist and traditional shops can still be found in many towns, but although some thrive, they are a dying breed. Among the most common are:

- **Baker** – Bakeries are very popular in England and stock a range of breads and pastry goods as well as cakes, flans and biscuits. There are no separate cake or patisserie shops in England as in some other countries.
- **Butcher** – A traditional butchers shop sells all kind of meat, game, offal, home-made sausages and other meat and dairy products, and generally offers a wider selection and better quality than a supermarket.
- **Card and gift shop** – Card and gift shops stock a range of greetings cards, plus wrapping paper, calendars, stationery and a selection of gifts.
- **Clothes boutique** – Many towns have independent clothes boutiques, stocking a range of niche labels and offering a more personal service than the high street chain stores.
- **Delicatessen** – Known as 'delis', these shops stock a range of English and continental meats, cheeses, meat and fish products, and other speciality foodstuffs.
- **Fishmonger** – Sells fresh fish, shellfish and fish products. They are few and far between nowadays, as the English don't generally eat a lot of fish (apart from fried fish), so it tends to be expensive.

- **Florist** – Most large supermarkets sell flowers, but florists stock a much wider and more exotic range of blooms, provide a delivery service (usually through Interflora), and can create bouquets and arrangements for parties and weddings to order.
- **Greengrocer** – A greengrocer sells fruit and vegetables, although they are rare nowadays outside food markets, and generally don't sell as wide a range as supermarkets. However, their produce is more likely to be local and fresh.
- **Hardware store or Ironmongers** – A hardware or ironmongers stores sells tools, household goods, kitchenware, wood (usually cut to size), paints, and all kinds of hardware and DIY supplies.
- **Music shop** – Independent music shops are particularly popular with younger people. Run by knowledgeable staff, they stock specialist music, hard-to-find albums and singles, and may also offer second-hand merchandise.
- **Newsagent** – A newsagent traditionally sold newspapers, magazines, cigarettes, sweets and soft drinks, but nowadays is more likely to be a convenience store or mini-market selling a bit of everything and open all hours.

You can find shops in any town in England by using online search directories such as UpMyStreet (www.upmystreet.com) and Yell (www.yell.com).

Famous Stores

The following is a selection of Britain's favourite and most famous stores.

Boots

Boots Company plc, widely known as simply Boots or Boots the Chemists, is one of the UK's most ubiquitous chain stores, with outlets in most high streets throughout the country – a total of 2,500, no less. In recent years, they have diversified their business from a traditional pharmacy to one offering one-hour photo-processing, opticians, and home appliances in their major stores. They stock an excellent range of cosmetics, hair products and perfumes.

> **Personal Shoppers**
>
> **Many of the UK's leading department stores provide a free personal shopper service, covering fashion, gifts and sometimes homewares. You can also hire a freelance independent personal shopper by the hour.**

Debenhams

Debenhams is a retailer with a chain of 135 department stores in the UK and Ireland. It's best known for its fashion, and sells a range of designer and own-label clothes at affordable prices. Part of Debenhams's appeal is its concessions, which are 'shops-in-shops' and which can be found in most Debenhams stores.

Fenwicks

Fenwick, founded 1882 in Newcastle-upon-Tyne (still its flagship store and headquarters), is an independent chain of stores in Canterbury, Leicester, London (Bond Street and Brent Cross), Tunbridge Wells, Windsor and York. It also owns the Bentalls stores in Bracknell and Kingston-upon-Thames. Most stores (the exception is Newcastle) focus on fashion and household goods.

Fortnum & Mason

Fortnum & Mason (usually referred to simply as 'Fortnums') is one of England's oldest and most renowned department stores; it was founded in 1707 and celebrated its 300th anniversary in 2007. Situated in Piccadilly, London, its fame rests almost entirely on its upmarket food hall, though only one of its several floors is devoted to food. It's also the location of a celebrated tea shop. If it's excellent and/or expensive, it will be sold here. Famous for its luxury food hampers – just the job for the races (Ascot, Epsom, etc.), polo, Glyndebourne and *fête champêtre* (garden parties).

Harrods

Harrods is the most famous department store in the world, and one of the largest. Situated in Knightsbridge in London, it occupies a 4.5 acre (1.82ha) site, with over one million ft2 (305,000m2) of selling space and more than 330 departments. Harrods caters to upmarket customers, and is said to be able to provide **anything** a customer wants – its motto is *Omnia*

Omnibus Ubique – 'All Things for All People, Everywhere'. Of particular note is its world-famous Food Hall, where you can taste many products before buying.

Harvey Nichols

Harvey Nichols ('Harvey Nicks'), founded in 1813 as a linen shop, is an upmarket department store chain, with its original store in London's Knightsbridge, and other stores in Birmingham, Edinburgh, Leeds and Manchester (plus a number overseas). It offers many of the world's most prestigious brands in womenswear, menswear, accessories, beauty, food, and homewares, and attracts younger shoppers than its main rival Harrods, which tends to be more expensive. The London store also has a renowned restaurant, bar and café, which have become destinations in their own right, and are a favourite meeting place for savvy shoppers.

John Lewis

The department store, John Lewis, recently topped a survey of the most popular English retailers, carried out by consumer magazine 'Which?' The chain scored especially highly with customers on its products and customer service, and offers solid good value (its motto used to be 'Never knowingly undersold'), an unconditional returns policy, and a general feeling of good taste rather than showy fashion.

One of the John Lewis Partnership's most unusual aspects is that it's a limited public company that's held in trust on behalf of its employees (called 'partners') – who have a say in the running of the business, and receive an annual share of the profits. John Lewis stores sell a wide range of goods including upholstery, lighting, electrical items, clothes, toys, beauty products and kitchenware. It's also one of the UK's favourite electrical retailers, the owner of Peter Jones and Waitrose supermarkets (see below), and one of the UK's foremost internet retailers (💻 www.johnlewis.com).

The only downside to John Lewis is that it has less than 30 stores nationwide, although it has plans to open another 11 by 2013.

> **'I love to shop after a bad relationship. I buy a new outfit and it makes me feel better. Sometimes, when I see a really great outfit, I'll break up with someone on purpose.'**
>
> Rita Rudner (American comedienne & writer)

Liberty

Liberty is a celebrated store in Regent Street, London, founded by Arthur Lasenby Liberty in 1875, to sell ornaments, fabrics and miscellaneous art objects from Japan and the Far East. Nowadays, it sells fashions, cosmetics, accessories and gifts, in addition to homewares and furniture. Liberty has a distinctive style, and is famous for producing its own beautiful and luxurious fabrics. The shop is noted for its intimate feel, being unlike a typical large department store, with stairs and decorative elevators instead of escalators.

Marks & Spencer

Marks & Spencer (variously known as M&S, Marks and Sparks or simply Marks) is an English institution – it came third in a 'Which' consumer survey of the UK's best retailers – with a reputation for high quality products and customer service. M&S lingerie is particularly popular, and most English women own at least some items of M&S underwear! It's one of the most widely-recognised chain stores in the UK, and the largest clothing retailer, as well as being a multi-billion pound food retailer.

Their food range is more expensive than most stores, but it offers unrivalled quality and reliability. It also sells homewares such as bed linen, but this is far smaller than the other two ranges.

Peter Jones

Peter Jones (known as PJs to its fans) is one of the largest and best-loved department stores in London (Sloane Square), and has been part of the John Lewis Partnership since the 1920s. It's seen as rather an exclusive store, although its stock and decor are no different from other John Lewis stores, and a cut above the partnership's other central London department stores (which is why it has retained its original name).

Selfridges

Selfridges is a chain of department stores founded by American entrepreneur Harry Gordon Selfridge, who opened a large store in London's Oxford Street in 1909. Selfridge was a pioneer in terms of department store marketing and retailing, and is popularly held to have coined the phrase 'the customer is always right', which he used regularly in his advertising. In addition to its London flagship store in Oxford Street, one of London's largest, Selfridges also has stores in Birmingham and Manchester.

Waitrose

Waitrose is the supermarket division of the John Lewis Partnership, and came second to its parent company in a *Which?* magazine customer

> **'Extravagance is everything you buy that is of no earthly use to your wife.'**
>
> Franklin Adams (American columnist & writer)

satisfaction survey. It's the UK's most popular supermarket, although one of its smallest, with fewer than 200 branches. Like the partnership's department stores (see above), Waitrose is targeted at the middle class market, emphasising quality food and customer service rather than low prices (their slogan is 'Quality food, honestly priced'). Waitrose offer a number of special services including home deliveries, a party service and online shopping (www.waitrose.com).

WH Smith

W H Smith (colloquially known as Smiths) is a British retailer with it headquarters in Swindon. It's best-known for its chain of high street, railway station and airport 'newsagent' shops selling newspapers, magazines, books, stationery and entertainment products. It's one of the UK's most omnipresent stores with almost 750 outlets, and offers an unrivalled range of magazines and trade newspapers; however, its range of books isn't as good as dedicated bookshops, such as Waterstones.

Supermarkets

Most English people buy most of their food in supermarkets, and the country is home to several large chains. The largest is Tesco (whose profits were £2.2bn in 2006) followed by Sainsburys, Asda,

Guildford, Surrey

Morrisons, Waitrose, Lidl and Aldi. Asda stocks a good range of clothes, and, along with Aldi and Lidl, offers the lowest prices and best value. Waitrose is more expensive, but is the most popular with customers, and has a reputation for high-quality products. Although it isn't a supermarket, Marks & Spencer also offers a wide range of excellent, if pricey, food. There are no hypermarkets in England, although some supermarkets are huge.

Self-Service Tills

In recent years, supermarkets have introduced self-service tills, where you scan your own goods. Self-service checkouts are already used in a number of supermarkets where shoppers use a hand-held scanner, running it over the barcode of each product before placing it in their trolley. The list is then downloaded from the scanner at the till, where payment is made. There are spot checks to ensure that people don't fail to scan any items.

Marks & Spencer's self-service checkouts have a touch-sensitive computer screen, and the shopper passes products over the barcode scanner before placing them in bags (the till also weighs fruit and vegetables). A picture of the product appears on the screen each time it is passed over the scanner, to reassure the shopper that it's the correct item. Shopping is also weighed after it's added up, to ensure that the weight tallies with the products scanned. The shopper then pays the total amount into the machine.

Cashback

In many shops, particularly supermarkets, when you're paying with a debit card you can request some 'cash back'. You can ask for an amount (the limit is usually £50) to be added to your bill, which is given to you with your receipt. If you only need a small amount of cash, this saves you going to an ATM (fee-free ATMs are rare in some areas).

Although many shoppers initially enjoy the novelty, the early verdict is that it doesn't (yet) speed up shopping, and is perhaps more for the stores' convenience than the shopper's.

MARKETS

Most small towns have markets on one or two days a week (Fridays and Saturdays are most popular), and in cities, there may be a permanent daily market. Markets are cheap, colourful and interesting, and often

a good place for shrewd shopping; although you must sometimes be careful what you buy and be wary of counterfeit goods.

Items on sale include fresh fruit and vegetables, foods from specialist retailers, clothes, handicrafts, household goods and second-hand books, records, antiques and bric-a-brac. Farmers' markets (see below), where producers sell directly to the public, are popular, and are held weekly in many towns.

Check with your local library, council or Tourist Information Centre (TIC) for information about local markets.

Farmers' Markets

A farmers' market is a market where farmers, growers or producers from the local area sell their own produce direct to the public. All products sold should have been grown, reared, caught, brewed, pickled, baked, smoked or processed by the stallholder. However, you should be wary, as some people at farmers' markets have been found to be selling produce grown using chemicals, labelled as 'organic' produce, and even re-selling mass-produced and imported fruit and vegetables.

Some of the best farmers' markets are certified by FARMA, the National Farmers' Retail & Markets Association (💻 www.farma.org.uk), who independently assess and certify farmers' markets around the country to make sure that they're the 'real deal'.

To find farmers' markets in your area, see 💻 www.farmersmarkets.net and 💻 http://thefoody.com/regionalfm.html.

BUYING FOOD & ALCOHOL

Fresh Produce

It can be surprisingly difficult to buy fresh local produce in England – 95 per cent of fruit and 50 per cent of vegetables are imported, or have been kept in cold storage by supermarkets for years. Most produce is sold loosely by weight, but it's becoming increasingly popular to package fruit and vegetables in plastic, which makes ascertaining its freshness difficult. In most supermarkets, loose fruit and vegetables are weighed by the cashier at the check-out.

It's worth looking for seasonal English produce, or asking the

'Food miles' is a recent buzzword coined to describe the distance food travels before it reaches a retailer. The centralised systems used by English supermarkets create ridiculous situations where goods can sometimes be transported hundreds of miles for packaging, only to be sent back to stores that are a stone's throw from where the produce was first collected.

Metric/Imperial Conversion

Weight

Imperial	Metric	Metric	Imperial
1 UK pint	0.57 litre	1 litre	1.75 UK pints
1 US pint	0.47 litre	1 litre	2.13 US pints
1 UK gallon	4.54 litre	1 litre	0.22 UK gallon
1 US gallon	3.78 litres	1 litre	0.26 US gallon

Capacity

Imperial	Metric	Metric	Imperial
1 UK pint	0.57 litre	1 litre	1.75 UK pints
1 US pint	0.47 litre	1 litre	2.13 US pints
1 UK gallon	4.54 litres	1 litre	0.22 UK gallon
1 US gallon	3.78 litres	1 litre	0.26 US gallon

Note: An American 'cup' = around 250ml or 0.25 litre.

manager to supply it, as truly fresh fruit and vegetables have far more flavour and taste than produce with more air-miles than a commercial pilot.

Foreign Food

A huge range of foreign foods can be found in England. Some of the most popular foreign cuisines are Italian, Thai, Indian and Chinese. Large supermarkets stock a wide range of speciality ingredients and ready-made sauces, which make it possible to whip up a Thai green curry or Chinese meal in double-quick time.

Meat

Meat sold in English supermarkets usually comes neatly filleted, minced or trussed and plastic-wrapped. If you prefer to choose your cut of meat, traditional butchers shops are found in many towns, where butchers prepare cuts of meat to your specifications, including boning, filleting or mincing.

Milk

Milk is sold in supermarkets and local grocery and convenience stores. Most English drink fresh milk, and few buy UHT or sterilised long-life versions, which are considered inferior, especially in tea! Milk is sold by the pint, which is equivalent to 0.568 litres.

Organic Food

Sales of organic foods are booming in England and nowadays it's relatively easy to find. Supermarkets stock a wide range of organic foods, including fruit and vegetables, meat, milk, breakfast cereals and biscuits. Mothers in particular seem to have embraced the organic trend, and around half of all baby food sold is organic. On the negative side, organic food is generally up to a third more expensive than non-organic – and a lot of it isn't strictly organic.

There are different forms of organic, some of which are stricter than others. To ensure that food really is organic, look for an accreditation body on the product: the Soil Association (💻 www.soilassociation.org) is the main one in England.

Alcohol

Alcohol can be purchased in England from a variety of stores, including supermarkets, off licences (called liquor stores or bottle shops in other countries), convenience stores and garages. There are no restrictions on what stores can sell, and all stores licensed to sell alcohol can sell beer, wine and spirits.

Nobody under the age of 18 is permitted to buy alcohol (retailers are supposed to ask for identification if a buyer looks

Food but not Food

apple of one's eye – someone you like a lot or feel particular affection for

big cheese – an important person or leader

butter up – to get someone on your side, often to ask for a favour

eat humble pie – to admit that you're wrong and apologise

hot potato – a controversial issue

in a nutshell – briefly; in a few words

piece of cake – something easy to accomplish

spill the beans – to reveal a secret

take with a pinch of salt – to be wary about believing something

a bit fishy – suspicious; not what it seems

custard pie comedy – slapstick

under 21 – presumably if you look under 21, you could also be under 18?) and alcohol cannot be sold by convenience stores before 10am on Sundays.

Wine

Sales of wine have boomed in the last decade in England, with sales increasing by nearly a quarter between 1999 and 2004. However, the English aren't discerning consumers when it comes to wine, and most people buy wine by price rather than by the type or country of origin. Research shows that the English typically choose bottles that cost around £4, being reluctant to pay over this threshold, but distrusting the quality of anything cheaper! Having cottoned on to this, many supermarkets now offer wines for £3.99, which have allegedly been reduced from twice this price.

Along with Sweden, Finland and Ireland, the UK pays the highest duty on wine in Europe, between £1 and £1.35 a bottle – as duty is a fixed rate per bottle, more expensive wine is usually better value for money, as a larger percentage of the price is going on the wine. Off-licences (specialist alcohol or liquor stores) and supermarkets stock a wide range of wines, with so-called 'New World' varieties from Australia, South Africa, South America and the US the most popular.

CLOTHES

Sizes

When it comes to weights and measures, the English like to do things their own way, and it probably won't surprise you to learn that England has its own sizing system for clothes (see box). Manufacturers and stores interpret these in different ways, therefore it's common to find you need a particular size in one

Continental to UK/US Size Comparison

Women's Clothes

Continental	34	36	38	40	42	44	46	48	50	52
UK	8	10	12	14	16	18	20	22	24	26
US	6	8	10	12	14	16	18	20	22	24

Men's Shirts

Continental	36	37	38	39	40	41	42	43	44	46
UK/US	14	14	15	15	16	16	17	17	18	-

Shoes (Women's and Men's)

Continental	35	36	37	37	38	39	40	41	42	42	43	44
UK	2	3	3	4	4	5	6	7	7	8	9	9
US	4	5	5	6	6	7	8	9	9	10	10	11

shop, but a smaller or larger size in another. Many women's clothes shops now offer petite ranges for smaller women, as well as ranges for taller women and maternity collections. Most high street shops stock a wide range of sizes from 4 (US zero) to 20.

Men's shirts were traditionally classed by collar size rather than body size in the UK, although nowadays they are just as likely to come in small (S), medium (M), large (L) and extra large (XL) sizes. Needless to say, they often vary in collar, body and sleeve sizes, depending on the manufacturer. It's important to try on shirts before buying them, or ensure that you can return them if they don't fit.

Shoes

English stores carry a wide range of sizes for both men and women. Typically, you can expect to find up to size 8 (42) for women, and size 12 (46) for men, in most shops. You can also buy wide-fitting shoes in a number of stores and from mail order and online outlets.

Children's Clothes

Shops such as H&M, Primark and supermarkets sell a wide range of inexpensive children's clothes. The quality of cheap clothes isn't particularly high, but few parents mind when it's possible to buy an outfit for £10! School uniforms are sold in specialist shops and some supermarkets, which has brought prices down considerably.

As a rule, children don't dress formally in England; most wear casual clothes such as trainers, tops and trousers or skirts. At birthday parties and on special occasions, girls generally wear party dresses, and boys wear shirts, smart trousers and maybe a tie.

> **Clothes Alterations**
>
> **Many stores provide an alteration service for customers, which may be included in the price of a garment, but more often there's an extra charge. There are also tailors in most towns that specialise in doing alterations, as do some drycleaners.**

ANTIQUES & COLLECTIBLES

The UK has a lively antiques and collectibles market, worth hundreds of millions of pounds a year. Most towns have at least one antiques' shop, and in some small towns they can outnumber all the other shops combined. Antique street markets are also popular. Two of particular note in London are Camden Passage antiques market in north London, held on Wednesdays and Saturdays, and Portobello Road, the world's largest antiques fair, held on Saturdays.

Antiques and collectors' fairs are staged somewhere in England every day, and include everything from top quality (i.e. expensive) fairs organised by the British Antiques Dealers' Association (BADA, 💻 www.bada.org) and Antiques for Everyone (💻 www.antiquesforeveryone.co.uk) at the National Exhibition Centre, to vast fairs with thousands of stalls (e.g. 💻 www.dmgantiquefairs.com), and small collectors' fairs and jumble sales, with just a handful of amateur dealers.

Car boot sales (see 💻 www.carbootjunction.com), where people sell practically anything from the boots (trunks) of their cars, are popular throughout the UK, and the best place to find real bargains (and loads of junk). Ensure that you arrive early. Car boots are customarily held on Sundays, and are advertised in local newspapers and signposted on roads. Another place to pick up a bargain is at a garage (yard) sale, where homeowners dispose of their unwanted belongings.

Other popular venues are auctions, although it helps to be knowledgeable about what you're buying, as you will probably be competing with experts. The UK has some of the world's most famous auction houses, including Sotheby's, Christie's and Philips, all of which hold antique valuation days throughout the country. In addition to these prestige sales rooms, there are literally hundreds of smaller venues, and auctions are held virtually every day.

A comprehensive diary of antiques fairs and auctions is published in *Antiques Info* (💻 www.antiques-info.co.uk) and *Antiques Diary* (💻 www.antiquesdiaryonline.com) magazines.

ALTERNATIVE RETAIL

Ethical Shopping

In recent years, many English people have become more aware of ethical

issues with regard to the products they buy. Sales of 'fair trade' products, which ensure that the producers in developing countries are paid a fair and consistent price, have grown considerably in recent years. Examples of ethical retailers include the Body Shop, Oxfam and Traidcraft (💻 www.traidcraftshop.co.uk).

Online Shopping

Internet shopping is big business in England and growing fast – in 2005, some 24m people in the UK shopped over the internet and spent almost £20bn, a third more than in 2004. Most English retailers now offer online shopping services, with the majority using courier companies to deliver goods. Online supermarket shopping is also popular. There are many specialist online stores, some of which, such as Amazon and Viking, provide stiff opposition to high street stores.

With internet shopping, the world is literally your oyster, and savings can be made on a wide range of goods and services, including holidays and travel. Small, high-price, high-tech items (e.g. cameras, watches, and portable computers and software) can usually be bought more cheaply in the US or the Far East, with delivery in just a few days. However, you need to bear in mind that you may have to pay duty and VAT on goods purchased overseas (but not from an EU country).

> **To find the best UK deals on the web, you can use price comparison websites such as Kelkoo (💻 www.kelkoo.co.uk), Pricerunner (💻 www.pricerunner.co.uk) and Shopping (💻 www.shopping.com).**

Home Deliveries

Most department stores offer home delivery. Furniture and domestic appliances are usually delivered free of charge, and many companies include the installation of an appliance (e.g. fridge or washing machine) and the disposal of your old one in the price.

RETURNING GOODS

Under UK consumer law, you're entitled to your money back if there's a fault with a product, or goods are of unsatisfactory quality, not fit for their purpose or not as advertised. You must, however, be able to prove that the fault was present when the goods were sold, and the burden of proof is on you as the consumer.

Refunds

Shops aren't obliged to give you a refund if there's nothing wrong with

a product (i.e. if you've changed your mind about the purchase), although many do so as a goodwill gesture. If you're buying a present, it's best to ask about refund policies before buying. During sales, some shops will only provide credit note refunds, unless a product is faulty.

Repairs, Replacements & Compensation

If you buy goods that you later find are faulty, you're entitled to a repair as an alternative to a refund or replacement. If the goods cannot be repaired economically, you're entitled to a replacement or a refund.

Sale Goods

You have the same rights when you buy goods in a sale as at any other time, unless a fault was specifically mentioned at the time of the sale. It's illegal for retailers to display notices stating 'no refunds on sale goods'.

Guarantees

Under EU law, all electronic items and appliances have a guarantee of two years, during which you're entitled to free repair, although you may have to pay a 'call-out' fee for an engineer. If the item goes wrong within a month of purchase, you can take it back to the shop where you bought it, after which you usually have to take it to a service or repair centre. You're responsible for collecting an item when it has been repaired, or paying for it to be shipped to you.

> **'Shopping is better than sex. If you're not satisfied after shopping, you can make an exchange for something you really like.'**
>
> Adrienne Gusoff (American writer & humourist)

CONSUMER COMPLAINTS

If you need to make a complaint, you should act quickly. Contact the seller as soon as possible to explain the problem, and to say what you want done about it. You should also make your complaint in writing to the customer services manager, confirming any promise or response made. If the shop is part of a chain, you should write to the head office. Shops are legally obliged to give customers this information, and businesses operating under a different name from their legal one must publicly display their corporate name and address.

If you aren't sure about where you stand legally, you can check your rights before you confront the trader by contacting a consumer organisation such as Consumer Direct (☎ 08454-040506, 💻 www.consumerdirect.gov.uk) or your local Citizens' Advice Bureau (💻 www.citizensadvice.org.uk), both of which provide free advice.

Extended Warranties
Extended warranties, which are beloved by stores, are hardly ever worth the money. The chances of most electrical and electronic equipment going wrong are very remote, and when they do it's usually cheaper to throw them away and buy new items.

The Consumers' Association

The Consumers' Association is the most acclaimed and respected independent consumer organisation in the UK, with over a million members. It publishes an excellent monthly magazine (available on subscription only) entitled *Which?*, containing invaluable information about a wide range of goods and services; just about everything is tested at some time or another.

All tests are organised independently by the Consumers' Association, and cover financial services (e.g. insurance, banking, pensions and investment); cars; leisure products; food and health; household and domestic appliances; and items of public interest. Dangerous products are highlighted, best buys are recommended and, most importantly, you're told how to obtain your legal rights when things go wrong.

The Consumers' Association also publishes other consumer magazines, including *Which Money?*, *Computing Which?*, *Gardening Which?* and *Holiday Which?*, along with a wide range of books (☎ 01992-822800, 💻 www.which.co.uk).

VAT Refunds

All visitors residing outside the European Union are entitled to reclaim value added tax (VAT), which is charged at 17.5 per cent on most goods purchased in the UK. VAT on services such as hotels, restaurants and car hire cannot be reclaimed, although business travellers may be able to claim back certain elements of VAT, such as accommodation costs.

Shops operating under the Retail Export Scheme, which includes all major stores and chains, may display a 'Tax Free Shopping' sign in their shop windows. Most stores set a minimum purchase level, and you may be charged an administration fee (which is deducted from your refund) by the retailer or refund company for making a refund of VAT. When buying goods on which you plan to obtain a VAT refund, you must ask the retailer for a tax refund form.

Visitors leaving the UK for a **final** destination within the EU aren't eligible to receive VAT refunds under the scheme. Travellers must

Shopping Idioms

just the ticket – exactly what you want
off your trolley – mad
pay through the nose – pay over the odds/pay too much for something
shop lift – steal goods
shop someone – to tell someone in authority of someone else's wrongdoing
to be all over the shop – to be in complete disarray

leave the EU with the goods before the end of the third month following that in which they were purchased; for example, goods purchased on 31st March must be exported by 30th June.

When leaving the UK or the European Union, you simply show your purchases, receipts and passport to customs officials, and have the form stamped. All goods must be carried in your hand baggage; therefore for practical purposes the scheme doesn't apply to large items that cannot easily be carried.

There are several options for collecting the refund: immediate cash at a cash refund office (including airports and the London Visitor Centre, 1 Regent Street, London), the direct crediting of a credit card, a bank cheque sent to a your address abroad, or (for certain countries) a cash refund when you return home.

Several companies operate VAT refund schemes for non-EU visitors, including Global Refund (💻 www.globalrefund.com) and Premier Tax Free (💻 www.premiertaxfree.com).

Bodiam Castle, Sussex

10.
ODDS & ENDS

A country's culture is influenced by various factors and reflected in myriad ways. Among the principal influences are its geography, climate and religion, which are considered here along with miscellaneous cultural manifestations, including, crime, the national flag and anthem, government and international relations, pets, time difference, tipping and toilets.

'Conversation about the weather is the last refuge of the unimaginative.'
Oscar Wilde (Irish writer & wit).

CLIMATE

Discussing the weather is a national pastime, and there's almost nothing the English like more than complaining about their climate. For most of the year this involves bemoaning the rain, grey skies and cold. Then, when warm weather finally arrives – and vast numbers of the population turn lobster red – the nation grumbles about the sudden heat and 'unbearable' humidity.

The British media also loves a weather story. At the first glimpse of sun, hordes of tabloid photographers decamp to the coastline, hoping for shots of bikini-clad beauties to brighten up their pages. Come flood, snow, fog or wind, you can almost guarantee that the weather will be photographed and analysed at length in the following day's newspapers. A particular favourite of the media is the rare occasions when the temperatures in England nudge past those of popular foreign holiday destinations. A slew of smug headlines inevitably follow, proclaiming "England sizzles as scorching temperatures leave Europe in the shade!" or "Boiling Britain: temperatures top Tenerife and Tanzania!"

Surprisingly, given its star billing in conversations across the land, England actually has a temperate climate, and the mercury usually only varies by a few degrees from the north of the country to the south. However, the English climate is prone to some fairly impressive mood swings, and it's difficult to give a definitive guide to what the weather will be like during any month of the year. In recent years, temperatures have hit the high 30s in July and August, but it has also been known to snow in June!

The south tends to be milder than the north in winter, and is less likely to experience snow, which is rare near sea level in England, but more frequent on higher ground. Typically, it rains on about one day in three, although this varies considerably depending on where you are in the country. The Lake District is the wettest area, with an average of over 2,000mm of rain a year, while many other regions get less than 700mm a year.

Extreme Weather

England doesn't get much in the way of extreme weather, but it does seem that the traditional four seasons of spring, summer, autumn and winter are becoming increasingly blurred, a fact many people attribute to climate change. While the country is some way from being able to bask in a Mediterranean climate, there's a definite trend for warmer, wetter weather in England. Spring is arriving earlier, with daffodils (a traditional Easter flower) blooming in January, and that scourge of summer picnics, the bumblebee, spotted as early as Christmas time.

The highest temperature ever recorded was 38.5°C (101.3°F) in Kent, southern England on 10th August 2003, and the lowest -26.1°C (-15.0°F) in Shropshire on 10th January 1982. Another telling indication of how the country is warming up, is that England, never a traditional wine-growing country, now has over 300 vineyards. Tornados have also become more frequent in England in the past five years, with up to around 60 a year; in December 2006 a tornado struck a corner of north-west London, damaging over 100 houses. Flooding is becoming increasingly common, and is almost guaranteed somewhere whenever it rains heavily for a few days.

> **'For months the sky has remained a depthless grey. Sometimes it rained, but mostly it was just dull. It was like living inside Tupperware.'**
>
> Bill Bryson (American writer)

Seasonal Affective Disorder

Around half a million (mostly young) people suffer from Seasonal Affective Disorder (SAD) – a type of winter depression that appears between September and April (particularly from December to February). It's caused by a biochemical imbalance in the hypothalamus, due to the shortening of daylight hours and the lack of sunlight in winter. For many people, SAD is a seriously disabling illness, preventing them from functioning normally; while for others, it's a mild but debilitating condition causing discomfort, but not severe suffering (also called 'winter blues').

Symptoms include sleep problems, lethargy, overeating, depression, social problems, anxiety, loss of libido and mood changes. Most sufferers show signs of a weakened immune system during the winter, and are more vulnerable to infections and other illnesses. The good news is that it can be treated by light therapy (successful in up to 85 per cent of cases) and other remedies (a holiday in Barbados works wonders!). SAD symptoms tend to disappear in spring. For more information, contact the Seasonal Affective Disorder Association (💻 www.sada.org.uk).

CRIME

In general, England is a relatively safe place to live. Violent crime is rare in much of the country, and you can walk safely in most towns and cities at any time of the day or night; if you take care of your property and take precautions against crime, your chances of being a victim are small. The crime rate varies dramatically from area to area, and anyone coming to live in England should avoid high crime areas if possible.

For many English people, crime is the number one concern, and in some areas, people are afraid to leave the relative safety of their homes at any time of day or night. Many crimes are drug-related – the use of hard drugs (particularly cocaine and crack) is a major problem in most cities, where gangs increasingly use guns to settle their differences. The police warn people (particularly women) against walking home alone in dark and quiet areas at night.

> **'You know, in England, if you commit a crime, the police don't have a gun and you don't have a gun. So if you commit a crime: "Stop! Or I'll... say stop again".'**
>
> Robin Williams (American actor & comedian)

By far the biggest area of crime is property-related – burglary and car theft rates are the highest (per capita) in Western Europe. If you live or work in a major city and park your car there, you have a one in four chance of having it stolen or broken into. Fraud (which includes credit card fraud, tax evasion and VAT fraud) costs billions of pounds a year, and accounts for a larger sum than the total of all other robberies, burglaries and thefts put together.

On the plus side, recent figures from the British Crime Survey showed a slight reduction in the number of crimes recorded during 2005/06, and the risk of becoming a victim of crime has fallen from 40 per cent, at its peak in 1995, to 23 per cent in 2006.

FLAG & ANTHEM

The English Flag

The English Flag consists of a red cross on a white background with the cross having a width of one-fifth of the height of the flag. Its origins are unclear, but the flag made its first appearance during the Middle Ages, when the use of a red cross on a white background was a symbol of St George, the patron saint of England.

The English flag hasn't traditionally been used by the English, who preferred the Union Flag (see below) as a symbol of their country; however, in recent years, and coinciding with growing English (rather than British) sentiments, the English flag is seen increasingly, particularly on sporting occasions. During international football and rugby tournaments, the flag hangs from pub ceilings, flutters from car aerials and is painted on the faces of fanatical supporters.

The Union Flag

The Union Flag (it should only be called the 'Union Jack' when it's flown from the Jack Mast of a British ship) is an amalgamation of the English and Scottish flags and the flag of St Patrick, representing Northern Ireland. It consists of a blue background with two red crosses (one conventional, placed on top of a diagonal cross), both edged with white.

In its present form, the Union Flag first appeared in 1801, and is the national flag of the United Kingdom of Great Britain and Northern Ireland. It has semi-official, or official, status in many Commonwealth countries and

> **'The idea that Englishmen might favour the cross of St George over the Union Flag will never catch on. Where's the fun in having a flag about which nobody can complain that it is being flown upside down?'**
>
> Michael Bird (television writer)

appears on the Australian and New Zealand flags.

The Anthem

The English national anthem is *God Save the King/Queen* (depending on the current monarch) and is a patriotic hymn. There's no single authorised version, although the following verses are those with the best claim to be the 'standard' version:

God save our gracious Queen*,
Long live our noble Queen,
God save the Queen:
Send her victorious,
Happy and glorious,
Long to reign over us:
God save the Queen.

O Lord, our God, arise,
Scatter her enemies,
And make them fall.
Confound their politics,
Frustrate their knavish tricks,
On Thee our hopes we fix,
God save us all.

Thy choicest gifts in store,
On her be pleased to pour;
Long may she reign:
May she defend our laws,
And ever give us cause
To sing with heart and voice
God save the Queen.

* When the monarch is a man, 'Queen' becomes 'King', 'her' becomes 'his' and 'she' becomes 'he'.

The first verse is usually the only verse that is played/sung. The second verse is now considered 'politically incorrect' and never sung. The third verse is sung on rare occasions such as the Last Night of the Proms (see **Chapter 8**). The national anthem is also one of the two national anthems of New Zealand and the royal anthem of Canada, Australia and other Commonwealth countries.

GEOGRAPHY

England is the largest country in Great Britain, both in terms of size and population. Almost 85 per cent of the UK's inhabitants are packed into its 129,720km^2 (50,085mi^2), making it nine times as densely populated as the US. Bordered by Scotland to the north and Wales to the west, England's terrain is as changeable as its weather, from undulating hills and green fields to barren, windswept moorland. The country also has a good selection of sandy and pebble beaches.

None of England's geographical landmarks are record breakers on a worldwide scale; its highest mountain, Scafell, is just over 978m (3,205ft) above sea level and the largest lake, Windermere, 16km

(10mi) long. The longest river is the Thames, 346km (215mi) long, which bisects the city of London and supplies it with two-thirds of its drinking water. Once effectively an open sewer, the Thames is now one of the cleanest urban waterways in Europe, where salmon, seals and even dolphins have all been seen in recent years; in 2006, a 5.5m (18ft) bottle-nosed whale died after it became stranded in the river near Battersea Bridge.

London

England's largest city by far and one of the largest cities in the world, London is England's epicentre from which everything emanates. Bisected by the Thames, the giant metropolis stretches for around 48km (30mi) north and south of the river. With around 7.5m residents squeezed into its (premium-priced) environs, the city's population density is more than ten times that of any other English region.

> **Sir Robert Walpole is considered the first English Prime Minister. Walpole began chairing the cabinet in 1721-24 during the reign of George I, as the king could speak little English and had little interest in politics. Nowadays, the Prime Minister is the leader of the party with the majority of seats in the House of Commons.**

GOVERNMENT

The United Kingdom is a constitutional monarchy, under which the country is governed by the

Houses of Parliament

ministers of the crown in the name of the monarch (Queen Elizabeth II), who is head of the state and the government. Nowadays, the monarchy has no real power, and its duties are restricted to ceremonial and advisory ones only; although there are certain acts of government that require the participation of the sovereign, such as the opening and dissolving of parliament, and giving royal assent to bills.

Parliament

Parliament is the ultimate law-making authority in the country, and consists of two houses or chambers, the House of Commons and the House of Lords, which together comprise the Houses of Parliament. Parliament sits in the Palace of Westminster in London, built in the 19th century after the previous building was destroyed by fire. The roots of the UK's democratic traditions date from

1265 (when King Henry III was forced to acknowledge the first Parliament) and Westminster, which is often referred to as the 'mother of parliaments', and is the model for many democracies around the world.

The House of Commons is the assembly chamber for the 651 Members of Parliament (MPs), who are commoners, (i.e. not Lords or titled people), elected by the people of the UK in a general election, which is held every five years unless Parliament is dissolved earlier. Each MP represents an area called a constituency, of which there are 523 in England. If an MP resigns, retires or dies during the term of government, a by-election is held to choose a new MP. Any British national over the age of 21 can stand for election as an MP, with the exception of disqualified people, e.g. those sentenced to more than one year's imprisonment.

The government of the day is formed by the political party that wins the largest number of seats at a general election. If no party

Voting

All British and Commonwealth citizens over the age of 18, and resident in the UK, may vote in parliamentary elections, provided they're registered on the electoral register or roll. Electoral rolls are maintained by local authorities and are usually updated monthly. If you're registered on the electoral roll, you can obtain a credit rating, which is helpful when applying for a bank account, mortgage or loan.

has a clear majority, a coalition government may be formed between a number of parties. The head of the government is the Prime Minister (PM), who's the leader of the party with the majority of seats (or the leader of the principal party in a coalition), and who chooses an inner cabinet of around 20 ministers. The leader of the Opposition, who is head of the largest defeated party, appoints a shadow cabinet of shadow ministers, whose job is to respond to the government ministers in Parliament, and to act as the party's spokespeople. MPs who are members of the cabinet or shadow cabinet sit on the front benches (on opposite sides) of the House of Commons. All other MPs are known as 'backbenchers'.

INTERNATIONAL RELATIONS

The European Union

The UK joined the European Union (EU) in 1973, but it has always been seen as something of a reluctant member, and many English people resent what they see as the EU's interference in the UK's internal affairs. There's growing pressure from certain political sectors – such as the UK Independence Party (UKIP) – to withdraw from the EU, although this has virtually no support from the mainstream parties. The main areas where the UK hasn't seen eye to eye with EU policy include:

Budget Rebate

In 1984, the UK was awarded an annual budget rebate equivalent to 66 per cent of its net contribution in the previous year. The rebate was allowed because, at the time, the UK was paying a larger contribution to the EU budget than corresponded to the UK's level of prosperity. However, since the agreement was made, the UK has gone from being one of the poorest countries in the EU to one of the richest, and many EU members (not surprisingly) resent the fact that the UK continues to receive the rebate. However, the UK has refused to give up the rebate until there's a fundamental reform of the EU budget, due to be reviewed in 2008/9.

> **Constitution**
>
> **Unlike many countries, such as the US and Spain, the British constitution isn't set out in a single document, and the relationship between the state and its people is reliant on statute law, common law, and practices and conventions.**

Schengen Agreement

In 1995, the UK and Ireland were the only EU member states not to sign up to the Schengen agreement, which removed all internal border controls and implemented effective controls at the external borders of the EU, and introduced a common visa policy.

Single Currency

Along with Denmark and Sweden, the UK chose not to adopt the Euro when it was launched in January 1999 and nearly a decade later, the nation doesn't seem much closer to ditching the pound. However, many shops and businesses (and telephone boxes) in the UK accept euros as payment.

The World

The UK has enjoyed reasonably good relations with the rest of Europe since the Second World War, although there have been some high-profile clashes with France and Germany, most recently over the US-led war with Iraq.

> **'Once when a British Prime Minister sneezed, men half a world away would blow their noses. Now when a British Prime Minister sneezes nobody else will even say "Bless you".'**
>
> Bernard Levin (journalist & broadcaster)

The UK has varied relationships with the 53 member states of the Commonwealth of Nations, which was created out of the British Empire. The UK tends to side with EU countries rather than Commonwealth countries when disputes arise; for example, during the issue of French nuclear testing in the Pacific, the UK sided with France against Australia and New Zealand.

International Organisations

The UK is a founder member of the United Nations (UN), formed in 1945 along with China, France, Russia and the US, and is a permanent member of the UN Security Council. The UK is also a founder member of the North Atlantic Treaty Organisation (NATO), formed in 1949, which brings together the armies of member states.

The UK has a so-called 'special relationship' with the US, coined by Prime Minister Winston Churchill after he established a strong Anglo-American alliance with US President Franklin Roosevelt during World War II. However, subsequent British Prime Ministers have found sustaining the special relationship a daunting task, particularly as since Churchill's time, the UK has declined in influence, whereas the US has become the only world power. Not surprisingly, this means that the 'special relationship' is much more important to the UK than it is to the US, which doesn't need the UK's support to implement its foreign policy. In fact, many English people (and European countries) believe that the UK is merely America's poodle, with little real influence, and most English people would like to see the country less dependent on its larger Atlantic neighbour.

PETS

The UK has over 14m pet owners (including some 7m dog owners) and England is generally regarded as a country of animal lovers. Supporting this claim is the fact that the sum of money left in bequests to the Royal Society for the Prevention of Cruelty to Animals (RSPCA) far exceeds the amount left to the

National Society for the Prevention of Cruelty to Children. The English are almost uniquely sentimental about animals, even those reared for food, and protests about various forms of commercial cruelty to animals make regular headlines. The English are also prominent in international animal protection organisations that attempt to ban cruel sports and practices in which animals are mistreated (such as bullfighting).

The RSPCA is the main organisation for animal protection and welfare, and operates a number of animal clinics and welfare centres. Many English people are also concerned about the survival of wild animals, and there's even a British Hedgehog Preservation Society (BHPS), although they have yet to teach the creatures how to cross roads safely. There are over 40 animal shelters in the UK, including those run by the Cats Protection League, The Dogs Home (Battersea), the National Canine Defence League, the RSPCA and the Wood Green Animal Shelters.

> **'I once tried to smuggle my Peke, Pinkie Pankie Poo, past customs by wrapping him in my cloak. Everything was going fine until my bosom barked.'**
>
> Mrs. Patrick Campbell (British stage actress)

Dogs

After a series of vicious attacks on children, the government introduced a controversial ban on the ownership of certain breeds of dogs. These are mainly fighting breeds, and include pit bull terriers, Japanese tosas, dogo argentinos and fila brazilieros, all of which cannot be imported or bred in the UK (males must be neutered), and must be registered and muzzled in public. If the law is broken, a dog can be destroyed, and if it attacks anyone the owner is liable to a fine (and the dog is usually destroyed). You can be fined up to £400 (in addition to compensation) if your dog kills or injures livestock, and a farmer can legally shoot a dog that molests farm animals.

There is no dog registration or licence scheme in England.

RELIGION

England has a history of religious tolerance and in theory, every resident has freedom of religion without hindrance by the state or

Westminster Abbey, London

community. The English aren't particularly religious (church attendance has been falling for years), which perhaps explains their traditional tolerance towards the faiths of others. However, it isn't all happy families and there are some deep-seated pockets of discrimination. In recent years there have been some high-profile tensions with Muslim communities, particularly in the aftermath of the 9/11 and 2005 (7/7) London bombings.

There have also been disputes over religious freedom in schools. In 2004, a 15-year-old girl lost the legal battle to wear Islamic-style dress to school, and in March 2007 the government issued new uniform guidelines allowing schools to ban pupils from wearing full-face veils on the grounds of security, safety or learning. The guidelines recommended that efforts be made to accommodate religious clothing, but stressed the importance of teachers and pupils being able to make eye contact.

> **'Most Englishmen, if forced to into analysing their own creeds – which Heaven forbid – are convinced that God is an Englishman, probably educated at Eton.'**
>
> E.M. Delafield (author of *Diary of a Provincial Lady*)

English churches are among the oldest and most magnificent buildings in the world, particularly the great cathedrals, many dating from the 11th or 12th centuries.

TIME DIFFERENCE

The UK is on British Summer Time (BST) in summer and Greenwich Mean Time (GMT) in winter. The clocks go back at 1am on the last Sunday of October, and the change back to BST is made in the spring (usually at the end of March), when people put their clocks forward one hour. Time changes are announced in local newspapers and on radio and TV.

The time is given on the telephone 'speaking clock'(☎ 0871-789 3642), a service that dates from 1936), and displayed on televisions (e.g. teletext services) and computers. Before making international telephone calls or booking long-distance flights,

LONDON	CAPE TOWN	BOMBAY	TOKYO	LOS ANGELES	NEW YORK
Noon	2pm	5.30pm	9pm	4am	7am

you should check the local time difference, which is shown in the International Dialling section of telephone directories and online (🖳 www.timezoneconverter.com). The time difference between the UK (when it's noon GMT, the time on which the BBC World Service operates) and some major international cities is shown below:

In recent years, there has been talk about bringing British time into line with Central European Time (CET), of which the majority of people (some 95 per cent) in England, Wales and Northern Ireland approve (in Scotland around 85 per cent take the opposite view, as they would have even darker mornings). Arguments for adopting CET include increased road safety – research has shown that twice as many road accidents occur when people travel home in the dark as when they set out in the dark in the morning. The Royal Society for the Prevention of Accidents estimates that if the UK adopted CET, road casualties would be dramatically reduced. But this may never happen, as the UK is out of step with Europe on most other things (and seems to like it that way).

TIPPING

Most English are anti-tipping (but usually too timid not to leave a tip), and would like to see it abolished and replaced with a universal service charge. One of the reasons for this is because there are no clear rules as to who and when to tip, and this sometimes leads to embarrassing situations. Whether you tip or not, and how much, is a personal choice, and may depend on whether you think you've received exceptional service or good value for money.

It's usual to give tips to the following people:

- **Barmen** – it isn't customary to tip a barman in a pub, although you can offer to buy him a drink if you've been propping up the bar for a few hours. It is, however, customary to tip barmen in bars and hotels when drinks are served at a table.
- **Hairdressers** – tip £1 or £2 or 10 per cent of the bill, depending on the service;
- **Hotel staff** – tipping is more discretionary and depends on the type of hotel – the better the hotel, the more likely a tip will be expected. Most people tip hotel porters 50p to £1 per suitcase. Tips for a doorman who gets you a taxi are similar. Visit Britain recommends a tip of 10 to 15 per cent for hotel staff when service isn't included in the price;
- **Restaurant staff** – but only when service isn't included (see **Restaurants** below);

- **Taxi drivers** – a tip of around 10 to 15 per cent is normal, although many people just round the fare up to the nearest pound.

It's also common to tip cloakroom attendants and garage staff (who clean your car windscreen, or check the oil or tyre pressure).

Restaurants

There are no hard and fast rules for leaving a tip in a restaurant, and restaurant owners exploit this by paying their staff low wages on the expectation that tips will supplement their wages. If you don't tip a waiter he may not starve (unless the restaurant's food is particularly bad), but he may struggle to survive on his meagre salary. Many bills have 'service not included' printed on them, which is an open invitation for you to leave a tip. Even when service is included in the bill, this doesn't mean that the percentage added for service goes to the staff, although 'service included' deters most people from leaving a tip. Don't be shy about asking whether service is included, which should be shown on the menu.

Restaurant tips can be included in cheque or credit card payments or given as cash. The total on credit card counterfoils is often left blank, even when service was included in the price, to encourage you to leave a tip; don't forget to fill in the total before signing it.

TOILETS

Although public toilets are usually free and are better than many found on the continent, the general standard is pretty awful. The most sanitary (even luxurious) toilets are found in hotels, restaurants and department stores, and are for customers only. Toilets in public offices, museums and galleries are also usually clean; railway stations, bus stations, airports, multi-storey car parks and petrol stations generally have reasonably clean toilets; while pub toilets vary from bad to excellent. Toilets provided by

> **The English don't use the expressions 'powder room', 'wash room' or 'bathroom' (as in the US), but use 'toilet' or the colloquial 'loo' informally, and 'ladies' or 'gents' in more formal situations.**

local councils are located in towns, parks, car parks and on beaches, and are generally among the worst anywhere (the financial squeeze on local authorities in recent years has also meant the closure of many public toilets).

An increasing number of department stores, large supermarkets, large chemists (e.g. Boots), restaurants, pubs and public toilets for motorists provide nappy-changing facilities or facilities for nursing mothers (although legal, breastfeeding isn't usually done in public in England). Many shopping centres have special toilets for the disabled, as do airports and major railway stations. However, most public toilets for motorists aren't accessible to disabled drivers.

Charges

There's a charge of 20p to use toilets at London's mainline rail stations and in some department stores. Entrance is through a turnstile or via a coin machine on the door. A change machine isn't usually provided (and naturally the attendant will be absent when you're desperate and don't have the right coin). Some public toilets require payment of 10p or more.

> **'How lucky you English are to find the toilet so amusing. For us, it is a mundane and functional item. For you it is the basis of an entire culture.'**
>
> (from the BBC comedy series *Blackadder*)

Fittings

Toilets are fitted with a variety of flushing methods, including chains to pull, buttons to push (located on the toilet or wall), knobs to pull and foot buttons to tread on. Some even flush automatically. Men's urinals may have a knob to be pushed, pulled or trodden on (which many people neglect to do), although most are automatic.

Expect to come across a variety of hand-washing facilities (or none at all) which include wash basins with knobs you hold down to obtain water (usually cold or scalding hot); soap in the form of a bar, or liquid or powder from a dispenser; disposable paper towels, roll linen towels and hot air dryers, which may operate manually via a button or automatically (and which always stop just before your hands are dry). But be warned: public toilets often provide no soap or hand-drying facilities and may even have no running water or toilet paper.

Glastonbury Tor, Somerset (© www.michaelmathias.co.uk)

Goldfinch

APPENDICES

APPENDIX A: USEFUL ADDRESSES

In England

Listed below are the contact details for the embassies and high commissions (Commonwealth countries) of the main English-speaking countries in London. A full list of embassies and consulates in London is published in *The Diplomatic List* (The Stationery Office) and available online from the Foreign & Commonwealth Office website (🖳 www.fco.gov.uk).

Australia: Australian High Commission, Australia House, Strand, London WC2B 4LA (☎ 020-7379 4334, 🖳 www.uk.embassy.gov.au).

Canada: Canadian High Commission, Macdonald House, 1 Grosvenor Square, London W1K 4AB (☎ 020-7258 6600, 🖳 www.international.gc.ca/canada-europa/united_kingdom).

Ireland: Irish Embassy, 17 Grosvenor Place, London SW1X 7HR (☎ 020-7235 2171).

New Zealand: New Zealand High Commission, New Zealand House, 80 Haymarket, London SW1Y 4TQ (☎ 020-7930 8422, 🖳 www.nzembassy.com/uk).

South Africa: South Africa House, Trafalgar Square, London WC2N 5DP (☎ 020-7451 7299, 🖳 www.southafricahouse.com).

USA: American Embassy, 24 Grosvenor Square, London W1A 1AE (☎ 020-7499 9000, 🖳 www.usembassy.ork.uk).

Abroad

A full list of British diplomatic missions abroad is available from the Foreign & Commonwealth Office website (🖳 www.fco.gov.uk).

Australia: British High Commission, Commonwealth Avenue, Yarralumla, Canberra, ACT 2600 (☎ +61-2-6270 6666, 🖳 www.britaus.net).

Canada: British High Commission, 80 Elgin Street, Ottawa K1P 5K7 (☎ 1-613-237 1530, 💻 www.britainincanada.org).

Ireland: British Embassy, 29 Merrion Road, Ballsbridge, Dublin 4 (☎ +353-1-205 3700, 💻 www.britishembassy.ie).

New Zealand: British High Commission, 44 Hill Street, Wellington 1 (☎ +64-4-924 2888, 💻 www.britain.org.nz).

South Africa: British High Commission, 255 Hill Street, Arcadia 0002, Pretoria (☎ +27-12-421 7500, 💻 www.britain.org.za).

USA: British Embassy, 3100 Massachusetts Avenue NW, Washington DC 20008 (☎ +1-202-6500, 💻 www.britainonusa.com).

The business hours of embassies vary and they close on their own country's national holidays as well as on Australian public holidays. Always telephone to confirm opening hours before visiting.

APPENDIX B: FURTHER READING

The books listed below are just a selection of the hundreds written about England. The publication title is followed by the author's name (where applicable) and the publisher (in brackets).

Culture

A Class Act: The Myth of Britain's Classless Society, Andrew Adonis & Stephen Pollard (Hamilton)

Debrett's New Guide to Etiquette and Modern Manners, edited by John Morgan (Headline)

England in Particular: A Celebration of the Commonplace, the Local, the Vernacular and the Distinctive, Sue Clifford & Angela King (Hodder)

England, My England: A Treasury of All Things English, Gerry Hanson (Robson Books)

The English, Jeremy Paxman (Michael Joseph)

The English Companion: An Idiosyncratic A-Z of England and Englishness, Godfrey Smith (Old House)

How to be a Brit, George Mikes (Andre Deutsch)

Littlejohn's Britain, Richard Littlejohn (Hutchinson)

The Lore of the Land: A Guide to England's Legends, Jennifer Westwood & Jacqueline Simpson (Penguin)

I Never Knew That About England, Christopher Winn (Ebury Press)

Notes from a Small Island, Bill Bryson (Doubleday)

Watching the English: The Hidden Rules of English Behaviour, Kate Fox (Hodder & Stoughton)

We British: Britain Under the Moriscope Erik Jacobs & Robert Worcester (Weidenfeld & Nicholson)

The Xenophobe's Guide to the English, Antony Miall & David Milsted (Oval Books)

History

Blood of the Isles, Bryan Sykes (Bantam)

Britain AD: A Quest for Arthur, England & the Anglo-Saxons, Francis Pryor (Element)

History of Britain (3 Volumes), Simon Schama (BBC Worldwide)

A History of Modern Britain, Andrew Marr (Macmillan)

Homo Brittanicus: The Incredible Story of Human Life in Britain, Chris Stringer (Allen Lane)

How we Built Britain, David Dimbleby (Bloomsbury)

London in the Nineteenth Century: A Human Awful Wonder of God, Jerry White (Jonathan Cape)

The Oxford History of Britain, Kenneth.O. Morgan (Oxford University Press)

The Rough Guide History of England, Robin Eagles (Penguin Books)

Language

The Adventure of English, Melvyn Bragg (Sceptre)

The Cambridge Encyclopaedia of the English Language, David Crystal (Penguin)

The Concise Oxford English Dictionary (OUP)

Eats, Shoots & Leaves: The Zero Tolerance Approach to Punctuation, Lynne Truss (Profile Books)

The English Language: A Guided Tour of the Language, David Crystal (Penguin)

Mother Tongue: The English Language, Bill Bryson (Penguin)

The Stories of English, David Crystal (Penguin)

Literary classics

Bleak House; Great Expectations; Oliver Twist, Charles Dickens (Penguin Popular Classics)

The Canterbury Tales, Geoffrey Chaucer (Penguin Classics)

Complete Works, William Shakespeare (Wordworth Royals)

Far from the Madding Crowd; The Mayor of Casterbridge; Tess of the D'Urbervilles, Thomas Hardy (Penguin Popular Classics)

Jane Eyre, Charlotte Bronte (Penguin Popular Classics)

Middlemarch; Mill on the Floss, George Eliot (Penguin Popular Classics)

North and South, Elizabeth Gaskell (Penguin Popular Classics)

The Pilgrim's Progress, John Bunyan (Oxford World's Classics)

Pride and Prejudice; Sense and Sensibility; Mansfield Park, Jane Austen (Penguin Popular Classics)

Tom Jones, Henry Fielding (Wordsworth Classics)

Vanity Fair, William Makepeace Thackeray (Penguin Popular Classics)

Wuthering Heights, Emily Bronte (Penguin Popular Classics)

Living & Working

Buying, Selling & Letting Property, David Hampshire (Survival Books)

Buying or Renting a Home in London, David Hampshire & Sue Harris (Survival Books)

Living and Working in Britain, David Hampshire (Survival Books)

Living and Working in London, edited by Di Tolland (Survival Books)

Top Towns (Guinness Publishing)

Modern Classics

Animal Farm; The Road to Wigan Pier; **Down and Out in Paris and London; and 1984**, George Orwell (Penguin Books)

Brighton Rock; The End of the Affair; The Heart of the Matter, Graham Greene (Vintage Classics)

Fever Pitch; High Fidelity; About a Boy, Nick Hornby (Penguin Books)

The French Lieutenant's Woman; The Collector, John Fowles (Vintage Classics)

The Handmaid's Tale, Margaret Atwood (Vintage)

Howard's End, E. M. Forster (Penguin Twentieth Century Classics)

Mrs Dalloway; A Room of One's Own, Virginia Woolf (Wordsworth Classics)

Rebecca; Jamaica Inn, Daphne Du Maurier (Virago Modern Classics)

Sons and Lovers; Women in Love, D.H. Lawrence (Penguin Popular Classics)

White Teeth; **On Beauty**, Zadie Smith (Penguin Books)

Tourist Guides

AA Explorer Britain (AA Publishing)

Baedeker's AA Great Britain (Baedeker/AA)

Blue Guide England, Ian Ousby (A&C Black)

Bollocks to Alton Towers: Uncommonly British Days Out, Jason Hazeley & Others (Penguin)

Britain Travel Survival Kit (Lonely Planet)

The Complete Guide to London (Nicholson)

England, David Else (Lonely Planet)

Eyewitness Travel Guide London (Dorling Kindersley)

The Good Weekend Guide (Vermillion)

Let's Go: London (Pan)

Michelin Green Guide to Great Britain (Michelin)

Reader's Digest Touring Guide to Britain (Reader's Digest)

Rough Guide to England (The Rough Guides)

Time Out London Guide (Time Out)

Weekend Breaks in Britain (Which? Books)

Welcome to Britain (Collins)

Miscellaneous

A-Z London Guide (Geographers)

Black Diamonds: The Rise and Fall of a Great British Dynasty, Catherine Bailey (Viking)

Britain in Figures (The Economist)

Coast, Christopher Somerville (BBC Books)

The Coast Road: A 3,000 mile journey round the edge of England, Paul Gogarty (Robson Books)

Cool Camping England, Jonathan Knight (Punk Publishing)

Eating for England: The Delights and Eccentricities of the British at Table, Nigel Slater (Fourth Estate)

English Cathedrals, Edwin Smith & Olive Cook (Herbert Press)

English Food, Jane Grigson & Others (Penguin)

England's Thousand Best Churches & England's Thousand Best Houses, Simon Jenkins (Allen Lane)

Food for Thought: A Culinary Tour of the English Garden, Simon Courtauld (Think Publishing)

Gardens Through Time: 200 Years of the English Garden, Diarmuid Gavin & Jane Owen (BBC)

The Good Walks Guide (Which? Books)

Great British Menu – Traditional Recipes (Dorling Kindersley)

The Guinness UK Data Book (Guinness Publishing)

The Lost Villages of England, Leigh Driver & Stephen Whitehorne (New Holland)

The New British State (The Times)

A Picture of Britain, David Dimbleby (Tate)

Pubs and Inns of England and Wales, Alistair Sawday & David Hancock (Alistair Sawday)

Seven Centuries of English Cooking, Maxine de la Falaise (Grove Press)

Statlas UK (Ordnance Survey)

Whitaker's Almanack (The Stationery Office)

A Year in the Life of an English Meadow, Polly Devlin & Others (Frances Lincoln)

APPENDIX C: USEFUL WEBSITES

Below is a list of websites of interest to anyone wishing to learn more about England and the English.

Business

British Business (www.britishbusinesses.com) – online UK business directory.

Business Link (www.businesslink.org) – Includes hot topics, latest news, plus e-commerce and e-business pages.

Culture

All About English Culture (www.allinfoaboutenglishculture.com) – Your key to the fads, foibles and eccentricities of cultural England.

Black Britain (www.blackbritain.co.uk) – Jobs and career pages along with helpful feature pages on ethnic issues.

British Empire (www.britishempire.co.uk) – Timelines, maps, biographies, and articles on various aspects of British and imperial history, culture, technology and armed forces.

British Life & Culture (www.woodlands-junior.kent.sch.uk/customs) – A wealth of cultural information from the children of Woodlands Junior School.

British Museum (www.thebritishmuseum.ac.uk) – Houses a vast collection of world art and artefacts.

Enjoy England (www.enjoyengland.com) – The official website for tourism in England.

Ethnic Pages (www.ethnic-pages.co.uk) – A useful insight into multicultural Britain, including books, music, arts and crafts, dance and disabilities.

Icons (www.icons.org.uk) – A portrait of England.

Victoria & Albert Museum (www.vam.ac.uk) – The website of one of England's most celebrated museums, established in 1857.

We are the English.com (www.wearetheenglish.co.uk/quotes/quotes10.html) – A celebration of English heritage.

Wikipedia (💻 http://en.wikipedia.org/wiki/England) – the English pages of the free online encyclopaedia.

Education

British Council (💻 www.britishcouncil.org) – The UK's international organisation for educational opportunities and cultural relations.

Department for Children, Schools and Families (💻 www.dfes.gov.uk) – The DCSF is responsible for improving the focus on all aspects of policy affecting children and young people, as part of the Government's aim to deliver educational excellence.

Education UK (💻 www.educationuk.org) – Everything foreign students need to know about education in the UK (from the British Council).

English in Britain (💻 www.englishinbritain.co.uk) – Online database of over 1,600 British Council Accredited English language courses, at over 300 schools.

Learn English (💻 www.learnenglish.org.uk) – Learn English online with the help of this free website from the British Council.

Office for Standards in Education (💻 www.ofsted.gov.uk) – The government department responsible for inspecting and regulating education and schools in England.

Student Accommodation (💻 www.accommodationforstudents.com) – A search engine for students seeking accommodation in and around the UK's major cities.

Government

10 Downing Street (💻 www.number-10.gov.uk) – official website of the British Prime Minister.

Crime Reduction (💻 www.crimereduction.gov.uk) – A government site providing crime statistics and advice on avoiding and preventing crime.

Directgov (💻 www.direct.gov.uk) – Portal to public service information from the UK Government, including directories, online services, and news and information of relevance to specific groups.

Government Gateway (💻 www.ukonline.gov.uk and www.gateway.gov.uk) – Access to over 1,000 government websites. Government

Gateway is a centralised registration service that enables you to sign up for online government services.

National Health Service (💻 www.nhsdirect.nhs.uk) – Your gateway to government health information, services and assistance.

National Statistics (💻 www.statistics.gov.uk) – the government agency that produces and disseminates social, health, economic, demographic, labour market and business statistics.

UK Government Guide (💻 www.ukgovernmentguide.co.uk) – An easy way to access local UK government websites.

UK Parliament (💻 www.parliament.uk) – the official parliament website.

UK Visas (💻 www.ukvisas.gov.uk) – All you need to know about UK visas.

Webmesh (💻 www.webmesh.co.uk/government.htm) – Links to government departments.

Living & Working

Accommodation London (💻 www.accommodationlondon.net) – Help with finding a place to live in London, with text in English, French, Spanish, Italian and Swedish.

Environment Agency (💻 www.environment-agency.gov.uk) – Check the occurrence of flooding and other natural hazards in an area.

Get A Map (💻 www.getamap.co.uk) – Free downloadable Ordnance Survey neighbourhood maps.

Home Check (💻 www.homecheck.co.uk) – Local information about the risks of flooding, landslip, pollution, radon gas, landfill, waste sites, etc. Also provides general information about neighbourhoods.

Hometrack (💻 www.hometrack.co.uk) – Online property reports.

Home Pages (💻 www.homepages.co.uk) – Comprehensive property database and information about buying and selling property.

Jobcentre (💻 www.jobcentreplus.gov.uk) – The government website for job seekers, with advice on job hunting, training, recruitment and benefits.

Knowhere (💻 www.knowhere.co.uk) – An alternative look at over 2,000 UK towns.

The Move Channel (💻 www.themovechannel.com) – General property website containing everything you need to know about moving house.

My Village (💻 www.myvillage.com) – Community sites for London and 20 other cities.

Neighbourhood Statistics (💻 http://neighbourhood.statistics. gov.uk) – Contains a wide range of statistics for neighbourhoods in England and Wales.

Proviser (💻 www.proviser.com) – Local property prices and street maps for England and Wales.

Property Live (💻 www.propertylive.co.uk) – The National Association of Estate Agents' property website.

Right Move (💻 www.rightmove.co.uk) – Buying, selling and letting property.

Scoot (💻 www.scoot.co.uk) – Find essential services for homeowners.

UK Online (💻 www.ukonline.gov.uk) – Comprehensive information about local services and neighbourhoods, including schools, health, housing and crime statistics.

Up My Street (💻 www.upmystreet.co.uk) – Information about neighbourhoods, including property prices, local services, schools, local government, etc..

Media

BBC (💻 www.bbc.co.uk) – Excellent, comprehensive website from one of Britain's great institutions – www.bbc.co.uk/england provides local news, sport, entertainment and debate for England.

British Papers (💻 www.britishpapers.co.uk) – links to the websites of all British newspapers that are online.

Loot (💻 www.loot.com) – Log on to buy and sell virtually anything under one roof.

This is England (www.thisengland.co.uk) – the website of *This is England* magazine.

Time Out (💻 www.timeout.com). Weekly entertainment guide.

What's On (www.whatsoninlondon.co.uk). Weekly entertainment guide.

Which? Magazine (www.which.net). Monthly consumer magazine, available on subscription.

Miscellaneous

Advice Guide (www.adviceguide.org.uk) – Established by the Citizens' Advice Bureau (CAB), with down-to-earth advice, including information about civil rights, benefits and the legal system.

BBC Weather (www.bbc.co.uk/weather) – Provides UK and worldwide weather services and maps for temperature, wind, satellite, lighting, pressure and radar.

Britannia (www.britannia.com/history) – The internet's most comprehensive information resource for the times, places, events and people of British history.

British Library (www.bl.uk) – Search the BL catalogues, order items for research, view exhibitions, etc.

British Monarchy (www.royal.gov.uk) – Official website of the British Monarchy.

Football Association (www.thefa.com) – The Official Website of the England Team, The FA Cup and football (soccer) at all levels in England.

Consumers' Association (www.which.net) – The UK's consumer watchdog, which publishes the monthly *Which?* consumer magazine.

John Lewis (www.johnlewis.com) – The website of Britain's favourite retailer.

Medical Care (www.med4u.co.uk) – The leading UK online medical service. Obtain health advice and a second opinion with ease.

Premier League (www.premierleague.co.uk) – Official website of England's top soccer league.

Price Runner (www.pricerunner.co.uk) – Compare UK prices of a wide range of goods and services, online.

Shopping Net (www.shopping.net) – The UK's most comprehensive shopping website, which allows you to search thousands of websites for products and services at the best prices.

Sports Link (💻 www.sportslink.co.uk) – Lists sports and leisure facilities throughout the UK.

This Is Money (💻 www.thisismoney.co.uk) – Data and statistics on money matters as well as useful money guides.

UK Weather (💻 uk.weather.com) – Provides a ten-day summary forecast for cities, with maps for shorter periods ahead.

Travel

At UK (💻 www.atuk.co.uk) – The foremost UK travel search engine and directory.

British Airways (💻 www.britishairways.com) – The website of Britain's largest airline.

Multimap (💻 www.multimap.co.uk) – Invaluable resource for finding your way around if you haven't got an 'A–Z'.

National Express (💻 www.nationalexpress.com) – The UK's largest scheduled coach travel company.

National Rail (💻 www.nationalrail.co.uk) – For when you want to get out of London. Timetables, special offers and a journey planner for all the UK's railway services.

Public Transport Information (💻 www.pti.org.uk) – Covers all travel by rail, air, coach, bus, ferry, metro and tram within the UK (including the Channel Islands, Isle of Man and Northern Ireland), and between the UK and Ireland.

Rail (💻 www.rail.co.uk) – The best independent rail information, including timetables.

Streetmap (💻 www.streetmap.co.uk) – Another invaluable resource for finding your way around.

Transport For London (💻 www.tfl.gov.uk) – Everything you need to know about London's public transport systems.

Travel Britain Guide (💻 www.travelbritain.com) – Travel and Tourism Deals and Resources Pages for travel and entertainment resources in the UK.

Travel Line (💻 www.traveline.org.uk) – The UK's premier website for impartial information on planning a journey by bus, coach or train.

Virgin Atlantic (💻 www.virgin-atlantic.com) – The website of Britain's best airline.

Tourism

English Heritage (💻 www.english-heritage.org.uk) – The organisation responsible for protecting and promoting the historic environment, officially known as the Historic Buildings and Monuments Commission for England.

Itchy London (💻 www.itchylondon.co.uk) – Online version of the city guidebook, with reviews of bars, clubs and pubs and suggestions for places to go out.

London (💻 www.londonby.com or www.londonnet.co.uk) – Two of the most comprehensive London websites for both residents and visitors.

London Town (💻 www.londontown.com) – Comprehensive site featuring articles and reviews of restaurants, films and theatre shows, hotel and travel bookings and general information.

National Trust (💻 www.nationaltrust.org.uk) – The website of one of Britain's most beloved charitable institutions that looks after some 350 historic houses, gardens, industrial monuments and mills, all of which are open to the public.

Restaurant.co.uk (💻 www.restaurants.co.uk) – One of the UK's most comprehensive restaurant search portals.

Reception Bell (💻 www.receptionbell.com) – A comprehensive guide to UK travel accommodation.

This Is London (💻 www.thisislondon.com) – General information from the *Evening Standard* newspaper.

Toptable (💻 www.toptable.co.uk) – Online restaurant booking service, offering deals such as two-for-one offers and tables at hard-to-book London restaurants.

UK Travel (💻 www.uktravel.com) – Comprehensive UK travel information.

Visit Britain (💻 www.visitbritain.com) – The official site of the British Tourist Authority.

Visit England (💻 www.visitengland.com) – The website of the English Tourist Board.

Welcome to London (💻 www.welcometolondon.com) – London's most widely read online visitor magazine.

APPENDIX D: ENGLISH DIALECTS

This appendix includes a selection of words from some of England's most colourful slang, including Cockney Rhyming Slang, Geordie, Scouse and Brummie. Most English regions have local dialects or unique words, although English speakers will understand most people – unless they have a very thick accent, in which case you may understand nothing at all!

Cockney Rhyming Slang (East London)

Cockney rhyming slang is the colloquial language of the East of London. A true Cockney is someone born within the sound of Bow Bells (St Mary-le-Bow Church in Cheapside, London). However, nowadays the term is loosely applied to many born outside this area, provided they have a Cockney accent or a Cockney heritage (see also **Chapter 5**).

There are many online sources of Cockney slang including, www.cockneyrhymingslang.co.uk, www.phespirit.info/cockney and www.bbc.co.uk/dna/h2g2/A649.

Abergavenny: penny
Adam and Eve: believe
Alan Whickers: knickers
Alligator: later
Apple Fritter: bitter (beer)
Apples and Pears: stairs
April Fool: stool or tool
April Showers: flowers
Army & Navy: gravy
Artful Dodger: lodger
Babbling Brook: cook
Bacon and Eggs: legs
Ball of Chalk: walk
Bangers and Mash: cash
Barn Owl (barney): row (argument)
Barnet Fair: hair
Bath Bun: son
Big Ben: ten
Big Dippers: slippers
Billy Goat: coat
Boat Race: face
Bob Hope: soap
Battle Cruiser: boozer (pub)
Bo-peep: sleep
Bow and Arrow: sparrow
Brahms and Lizst: pissed (drunk)
Brass Band: hand
Brass Tacks: facts
Bread and Honey: money
Britney Spears: beers
Brown Bread: dead
Bubble Bath: laugh
Bubble and Squeek: Greek
Butcher's Hook: look
Cain and Abel: table
Cash and Carried: married
Cat and Mouse: house
Cherry Ripe: pipe
Chevy Chase: face
Chew the Fat: chat

China plate: mate
Clothes Peg: egg
Cock Sparrow: barrow
Cream Crackered: knackered (tired/broken)
Currant Bun: sun, son
Custard and Jelly: telly
Daisy Roots: boots
Danny Marr: car
Day and Night: light
Dickory Dock: clock
Dicky Bird: word
Ding Dong: song
Dog and Bone: telephone
Donkey's Ears: years
Drum 'n' Bass: face
Earwig: twig (understand)
East and West: vest
Elephant & Castle: parcel
Elsie Tanner: spanner
Flowery Dell: cell (prison)
Frog & Toad: road
Garden Gate: mate
Ginger Beer: queer (homosexual)
Gipsy's Warning: morning
Gold Watch: scotch
Grasshopper: copper (policeman)
Greengages: wages
Ha'penny Dip: ship
Half Inch: pinch
Ham and Eggs: legs
Hank Marvin: starving (hungry)
Harry Lime: time
Hit and Miss: kiss
Irish Jig: wig
Isle of Wight: light, right
J. Arthur Rank: bank, wank
Jack and Jill: hill
Jack Tar: bar
Jam Jar: car
Jimmy Riddle: piddle (urinate)
Joanna: piano
Khyber Pass: arse, glass
King Lears: ears
Lady Godiva: fiver (five pounds)
Lee Marvin: starving
Left in the Lurch: church
Lemon and Lime: crime
Lemon Squeezy: easy
Loaf of Bread: head
Lollipop: shop
Loop the Loop: soup
Mickey Mouse: house
Mince Pies: eyes
Moby Dick: sick
Mork & Mindy: windy
Mother Hubbard: cupboard
Mutt and Jeff: deaf
Mystic Megs: legs
Nanny Goat: boat, coat
Ned Kelly: telly
Nellie Dean: queen (homosexual)
Noah's Ark: lark
North and South: mouth
Oedipus Rex: sex
Oily Rag: fag
Oliver Twist: pissed
One Time Looker: hooker
Pat Malone: alone, own
Pen and Ink: stink
Peter Pan: can (prison)
Pick and Mix: sticks (countryside)
Pig's Ear: beer
Pinch (steal): half Inch
Plates of Meat: feet
Pony: £25
Pony & Trap: crap
Pork Pies (porkie pies): lies
Rabbit & Pork: talk
Radio Rental: mental

Maybe it's Because I'm a Londoner
(words & music by Hubert Gregg)

Maybe it's because I'm a Londoner, that I love London so.
Maybe it's because I'm a Londoner that I think of her wherever I go.
I get a funny feeling inside of me just walking up and down.
Maybe it's because I'm a Londoner that I love London Town.

Rhythm and Blues: shoes
Robin Hood: good
Rosie Lee: tea
Round the Houses: trousers**Ruby**
Murray: curry
Saucepan Lid: kid
Septic Tank: Yank
Sexton Blake: fake
Sky Rocket: pocket
Steam Tug: do something stupid (steam tug = Mug = Fool)
Sweeney Todd: flying squad (police)
Syrup of Figs: wig
Tea Leaf: thief
Tick-tock: clock
Tit for Tat (titfer): hat
Todd Sloane: alone, own
Tom Foolery: jewellery
Trick Cyclist: psychiatrist
Trouble and Strife: wife
Turtle Doves: gloves
Two and Eight: state (of anguish)
Uncle Dick: sick
Vera Lynn: gin
Weasel & Stoat: coat
Whistle and Flute: suit
Widow Twanky: hanky

Geordie (Tyneside)

Geordie is the dialect of Newcastle (Tyneside) and the northeast of England (Northumberland and Durham). For more information, see www.northeastengland.talktalk.net. The song *Blaydon Races* (see page 237) is the unofficial anthem of the Geordies.

Aad: old
Agyen: again
Ahint: behind
Alang: along
Alreet: alright
Amang: among - of Anglo-Saxon origin
Aw: I - me as in Aw went te Blaydon races
Axe: ask from the Anglo-Saxon Acsian 'to ask'.
Aye: yes
Baccy: tobacco
Bairn: a child - Anglo-Saxon and Viking
Bait: food taken to work
Bank: a hill
Beor: beer
Beuk: a book
Blaa: blow
Blaa Oot: heavy drinking session
Boggle: a ghost or spectre.

Bonny: beautiful - from the French Bon
Bord: bird
Borst: burst
Bourn: a stream
Bullet: a sweet - a word of French origin.
Burr: the name given to the strange Northumbrian pronunciation of the R sound.
But: a kind of spoken full stop or 'period.
Canny: cagey, careful, shrewd. Can also mean good, nice and very, among other things.
Card: cold
Chorch: church
Claes: clothes - Anglo-Saxon
Clarty: dirty
Clivvor: clever
Crack: to talk from Durtch Kraaken
Da: dad - father
Dede: dead
Dee: do
Divvent: do not.
Doon: down
Eee: eye
Fettle: good condition
Fower: four
Gadgie: an old man
Gan (Gannin): go (going) from the Anglo Saxon word for go.
Ganzie: a jumper/sweater
Hinny: honey - a term of endearment.
Hoos: house
Howay: come on – 'howay' or 'h'way the lads' is chanted at football matches.
Ket: a sweet or something that is nice
Kidda: a term of endearment.
Ma: mother
Mac': make
Mair: more
Man: frequently used at the end of a sentence
Mebbees: may be or Perhaps
Neet: night.
Nyem: name
Ower: over
Pet: a term of endearment.
Poliss: policeman
Reet: right
Sark: a shirt
Sel': self
Sooth: south
Stottie: a kind of flat cake-like bread
Tab: a cigarette
Tak': take
Tatie: potato
Te': to
Telt: told
Thowt: thought.
Toon: town
Tret: treated
Tyke: a Yorkshireman
Us: me
Wag: playing the wag is playing truant
Wark: work
Wes: was
Yem: home
Yen: one
Yersel': yourself

Blaydon Races
(chorus, by Geordie Ridley)

Oh me lads, you should've seen us gannin
Passing the folks along the road
And all of them were starin'
All the lads and lasses there
They all had smilin' faces
Gannin along the Scotswood Road
To see the Blaydon races.

Scouse (Merseyside)

Scouse is the accent and dialect of English spoken in the north-western city of Liverpool and in some adjoining urban areas of Merseyside. For more information see 💻 http://24carat.co.uk/scousedictionaryframe.html, 💻 www.mikekemble.com/mside/scouse1.html and 💻 http://louisville.edu/~tavan001/Merseytalk.html.

The song, *You'll Never Walk Alone* (see page 239), written by Oscar Hammerstein II and Richard Rogers, was adopted as the anthem of Liverpool Football Club in the '60s after the song was a big hit by the Liverpool band, Gerry & The Pacemakers.

Antwaccky: ancient, very old
Any Road: anyway, whatever
Ar Kid: my brother
Away for Slates: make a hurried exit
Back Bog: back yard privy (toilet)
Backie: riding on the back of someone's bike
Bangeroo: a pig
Banny Mug: thick brown pottery
Barm Cake: yeast cake; a foolish person
Basil Belly: fat man
Bed-wetter: an early riser
Beer Can Head: Birkenhead (town south of the River Mersey opposite Liverpool and linked by a tunnel)
Bevvy: a beer
Binbagged: thrown out by your mate
Binhead: a dim-witted person
De Bizzies: police
Blad: newspaper
Blind Scouse: quasi-vegetarian, meatless stew
Blocked: stoned on drugs
Blocker: bowler hat
Blue Nose: Everton football fan
Bone Orchard: cemetery
Boyanks: string that navvies tied around legs to stop mud or clay
Buttie, Butty: sandwich, bread and butter
Casey: leather football
Chocker: full
Chuck: bread

Cogger: left footer, Catholic
Corksucker: an American
Council Pop: water
Cow Juice: milk
Crozzy: riding on the crossbars (bike)
Da: father
Darrafact: is that so?
Delf: cups, saucers and plates
Dem: they, those
Desert Wellies: sandals
Dibbins: money thrown into the ring for amateur boxers
Diddyman: small person
Dicky's Meadow: in real trouble, e.g. 'you're in Dicky's meadow'
Dimps: recently discarded cigarette butts still with a few "drags" left in them
Donky Stone: used to clean front doorsteps
Don't Let On You're Bandy: keep your own counsel
Dowse: keep a lookout for the police (usually when playing pitch and toss)
Exey Cosher: newspaper street seller
First Wet: after a haircut, friends wet fingers and hit you on the head
Getting Off At Edge Hill: simple inexpensive method of contraception, the withdrawal method
High Rip: gang of women who used to rob sailors
Hug Me Tight: a tight blouse
In The Cut: the Leeds/Liverpool canal.
Jacks 'n Ollies: five stone (kid's game)
Jigger: typical location for knee-trembler
Kinnell: expression of surprise
Kirkby Kiss: head butting an opponent in the face.
La: lad, young man
Latch-lifter: (paid) first drink, having enough money to go to the pub
Leg It: scarper, run away
Mitts: hands
Mug You: pay for or treat your mate (usually to a drink)
Nesh: feels the cold
Notecracker: someone who would change a seaman's advance money order
Nudger: baguette
The Nugget: a full weekend's work on the docks
Ollies: marbles
De One-eyed City: Birkenhead
One Ton Heavy On: boys' street game (like leapfrog)
De Onion Patch: Anfield football ground
Paddy's Wigwam: the Catholic Cathedral
Pobs: sloppy baby food made from bread and milk
De Pool: the City of Liverpool
Red Raddle: colour the tiles/front step
Scaldy: swimming hole, part of canal warm with industrial effluent
Scoop: pint, usually of beer. From when beer was "scooped" out of barrels.
Scran: food
Scuffers: police
Shaddle: moving plank of wood

in children's playground
Shirt Lifter: homosexual
Splosh: money
The Stick: old name for the Landing Stage
Stickie Lice: a liquorice root (to eat)
Sub: loan
Ta Wack: thanks, most grateful
Tanner Meg: a small rubber football
Togo: sugar
Tramstopper: large slice of bread
Ullo Dur!: greetings! Pleased to make your acquaintance
Vatican: the new VAT Office in Liverpool
Wack: sir
Wear The Fox Hat: enquiry as to geographical location
Webs: feet
Welt: tea break
Wingy: person with one arm
Yis: yes
Y'know Like: meaningless interjection
Yer Wha?: you what?, did I her you correctly?
Yews: you (plural)

You'll Never Walk Alone
(Words and Music Oscar Hammerstein II and Richard Rogers)

When you walk through a storm, hold your head up high
And don't be afraid of the dark.
At the end of the storm there's a golden sky
And the sweet, silver song of a lark.

Walk on through the wind, walk on through the rain,
Though your dreams be tossed and blown.
Walk on, walk on with hope in your heart,
And you'll never walk alone.

You'll never walk alone.
Walk on, walk on with hope in your heart,
And you'll never walk alone.
You'll never walk alone.

Brummie (Birmingham)

A selection of Birmingham (Brummie) and Black Country slang words and phrases are listed below. For more information see www.virtualbrum.co.uk/slang.htm.

Ackers: money
Adu: how are you?
Aafpast: half past the hour
Ahr: yes
Arf soaked: stupid
Alloy: friend
Anroadup: anyhow, anyway
Avon: light commercial vehicle, van
Bin: been
Blartin: crying
Blastid: damn, bloody (mild expletive)
Bosta: large
Bostin: terrific, excellent
Bosti Fittle: good food
Bug Hutch: local cinema
Caggy-handed: left-handed
Canting: talking
Chimley: chimney
Copolt: take hold of this
Cor: cannot
Cut: canal
Donnies: hands
Doolally: barmy, crackers
Duck: woman (can also be a man)
Fake: cigarette
Fizzog: face
Gaffer: boss
Gerraway: really?
Gerron Me Wick: fed up with someone
Gerrout: I am gobsmacked (incredulous)
Giya: give you
Glarnies: marbles
Guzz: goes
Guzzunda: a bedpan ?
Horse Pickle: hospital
Kaliye: sherbert
Kayliyed: intoxicated
Lard 'ed: stupid, thick
Larpom: toilet
Mardy: grumpy, in a bad mood
Miskins: dustbins
Misses: wife
Mizzly: cold and wet weather
Mooch: look
Morkins: someone stupid
Mucker: mate, good friend
Nah: no
Oh-ahrr: yes, certainly
On a Loin: angry, annoyed
Out Door: off licence (liquor store)
Orse Rowed: thoroughfare
Otchin: method of propulsion used by babies
Palaver: a vexing situation
Parky: cold, chilly
Rezza: reservoir
Rocks: sweets
Roit Bosta: something very good
Safta: this afternoon
Scrubba: prostitute
Sukka: frozen confectionary on a stick (lollipop)
Summat: something
Tennarf: I agree
Ta Rah: goodbye
Tay: it is not
Tussock: irritating cough

Waggin it: playing truant
Wamul: dog
Wench: girl
Worroh: hello
Wotcha: what have you got
Wudden 'ill: stairs
Wum: home
Yampy: daft, stupid
Yow No: you know, assumption of understanding

APPENDIX E: MAP OF ENGLAND

The map of England opposite shows the counties, which are listed below in alphabetical order. The list shows the abbreviations (in brackets) that ae in common use for some counties. There is a geographical map on page 6.

Bath & Northeast Somerset
Bedfordshire (Beds.)
Berkshire (Berks.)
Buckinghamshire (Bucks.)
Cambridgeshire (Cambs.)
Cheshire
Cleveland
Cornwall
Cumbria
Derbyshire (Derby)
Devon
Dorset
Durham
East Sussex (E. Sussex)
Essex
Gloucestershire (Glos)
Greater Manchester
Hampshire (Hants.)
Hereford &
Worcestershire (Worcs.)
Hertfordshire (Herts.)
Isle of Wight
Kent
Lancashire (Lancs.)
Leicestershire (Leics.)
Lincolnshire (Lincs.)
London
Merseyside
Norfolk
North Yorkshire (N.Yorks)
Northamptonshire (Northants)
Northumberland
Nottinghamshire (Notts.)
Oxfordshire (Oxon)
Shropshire (Salop)
Somerset
South Yorkshire (S. Yorks.)
Staffordshire (Staffs.)
Suffolk
Surrey
Warwickshire (Warks.)
West Midlands
West Sussex (W. Sussex)
West Yorkshire (W. Yorks.)
Wiltshire (Wilts.)

SCOTLAND
ATLANTIC OCEAN
NORTH SEA
NORTHERN IRELAND
NORTHUMBERLAND
TYNE & WEAR
CLEVELAND
CUMBRIA
DURHAM
NORTH YORKSHIRE
ISLE of MAN
IRISH SEA
LANCASHIRE
WEST YORKSHIRE
GREATER MANCHESTER
SOUTH YORKSHIRE
MERSEYSIDE
REPUBLIC OF IRELAND
CHESHIRE
DERBYSHIRE
NOTTINGHAMSHIRE
LINCOLNSHIRE
STAFFORDSHIRE
NORFOLK
SALOP
LEICESTERSHIRE
W. MIDLANDS
CAMBRIDGESHIRE
WARWICKSHIRE
NORTHAMPTONSHIRE
SUFFOLK
WALES
HEREFORD AND WORCESTERSHIRE
BEDFORDSHIRE
HERTFORDSHIRE
ESSEX
GLOUCESTERSHIRE
OXFORDSHIRE
BUCKINGHAMSHIRE
LONDON
WILTSHIRE
BERKSHIRE
SURREY
KENT
ATLANTIC OCEAN
SOMERSET
HAMPSHIRE
WEST SUSSEX
EAST SUSSEX
DEVON
DORSET
ISLE of WIGHT
CORNWALL
ENGLISH CHANNEL
ISLES of SCILLY

A Seat with the Gods (© www.michaelmathias.co.uk)

INDEX

A

B

C

D

E

F

G

H

I

T

UV

W

Survival Books was established in 1987 and by the mid-'90s was the leading publisher of books for people planning to live, work, buy property or retire abroad.

From the outset, our philosophy has been to provide the most comprehensive and up-to-date information available. Our titles routinely contain up to twice as much information as other books and are updated frequently. All our books contain colour photographs and some are printed in two colours or full colour throughout. They also contain original cartoons, illustrations and maps.

Survival Books are written by people with first-hand experience of the countries and the people they describe, and therefore provide invaluable insights that cannot be obtained from official publications or websites, and information that is more reliable and objective than that provided by the majority of unofficial sites.

Survival Books are designed to be easy – and interesting – to read. They contain a comprehensive list of contents and index, and extensive appendices, including useful addresses, further reading, useful websites and glossaries to help you obtain additional information as well as metric conversion tables and other useful reference material.

Our primary goal is to provide you with the essential information necessary for a trouble-free life or property purchase and to save you time, trouble and money.

We believe our books are the best – they are certainly the best-selling. But don't take our word for it – read what reviewers and readers have said about Survival Books at the front of this book.

Other Survival Books

Investing in Property Abroad: Essential reading for anyone planning to buy property abroad, containing surveys of over 30 countries.

The Best Places to Buy a Home in France/Spain: Unique guides to where to buy property in France and Spain, containing detailed regional profiles and market reports.

Buying, Selling and Letting Property: The best source of information about buying, selling and letting property in the UK.

Earning Money From Your Home: Income from property in France and Spain, including short- and long-term letting.

Foreigners in France/Spain: Triumphs & Disasters: Real-life experiences of people who have emigrated to France and Spain, recounted in their own words.

Making a Living: Comprehensive guides to self-employment and starting a business in France and Spain.

Renovating & Maintaining Your French Home: The ultimate guide to renovating and maintaining your dream home in France.

Retiring in France/Spain: Everything a prospective retiree needs to know about the two most popular international retirement destinations.

Running Gîtes and B&Bs in France: An essential book for anyone planning to invest in a gîte or bed & breakfast business in France.

Rural Living in France: An invaluable book for anyone seeking the 'good life', containing a wealth of practical information about all aspects of French country life.

Shooting Caterpillars in Spain: The hilarious and compelling story of two innocents abroad in the depths of Andalusia in the late '80s.

Wild Thyme in Ibiza: A fragrant account of how a three-month visit to the enchanted island of Ibiza in the mid-'60s turned into a 20-year sojourn.

For a full list of our current titles, visit our website at
www.survivalbooks.net

Photo Credits

www.shutterstock.com:

pages 12 (© Sharon Kingston), 14 (© Jo Ann Snover), 15 (© Countyroad), 16 (© Charlie Bishop), 17 (© Graham Tomlin), 19 (©Alexander Gitlits), 20 (© Christine Nichols), 21 (© Iofoto), 26 (© Aga), 31 (© Yuri Arcurs), 33 (© Yuri Arcurs), 34 (© Mark William Penny), 35 (© gary718), 38 (© Darren Baker), 39 (© Eduardo Jose Bernardino), 41 (© Vladislav Gurfinkel), 42 (© Richard Waite), 44 (© Girish Menon), 46 (© Deetone), 47 (© Gary James Calder), 48 (© Charlie Bishop), 49 (© Paul Cowan), 50 (© Gordan Ball LRPS), 51 (© Mary Lane), 53 (© Mark William Richardson), 56 (© Robert Mackenzie), 57 (© Peter Elvidge), 60 (© Tom Grundy), 64 (© Cornel Achirei), 65 (© Thomas Sztanek), 66 (© Ian Holland), 67 (© Timothy Large), 69 (© Robert J Beyers II), 72 (© Gelpi), 73 (© Mashe), 74 (© Prism_68), 77 (© Anette Linnea Rasmussen), 80 (© Jim Mills), 82 (© Kenneth V. Pilon), 84 (© Vasyl Helevachuk), 85 (© dwphotos), 86 (© ronfromyork), 87 (© Alex James Bramwell), 88 (© Peter Guess), 92 (© Gabriel Moisa), 93 (© Lev Olkha), 96 (© Liudmila Korsakova), 97 (© Lance Bellers), 99 (© Pres Panayotov), 101 (© unknown), 102 (© Michael Gerrard), 105 (© Stephen Aaron Rees), 106 (© Bruce Amos), 108 (© Thomas Owen Jenkins), 109 (© Ant Clausen), 110 (© iofoto), 111 (© Stephen Finn), 113 (© Christopher Ewing), 114 (© Grigiry Iofin), 115 (© UltraOrto, S.A.), 116 (© Andrew Kua Seng How), 118 (© Joe Gough), 121 (© Colin & Linda McKie), 123 (© Bouzou), 124 (© Andres Rodriguez), 127 (© Adam Borkowski), 134 (© Timothy Passmore), 136 (© Peter Gudella), 138 (© David Burrows), 139 (© Massimiliano Lamagna), 140 (© Guy Erwood), 141 (© Stephen Aaron Rees), 144 (© Markabond), 145 (© Paul Cowan), 146 (© William Casey), 147 (© Fred Goldstein), 149 (© Kevin Britland), 152 Harvey Fitzhugh), 154 (© Tischenko Irina), 155 (© Paddington), 156 (© Joshua Haviv), 157 (© Joe Gough), 158 (© Mauro Bighin), 162 (© Guy Erwood), 163 (© Jerome Whittingham), 164 (© kd2), 168 (© Catnao), 169 (© Vertes Edmond Mihai), 173 (© Chris Mole), 174 (© ARphotography), 175 (© Chris Mole), 176 (© Paul Cowan), 177 (© Chunni4691), 178 (© Chris Mole),